D0002360

HEALTH DATA IN THE INFORMATION AGE

USE, DISCLOSURE, AND PRIVACY

MOLLA S. DONALDSON and KATHLEEN N. LOHR, *Editors*

Committee on Regional Health Data Networks

Division of Health Care Services

INSTITUTE OF MEDICINE

NATIONAL ACADEMY PRESS
Washington, D.C. 1994

National Academy Press • 2101 Constitution Avenue, NW • Washington, DC 20418

NOTICE: The project that is the subject of this report was approved by the Governing Board of the National Research Council, whose members are drawn from the councils of the National Academy of Sciences, the National Academy of Engineering, and the Institute of Medicine. The members of the committee responsible for this report were chosen for their special competencies and with regard for appropriate balance.

This report has been reviewed by a group other than the authors according to procedures approved by a Report Review Committee consisting of members of the National Academy of Sciences, the National Academy of Engineering, and the Institute of Medicine.

The Institute of Medicine was chartered in 1970 by the National Academy of Sciences to enlist distinguished members of the appropriate professions in the examination of policy matters pertaining to the health of the public. In this, the Institute acts under both the Academy's 1863 congressional charter responsibility to be an adviser to the federal government and its own initiative in identifying issues of medical care, research, and education. Dr. Kenneth I. Shine is president of the Institute of Medicine

Support for this project was provided by the John A. Hartford Foundation, the American Health Information Management Association, Electronic Data Systems Corporation, and Science Applications International Corporation.

Library of Congress Cataloging-in-Publication Data

Institute of Medicine (U.S.). Committee on Regional Health Data
    Networks.
        Health data in the information age : use, disclosure, and privacy
    / Molla S. Donaldson and Kathleen N. Lohr, editors ; Committee on
    Regional Health Data Networks, Division of Health Care Services,
    Institute of Medicine.
        p. cm.
    Includes bibliographical references and index.
    ISBN 0-309-04995-4
    1. Medical records—Access control. 2. Confidential
communications—Physicians. 3. Medical informatics. I. Donaldson,
Molla S. II. Lohr, Kathleen N., 1941- . III. Title.
RA976.I48 1994
651.5′04261—dc20   94-2613
                                                        CIP

Printed in the United States of America

The serpent has been a symbol of long life, healing, and knowledge among almost all cultures and religions since the beginning of recorded history. The image adopted as a logotype by the Institute of Medicine is based on a relief carving from ancient Greece, now held by the Staatlichemuseen in Berlin.

Cover art: Woodcut of Galen, flanked by Hippocrates and Avicenna. Source: Galen, *Opera*, Lyon, 1528, vignette on title page. Courtesy of National Library of Medicine, Bethesda, Maryland.

iii

Study Staff, Division of Health Care Services

Karl D. Yordy, Director (until 10/1/93)
Kathleen N. Lohr, Director (as of 10/1/93), Study Director
Molla S. Donaldson, Study Director
Helen C. Rogers, Project Assistant

---

*Member, Institute of Medicine
†Served through June 23, 1993
‡Member, National Academy of Engineering

Preface

From the very first meetings, in the early 1970s, of the newly constituted Institute of Medicine (IOM) of the National Academy of Sciences, a major objective has been the engagement of the most important and difficult health and science policy issues from the public's or society's perspective. The Institute was created so that a broad-based and multidisciplinary membership could work across professions, within and without the health sciences, toward the solution of these complex and difficult problems.

From my personal experience as a staff member at the IOM during the first four years of its life, I can attest to the early recognition of the importance of the process of having a balanced, multidisciplinary committee working on the policy issues at hand. The assumption was that the sum of the parts of such a diverse group was surpassed by the synergy of the whole; more often than not, this positive learning experience also produced a useful document or report. In my personal experience with such groups, I cannot recall a failure either in the product and its value or in the process and its impact on the individuals participating. I must say, however, that the challenges facing this committee on regional databases were so great and our initial difficulties so intense in becoming clear about and comfortable with the seminal questions embedded in our charge that I was not optimistic about either our two-year experience together or the product that I could envision emerging.

Our challenges were formidable because the very nature of the "regional databases" was obscure to some, their potentials for good or harm were obscure to others, and the interweaving of such heavy strands of legal material with information technology, data management, security maintenance, and the substance of health services research made it exceedingly hard for many of us to get comfortable with our view and understanding of the completed policy tapestry.

But we did it! Never have I been on a committee with the dogged determination of this one; our relatively large committee seldom had a meeting wherein even one, let alone more than one, member was absent, and they stayed to the end. Never have I been on a committee wherein the doctors, scientists, data experts, lawyers, representatives of the public interest, and experts from the business world had such great expertise, such strong opinions, and such diverse perspectives.

The key to the success of this project, it seems to me, was the gradual emergence of a commonality in shared values. Somewhat to our collective surprise, we found ourselves unanimous in our acceptance of the following fundamental assumptions: (1) use of population-wide databases developed from individually collected, computerized personal health data has become a working reality; (2) potential benefits of such data sets used for financial, organizational, quality improvement, and research purposes to society are indeed great; (3) protection of the individual record from person-identifiable exposure must involve all possible behavioral, systematic, and technical security measures; (4) relevant data sets and analyses including hospital-, clinic-, and provider-specific data must be expeditiously made available to the public; and (5) bona fide researchers must have access to person-identifiable records in order to provide society with timely studies on health status and health care.

These five foundational elements were essential to the committee's collective thinking and its observations, conclusions, and recommendations as detailed in the report.

Once the committee came together around these ideas, it was able to move systematically through the myriad of policy implications that come from reasoning from basic principles. This could not have been accomplished without the indomitable persistence and prodigious intellectual work of Molla Donaldson and Kathleen Lohr. Karl Yordy made key contributions intermittently as was appropriate for an IOM division head.

Finally, it has become increasingly obvious to me (and I believe to the rest of the committee) that the future we see emerging before us, as a result of our participation in this study, has heavy implications for public education. In a way, developing an informed and sophisticated public is what regional databases and their analyses and reports are all about. The burden of these education efforts may fall primarily upon health database organizations, but in my view this responsibility belongs to all interested parties, institutions, and professions. The purpose of these new information technologies is to enhance the health status of society and to improve health care for the individual patient. We hope and trust that this report itself will contribute to public understanding of these complex but important matters.

Roger J. Bulger, M.D., F.A.C.P.
Chair

Acknowledgments

The Committee on Regional Health Data Networks wishes to acknowledge the assistance that they and the study staff received from many individuals and organizations during this study. Among these are a large number of individuals and organizations who met with members of the committee and staff during site visits and provided valuable insight into both the benefits to be gained and the obstacles to current efforts to establish and operate various kinds of health database organizations and regional networks.

The committee benefited from presentations by guests invited to three of its meetings. In March 1992 John P. Fanning, LL.B., Office of Health Policy and Evaluation, Office of the Assistant Secretary of Health, Department of Health and Human Services, spoke to the committee about privacy issues related to the disclosure of data from various kinds of databases. Lance J. Hoffman, Ph.D., Professor, Department of Electrical Engineering and Computer Science, George Washington University, gave an evening presentation on issues of security and inferential identification. In June 1992 the committee was joined by H. Jefferson Smith, Ph.D., of Georgetown University School of Business Administration; William Goss of the Health Care Management Program at General Electric; Robin Stults, R.R.A., of the University of Maryland Medical System; and Edward J. Hinman, M.D., of Lincoln National. All these participants discussed current practices in the use and protection of health information from their various perspectives (employers, providers, computer security experts, and insurers and third-party payers). Bert Tobin of Benton International also presented a working model of an information repository. At both this meeting and the next meeting in October 1992, Robert Belair, J.D., explored with the committee a range of legal and regulatory aspects of privacy and confidentiality. At the October meeting, the committee also heard from John Baker, Senior Vice President of Equifax, Inc., in Atlanta, Georgia, regarding the issues of privacy, confidentiality, and access in other databases.

The committee also wishes to acknowledge the organizations, institutions, and groups, listed in Appendix A, that participated in its five site visits. A considerable debt of gratitude is owed to the many individuals, too numerous to name here, who because of their association with those organizations gave the committee valuable insights into the many issues of use, disclosure, and privacy that make up the heart of the committee's report.

The study would not have been possible without the support of the John A. Hartford Foundation, and the consistent and enthusiastic encouragement from Richard Sharpe, the Foundation's Program Officer, is hereby acknowledged. Generous assistance was also provided by the American Health Information Management Association, Electronic Data Systems Corporation, and Science Applications International Corporation.

This study benefited from both previous and current IOM studies, including work by the Committee on Improving the Patient Record in Response to Increasing Functional Requirements and Technological Advances, the Committee on Employer-based Health Benefits, and the Committee on Assessing Genetic Risks. The committee is particularly appreciative of the assistance from Marilyn J. Field, Ph.D., and Jane Fullarton, M.P.H., the project directors for the latter two studies, who provided cogent presentations on privacy and confidentiality matters at one committee meeting.

Finally, and in particular, the committee would like to express its gratitude to the IOM staff who facilitated the work of the committee. We are grateful for the secretarial and logistical support provided by Helen Rogers and Donald Tiller and for the assistance during the report review and preparation stage of Claudia Carl and Michael Edington of the IOM's Office of Reports and Information; the steady help of Nina Spruill, Financial Associate for the Division of Health Care Services, was also greatly appreciated. Krys Krystynak, while a participant in the federal 1992 SES Candidate Development Program, spent some time at the IOM assisting on the study. Finally, the committee acknowledges its considerable debt to Karl Yordy, Director of the Division of Health Care Services through September 1993, for his unflagging guidance and support during this project.

Contents

HEALTH DATA
IN THE
INFORMATION AGE

Summary

An Institute of Medicine (IOM) study committee has examined the potential that existing and emerging health database organizations offer in improving the health of individuals and the performance of the health care system. *Health Data in the Information Age: Use, Disclosure, and Privacy* advances recommendations related to the public disclosure of quality-of-care information and the protection of the confidentiality of personal health information. The emergence of health database organizations—whether through national health reform, state legislative initiatives, commercial ventures, or local business, medical, and hospital association coalitions—provides the impetus to explore how such assembled patient-level health care information can be used appropriately.

THE PROBLEM

The desire to understand and improve the performance of the health system begets a need for better health data for several purposes: to assess the health of the public and patterns of illness and injury; identify unmet regional health needs; document patterns of health care expenditures on inappropriate, wasteful, or potentially harmful services; identify cost-effective care providers; and provide information to improve the quality of care in hospitals, practitioners' offices, clinics, and other health care settings.

This, in turn, motivates proposals for the creation and maintenance of comprehensive, population-based health care databases that can provide such information with ease and reliability. Considerable obstacles lie in the way of achieving these goals. Some relate to the content and structure of current health databases; others concern the difficulties and costs of creating and maintaining comprehensive databases. Furthermore, public health databases (e.g., those maintained by states) may themselves lack connections with one another. Other problems include the need to create longitudinal records to understand how patients fare "in the system as a whole"; the need to adjust for important characteristics about patients' sociodemographic circumstances or health status (risk and severity adjustment); and the need to have information on the health of the population as a whole, not just of those who use the health system. Finally, the need for information on both end results (the outcomes) of care as well as on the processes of care poses great challenges to database developers.

The current push for health care reform has made clear to many that the success of reform options—as well as the ability to assess the effect of a reformed system on the health of the public—depends on access to the kinds of data that too often are unavailable.

Finally, as the reasons for creating large health databases mount, so do the possibilities that such databases (or, more correctly, their users) will do harm to patients, providers (institutions, physicians, and others), payers (government, private insurers, and corporations), and the public at large. The balance between the advantages of such databases and their potential for harm, or at least unfairness, to some groups is not yet clear, and the question of whether and how such entities ought to evolve has not been explored.

Recently, diverse groups of researchers, business leaders, and policymakers at state and regional levels have begun to develop databases intended to overcome some of the problems cited above and to permit increasingly sophisticated analyses of community health needs, practice patterns, costs, and quality of care. The interests that have prompted such action cover a broad range: the need to control business costs attributable to health benefits, the desire to use technological and computer applications to decrease administrative costs of processing insurance claims, the wish of experienced health services researchers to exploit the potential of health databases to evaluate and improve health care, the responsibility of community leaders to plan expansion and contraction of health care facilities and services across the nation, and the need to transmit medical history information for an increasingly mobile population.

Coincident with these interests are the greatly enhanced electronic capabilities for data management in many aspects of daily life. Comprehensive computer-based health data files can be easily linked and information from those files moved instantaneously. Many observers believe that an unparalleled opportunity exists to apply computer technologies creatively to address many of the informational needs and data problems noted above. The report focuses on steps that might be taken to foster such action and progress through what the IOM committee terms *health database organizations*.

The committee uses *health database organization* (HDO) to refer to entities that have access to (and possibly control of) databases and a primary mission to publicly release data and the results of analyses done on the databases under their control. Although such entities do not yet exist, many are moving forcefully toward implementation. Prototypical HDOs have several characteristics; they

- operate under a single, common authority;
- acquire and maintain information from a wide variety of sources and put their databases to multiple uses;
- have files containing person-identified or person-identifiable data;
- serve a specific, defined geographic area;
- have inclusive population files;
- have comprehensive data with elements that include administrative, clinical, health status, and satisfaction information;
- manipulate data electronically; and
- support electronic access for real-time use.

For maximum accountability, protection, and control over access to person-identifiable data, HDOs will need an organizational structure, a corporate or legal existence, and a physical location. The value of HDOs and their databases might be said to be the timely provision of reliable and valid information to address all the major questions in health care delivery facing the nation today and in the coming years. The prospect of creating these entities has raised numerous issues, including (1) worries on the part of health care providers and clinicians about use or misuse of the information HDOs will compile and release, and (2) alarm on the part of consumers, patients, and their physicians about how well the privacy and confidentiality of personal health information will be guarded.

INSTITUTE OF MEDICINE STUDY

In early 1992 the IOM appointed a study committee to address these issues. The project took place during the 18 months before the Clinton administration introduced its Health Security Act in the fall of 1993; it was neither designed nor intended to reflect specifics of that or any of the other health care reform proposals that were debated beginning in late 1993. The study committee consisted of 16 individuals with expertise in administration of medical centers and academic health centers, the practice of medicine, administration of large (nonhealth) corporations, health insurance, utilization management, use of large administrative and research databases for research purposes, consumer services, health and privacy law, ethics, data security, informatics, and state health data organizations. In addition to meeting with experts in these areas and reviewing the literature, the committee conducted five major site visits; it met with groups developing HDOs in business coalitions and other organizations, practicing physicians and representatives of local medical societies, insurers and third-party claims administrators, health maintenance organizations, consumers, hospital administrators and hospital associations, researchers, state and county health officials, employers, and computer system developers. At the conclusion of the study, the report underwent formal external review following the procedures of the National Research Council and the IOM.

The IOM committee took as a given that a variety of HDOs were being created and moving into operational phases and focused on two primary issues. The first is public release of descriptive and evaluative data on the costs, quality, and other attributes of health care institutions, practitioners, and other providers. The second involves the risks to and opportunities for protecting the privacy and confidentiality of data that do (or may) identify individuals in their role as patients or consumers, not as clinicians or providers.

USES AND USERS OF INFORMATION IN HDOS

Chapter 2 examines users and uses of HDO data and issues related to data quality. The major users of HDOs include health care provider organizations and practitioners, patients, their families, community residents, academic and research organizations, payers and purchasers, employers, health agencies, and others. The committee emphasizes that HDOs ought not necessarily to satisfy all such claimants. It does acknowledge, however, that the mere existence of a database creates new demands for access and new users and uses. Consequently, those who establish health databases and HDOs may be creating something for which the end uses cannot always be anticipated. Large databases such as those maintained by HDOs will be dynamic; in the committee's view, policies regarding access to those databases should, therefore, be based on firm principles that are flexible enough to accommodate unavoidable changes and unanticipated uses.

Databases

A *database* is "a large collection of data in a computer, organized so that it can be expanded, updated, and retrieved rapidly for various uses." Although databases may eventually be linked (or linkable) to primary medical records held by health care practitioners, the report addresses databases composed of secondary records that are generated subsequent to the primary record or that are separate from any patient encounter. They are not intended to be *the* major source of information about specific patients for the treating physician. The committee was particularly interested in linked databases that have, at a minimum, two specific characteristics: (1) their linking involves movement of health data outside the care setting in which they have been generated and (2) they include person-identified or person-identifiable data.

Key Attributes of Databases

In reviewing the considerable variation in databases that might be accessed, controlled, or acquired by HDOs, the committee sought a simple way to characterize them by key attributes. It selected two critical dimensions of databases: *comprehensiveness* and *inclusiveness*.

Comprehensiveness. Comprehensiveness describes the completeness of records about patient care events. It refers to the amount of information one has on an individual both for each patient encounter with the health care system and for all of a patient's encounters over time.

Inclusiveness. Inclusiveness refers to which populations in a geographic area are included in a database. The more *inclusive* a database, the more it approaches coverage of 100 percent of the population that its developers intend to include. Databases that aim to provide information on the health of the community ought to have an enumeration of all residents of the community (e.g., metropolitan area, state) so that the information accurately reflects the entire population of the region, regardless of insurance category. Conversely, *inclusiveness* is reduced when membership is restricted to certain subgroups or when individuals expected to be in the database are missing.

Databases may be (and often are) designed to include only subsets of the entire population of a geographic area. The potential benefits of the database, however, will increase as the database moves toward being inclusive of the entire population of a defined geographic area.

Other Characteristics of Databases

The more comprehensive and inclusive they are, the more databases facilitate detailed and sophisticated uses. In turn, these attributes entail both greater anticipated benefits and possible harms. Factors determining the magnitude of either benefits or harms can depend on several properties of databases in addition to comprehensiveness and inclusiveness. Among the more important characteristics are linkage over time; the accuracy and completeness of data; whether the databases are under public- and private-sector control; and their origin (e.g., hospital discharge abstracts, self-completed questionnaires from patients, insurance claims, computer-based pharmacy files, computer-based patient records).

For purposes of this report, *person-identified data* contain pieces of information or facts that singly or collectively refer to one person and permit positive (or probable) identification of that individual. An obvious piece of identifying information is an individual's name. Other identifiers may be biometric, such as a fingerprint, a retinal print, or a DNA pattern. The committee uses *person-identifiable* to characterize information that definitely or probably can be said to refer to a specific person. It includes items of information (e.g., the fact of a physician visit on a given day) that will allow identification of an individual when combined with other facts (e.g., zip code of residence, date of birth, or gender). To render data non-person-identifiable, some data managers convert facts to a more general form before releasing those data to others. Concerns with person-identifiable data arise because of the ability of computers to combine and cross-match data in various databases. It is thus the more inclusive of these terms.

Throughout its discussions, the committee focused on *regional* databases—those that pertain to a *defined population* of individuals living in, or receiving health care in, some *specifiable geographic area.* Far-thinking experts envision a time when regional entities will be linked across the nation, even if their governance and operations remain close to home; this creates the very long-range view of a national health data repository (operated by either a single organization or a consortium of regional or state entities) as a federation of functionally linked databases from all regions of the country. Some proposed and developing HDO models are based on state legislation that requires submission of health data to a public agency. Other models are based on voluntary community cooperation and may be based on provider or local business coalitions.

Ensuring the Quality of Data

The real rewards from the development and operation of HDOs will depend heavily on the quality of their data, which must be reliable and valid for their intended purposes. Developers must ensure that the data in their systems are of high enough quality that analyses can be done in a credible, defensible manner. Success in meeting this responsibility will call for attention to the reliability, completeness, and accuracy of the data. Although the federal government may have to take the lead in standards development and improved coding systems, the committee urges HDOs to encourage and work toward national standards for coding and definitions for core data elements. Finally, the basic structure and content of these databases ought to be carefully designed from the beginning, but they must have sufficient capacity for expansion and change to accommodate the health care sector as it evolves in coming years.

To address these issues, the committee recommends that HDOs take responsibility for assuring data quality on an ongoing basis and, in particular, take affirmative steps to ensure: (1) the completeness and accuracy of the data in the databases for which they are responsible and (2) the validity of data for analytic purposes for which they are used (Recommendation 2.1, see Box S-1).

The absence of sufficient clinical information in most databases today leads investigators to acquire needed information through manual abstraction of relevant information in hospital records, but this approach is costly and time-consuming. Some means are needed to obtain this information more directly from patient records. The best method of enhancing the comprehensiveness of HDO databases and the accuracy and completeness of data elements is to move toward a computer-based patient record (CPR). This is admittedly a daunting task. Accordingly, the committee recommends that HDOs support and contribute to regional and national efforts to create computer-based patient records (Recommendation 2.2) including the development and adoption of relevant standards.

BOX S-1 COMMITTEE RECOMMENDATIONS

RECOMMENDATION 2.1 ACCURACY AND COMPLETENESS

To address these issues, the committee recommends that health database organizations take responsibility for assuring data quality on an ongoing basis and, in particular, take affirmative steps to ensure: (1) the completeness and accuracy of the data in the databases for which they are responsible and (2) the validity of data for analytic purposes for which they are used.

Part 2 of this recommendation applies to analyses that HDOs conduct. They cannot, of course, police the validity of data when used by others for purposes over which the HDOs have no a priori control.

RECOMMENDATION 2.2 COMPUTER-BASED PATIENT RECORD

Accordingly, the committee recommends that health database organizations support and contribute to regional and national efforts to create computer-based patient records.

(continued)

RECOMMENDATION 3.1 CONDUCTING PROVIDER-SPECIFIC EVALUATIONS

The committee recommends that health database organizations produce and make publicly available appropriate and timely summaries, analyses, and multivariate analyses of all or pertinent parts of their databases. More specifically, the committee recommends that health database organizations regularly produce and publish results of provider-specific evaluations of costs, quality, and effectiveness of care.

RECOMMENDATION 3.2 DESCRIBING ANALYTIC METHODS

The committee recommends that a health database organization report the following for any analysis it releases publicly:

• general methods for ensuring completeness and accuracy of their data;
• a description of the contents and the completeness of all data files and of the variables in each file used in the analyses;
• information documenting any study of the accuracy of variables used in the analyses.

RECOMMENDATION 3.3 MINIMIZING POTENTIAL HARM

The committee recommends that, to enhance the fairness and minimize the risk of unintended harm from the publication of evaluative studies that identify individual providers, each HDO should adhere to two principles as a standard procedure prior to publication: (1) to make available to and upon request supply to institutions, practitioners, or providers identified in an analysis all data required to perform an independent analysis, and to do so with reasonable time for such analysis prior to public release of the HDO results; and (2) to accompany publication of its own analyses with notice of the existence and availability of responsible challenges to, alternate analyses of, or explanation of the findings.

RECOMMENDATION 3.4 ADVOCACY OF DATA RELEASE: PROMOTING WIDE APPLICATIONS OF HEALTH-RELATED DATA

To foster the presumed benefits of widespread applications of HDO data, the committee recommends that health database organizations should release non-person-identifiable data upon request to other entities once those data are in analyzable form. This policy should include release to any organization that meets the following criteria:

• It has a public mission statement indicating that promoting public health or the release of information to the public is a major goal.
• It enforces explicit policies regarding protection of the confidentiality and integrity of data.

- It agrees not to publish, redisclose, or transfer the raw data to any other individual or organization.
- It agrees to disclose analyses in a public forum or publication.

The committee also recommends, as a related matter, that health database organizations make public their own policies governing the release of data.

RECOMMENDATION 4.1 PREEMPTIVE LEGISLATION

The committee recommends that the U.S. Congress move to enact preemptive legislation that will:

- establish a uniform requirement for the assurance of confidentiality and protection of privacy rights for person-identifiable health data and specify a Code of Fair Health Information Practices that ensures a proper balance among required disclosures, use of data, and patient privacy;
- impose penalties for violations of the act, including civil damages, equitable remedies, and attorney's fees where appropriate;
- provide for enforcement by the government and permit private aggrieved parties to sue;
- establish that compliance with the act's requirements would be a defense to legal actions based on charges of improper disclosure; and
- exempt health database organizations from public health reporting laws and compulsory process with respect to person-identifiable health data except for compulsory process initiated by record subjects.

RECOMMENDATION 4.2 DATA PROTECTION UNITS

The committee recommends that health database organizations establish a responsible administrative unit or board to promulgate and implement information policies concerning the acquisition and dissemination of information and establish whatever administrative mechanism is required to implement these policies. Such an administrative unit or board should:

- promulgate and implement policies concerning data protection and analyses based on such data;
- develop and implement policies that protect the confidentiality of all person-identifiable information, consistent with other policies of the organization and relevant state and federal law;
- develop and disseminate educational materials for the general public that will describe in understandable terms the analyses and their interpretation of the rights and responsibilities of individuals and the protections accorded their data by the organization;

(continued)

    • develop and implement security practices in the manual and automated data processing and storage systems of the organization; and

    • develop and implement a comprehensive employee training program that includes instruction concerning the protection of person-identifiable data.

RECOMMENDATION 4.3 RELEASE OF PERSON-IDENTIFIED DATA

The committee recognizes that there must be release of patient-identified data related to the processing of health insurance claims. The committee recommends, however, that a health database organization *not* release person-identifiable information in any other circumstances *except* the following:

    • to other HDOs whose missions are compatible with and whose confidentiality and security protections are at least as stringent as their own;

    • to individuals for information about themselves;

    • to parents for information about a minor child except when such release is prohibited by law;

    • to legal representatives of incompetent patients for information about the patient;

    • to researchers with approval from their institution's properly constituted Institutional Review Board;

    • to licensed practitioners with a need to know when treating patients in life-threatening situations who are unable to consent at the time care is rendered; and

    • to licensed practitioners when treating patients in all other (non-life-threatening) situations, *but only with the informed consent of the patient.*

Otherwise, the committee recommends that health database organizations not authorize access to, or release of, information on individuals with or without informed consent.

RECOMMENDATION 4.4. RESTRICTING EMPLOYER ACCESS

The committee recommends that employers not be permitted to require receipt of an individual's data from a health database organization as a condition of employment or for the receipt of benefits.

PUBLIC DISCLOSURE OF DATA ON
HEALTH CARE PROVIDERS AND PRACTITIONERS

Chapter 3 examines public disclosure of data on health care practitioners and providers and presents recommendations about how HDOs can ensure that such analyses are fair to those identified and to the public.

HDOs are presumed to have two major capabilities. One is the ability to amass credible descriptive information and evaluative data on costs, quality, and cost-effectiveness for hospitals, physicians, and other health care facilities, agencies, and providers. The other is the capacity to analyze data to generate knowledge and then to make that knowledge available for purposes of controlling the costs and improving the quality of health care—that is, of obtaining value for health care dollars spent. The committee characterizes the activities that HDOs might pursue to accomplish these goals as *public disclosure*, defined as the timely communication, or publication and dissemination, of certain kinds of information to the public at large. The aims are to improve the public's understanding about health care issues generally and to help consumers select providers of health care.

The committee stance favoring public disclosure takes two forms. One is that the HDOs ought *themselves* to carry out some minimum number of consumer-oriented studies and analyses and publish them routinely. The other is that HDOs must make appropriate data available for *others* to use in such studies and analyses, where the expectation is that the results of such work will be publicly disclosed.

Acceptance of HDO activities and products relating to public disclosure over time will depend in part on the balance struck for fairness to patients, the public in general, payers, and health care providers. Fairness to patients involves protecting their privacy and the confidentiality of information about them. Fairness to the public involves distributing the accurate and reliable information needed to make informed decisions about providers and health care interventions. Finally, fairness to providers entails ensuring that data and analyses are reliable, valid, and impartial, giving providers some opportunity to confirm data and methods before information is released to the public, and finding some means of publishing their perspectives when it is released.

Key Factors in Public Disclosure

Public disclosure is acceptable *only* when it (1) involves information and analytic results that come from studies that have been well conducted, (2) is based on data that can be shown to be reliable and valid for the purposes at hand, and (3) is accompanied by appropriate educational material.

Several elements are crucial to successful public disclosure of health-related information. Among the more significant are topics of analysis (e.g., hospital-specific death rates) and who is identified in such releases (e.g., health plans, institutional providers, and individual practitioners). The full report explores these matters in some detail.

In the committee's view, disclosure of information about larger aggregations of health care providers, such as hospitals, will generally be less prone to cause undeserved losses of reputation, income, or career than disclosure of information on specific individual practitioners. The committee takes the position that public disclosure is a valuable goal to pursue, to the extent that it is carried out with due attention to accuracy and clarity and does not undermine the quality assurance and quality improvement (QA/QI) programs that health care institutions and organizations conduct internally.

Analyses and Disclosure of Results

The committee recommends that HDOs produce and make publicly available appropriate and timely summaries, analyses, and multivariate analyses of all or pertinent parts of their databases. More specifically, the committee recommends that HDOs regularly produce and publish results of provider-specific evaluations of costs, quality, and effectiveness of care (Recommendation 3.1).

The subjects of such analyses should include hospitals, health maintenance organizations, and other capitated systems; fee-for-service group practices of all sorts; physicians, dentists, podiatrists, nurse-practitioners, or other independent practitioners; long-term-care facilities; and other health providers on whom the HDOs maintain reliable and valid information.

The intended audience for publication or disclosure is the public, not simply member or sponsoring organizations. Some HDOs may be based in the private sector, operate chiefly for the benefit of for-profit entities, and have no connection with or mandate from states or the federal government. In these cases, the imperative to make information and analytic results available to the public on a broad scale is less clear. In the committee's view, however, the charters and bylaws of such HDOs ought to include firm commitments to conduct consumer-oriented studies, and where state legislation is used to establish HDOs or similar entities (e.g., data commissions), the enabling statutes themselves should contain such requirements. If public funds are used to support the development of HDOs, public release of analyses should be required as a condition of funding.

Describing Analytic Methods

The committee recommends that an HDO report the following for any analysis it releases publicly:

• general methods for ensuring completeness and accuracy of data;
• a description of the contents and the completeness of all data files and of the variables in each file used in the analyses;

• information documenting any study of the accuracy of variables used in the analyses (Recommendation 3.2).

The committee expects HDOs to accompany public disclosure of provider-specific information with clear descriptions of the database (including documentation of its completeness, accuracy, and data sources), of methods of risk adjustment, and of appropriate uses by the public, payers, and government of the data and analyses—including notice of those uses of data and analyses that are *not* valid.

Minimizing Potential Harms

The committee has taken a strong pro-disclosure stance toward comparative, evaluative data. Disclosure proponents assume that such studies will be done responsibly, and the public has every right to expect that to be the case. The committee sees some potential for harm in public release of comparative or evaluative studies on costs, quality, or other measures of health care delivery, however, and did not wish to rely solely on marketplace correctives; it believes that a more protective stance is needed. To enhance the fairness and minimize the risk of unintended harm from the publication of evaluative studies that identify individual providers, the committee recommends that each HDO should adhere to two principles as a standard procedure prior to publication: (1) to make available to and upon request supply to institutions, practitioners, or providers identified in an analysis all data required to perform an independent analysis, and to do so with reasonable time for such analysis prior to public release of the HDO results; and (2) to accompany publication of its own analyses with notice of the existence and availability of responsible challenges to, alternate analyses of, or explanations of the findings (Recommendation 3.3). Feedback from providers may reveal problems with data quality and study methods that HDOs would want to remedy. This set of recommendations reflects what might be regarded as a fairness doctrine.

Releasing Data

HDOs might well serve as a major repository of data that will be accessible to other groups. To foster the presumed benefits of widespread applications of HDO data, the committee recommends that HDOs should release non-person-identifiable data upon request to other entities once those data are in analyzable form. This policy should include release to any organization that meets the following criteria:

- It has a public mission statement indicating that promoting public health or the release of information to the public is a major goal.
- It enforces explicit policies regarding protection of the confidentiality and integrity of data.
- It agrees not to publish, redisclose, or transfer the raw data to any other individual or organization.
- It agrees to disclose analyses in a public forum or publication.

The committee also recommends, as a related matter, that HDOs make public their own policies governing the release of data (Recommendation 3.4).

STRENGTHENING QUALITY ASSURANCE AND QUALITY IMPROVEMENT PROGRAMS THROUGH DATA FEEDBACK

HDOs could help to improve the quality of health care through direct assistance to health care institutions, facilities, and clinical groups by making available to providers and practitioners the data for or results of evaluative studies of their services and those of their peers.

The committee assumed such an activity would occur chiefly as a part of or as an adjunct to a formal QA/QI process that providers and plans might conduct. Information on identified providers and individual clinicians would be made available to organizations' QA/QI programs so that they could take constructive action.

Some readers may think that a tension will exist between public disclosure and such feedback for internal use, but the committee believes that both will be important tools available to HDOs to improve quality and foster informed choices in health care. Thus, it voices support for both functions, in the belief that one activity does not—or at least need not—discredit the other and that effective combination strategies can be designed.

CONFIDENTIALITY AND PRIVACY OF PERSONAL DATA

Chapter 4 of the IOM report examines privacy, confidentiality, and security of information about individuals or patients—what this committee refers to as person-identified or person-identifiable data.

Two somewhat distinct trends have led to increased access to the primary health record and subsequent concerns about privacy. One has to do with primary health records, however they are created and maintained, and the other involves health records stored electronically.

The increasing complexity of health care and the involvement of greater numbers of individuals in health care delivery has resulted in ever more people accessing the health record to deliver and document care. The primary health record serves many purposes beyond direct health care, and many parties external to the healing relationship seek person-identified information. Of particular concern is the confidentiality of health information that is stored electronically; the aggregation of information on individuals from diverse databases will make computer-based health data increasingly valuable and in need of protection from unauthorized access.

Existing ethical, legal, and other approaches to protecting confidentiality and privacy of personal health data offer some confidentiality safeguards, but major gaps and limitations remain. The committee's recommendations are intended to strengthen current protections for confidentiality and privacy of health-related data, particularly for information acquired by HDOs.

Privacy and Privacy Rights

The most general and common view of privacy conveys notions of withdrawal, seclusion, secrecy, or of being kept away from public view, but with no pejorative overtones. In public policy generally, and in health policy in particular, privacy takes on a special meaning, namely, that of *informational privacy*, "a state or condition of controlled access to personal information." Informational privacy is infringed, by definition, whenever another party has access to one's personal information by reading, listening, or using any of the other senses. Such loss of privacy may be entirely acceptable and intended by the individual, or it may be inadvertent, unacceptable, and even unknown to the individual.

This definition of privacy thus reflects two underlying notions. First, privacy in general and informational privacy in particular are always matters of degree. Rarely is anyone in a condition of complete physical or informational inaccessibility to others, nor would they wish to remain so. Second, although informational privacy may be valuable and deserving of protection, many thoughtful privacy advocates argue that it does not, in itself, have moral significance or inherent value.

Nonetheless, informational privacy has value for all in our society, and it accordingly has special claims on our attention. The most salient federal protections for privacy are the principles of fair information practices embodied in the Privacy Act of 1974. The act addresses the right to know about, challenge, control, and correct information about oneself in federal government databases.

Privacy Rights

No explicit right to privacy is guaranteed by the Constitution of the United States. The presumed right as the basis of a civil action is based on legal opinion written by Justice Louis D. Brandeis in 1890, and its constitutional status derives from various amendments to the Bill of Rights. The Constitution generally has not provided strong protection for the confidentiality of individual health care information; the constitutional protection for informational privacy is very limited and derived from case law interpreting the Constitution.

To assert a right is to make a special kind of claim. Rights designate some interests of the individual that are sufficiently important to hold others under a duty to promote and protect, sometimes even at the expense of maximizing or even achieving the social good. Two interests are widely cited as providing the moral justification for privacy rights: the individual's interest in autonomy and the instrumental value that privacy may have in promoting other valuable human goods.

Whether HDOs can achieve their potential for good in the face of their possible impact on privacy will likely turn on the interplay of three considerations. First, to what extent do HDOs provide important (and perhaps irreplaceable) health care benefits to the regions in which they operate, and perhaps to the nation? Second, how will adequate privacy safeguards be incorporated into the HDOs? Third, do the societal benefits resulting from the implementation of HDOs outweigh the privacy risks?

There cannot be much doubt that HDOs will serve legitimate societal interests. Nevertheless, because HDOs will represent one of the more comprehensive and sensitive automated personal record databases yet established, the system inevitably implicates interests protected by informational privacy principles.

Confidentiality

Confidentiality relates to disclosure or nondisclosure of information. Historically, a duty to honor confidentiality has arisen with respect to information disclosed in the context of a relationship such as that between a physician and a patient. When one is concerned about data disclosure, whether or not any relationship exists between a data subject and a data holder, an essential construct is that of *data confidentiality*. It is the status accorded data indicating that they are protected and must be treated as such.

Exceptions to confidentiality requirements are widely acknowledged. Situations exist in which sensitive health information about individuals must be disclosed to third parties. Such reporting requirements are justified by society's need for information. Examples include mandatory reporting of communicable diseases and gunshot wounds. Physicians and other health professionals may also be required to divulge personal health information under legal "compulsory process," which may take the form of subpoenas or discovery requests enforced by court order.

The most important exception to the rule of confidentiality, however, is that of disclosure authorized by consent of a patient or a patient representative in the course of applying for insurance, employment, or reimbursement for medical claims. Such disclosure may or may not be justifiable and acceptable to patients. In such a case, however, consent cannot be truly voluntary or informed. Such authorizations are often not *voluntary* because the patient feels compelled to sign the authorization or forego the benefit sought, and they are not *informed* because the patient cannot know in advance what information will be in the record, who will subsequently have access to it, or how it will be used. Although such consent procedures are a necessary adjunct to other autonomy protections, this committee generally does not regard these procedures as sufficient in themselves to protect sensitive information from inappropriate disclosure.

Legal and ethical confidentiality obligations are the same whether health records are kept on paper or computer-based media. Current laws, however, have significant weaknesses. First, and very important, the degree to which confidentiality is required under current law varies according to the holder of the information and the type of information held.

Second, legal obligations of confidentiality often vary widely within a single state and from state to state, making it difficult to ascertain the legal obligations that a given HDO will have, particularly if it operates in a multistate area. These state-by-state and intrastate variations and inconsistencies in privacy and confidentiality laws are well established among those knowledgeable about health care records law; they are worrisome because some HDOs will routinely transmit data across state lines.

Third, current laws offer individuals little real protection against redisclosure of their confidential health information to unauthorized recipients for a number of reasons. Once patients have consented to an initial disclosure of information (for example, to obtain insurance reimbursement), they have lost control of further disclosure. Information disclosed for one purpose may be used for unrelated purposes without the subject's knowledge or consent. Such redisclosure practices represent a yawning gap in confidentiality protection.

As a practical matter, policing redisclosure of one's personal health information is difficult and may be impossible. At a minimum, such policing requires substantial resources and commitment. With the use of computer and telecommunications networks, an individual may never discover that a particular disclosure has occurred, even though he or she suffers significant harm—such as inability to obtain employment, credit, housing, or insurance—as a result of such disclosure. Pursuing legal remedies may result in additional disclosure of the individual's private health information.

Further, federal law may preempt state confidentiality requirements or protections without imposing new ones. For example, the Employment

Retirement Insurance Security Act (ERISA) preempts some state insurance laws with respect to employers' self-insured health plans, yet ERISA is silent on confidentiality obligations.

Last, enforcing rights through litigation is costly, and money damages may not provide adequate redress for the harm done by the improper disclosure.

Security

In the context of health record information, confidentiality implies controlled access to and protection against unauthorized access to, modification of, or destruction of health data. In computer-based or computer-controlled systems, security is implemented when a defined system functions in a defined operational environment, serves a defined set of users, contains prescribed data and operational programs, has defined network connections and interactions with other systems, and incorporates safeguards to protect the system against a defined threat to the system, its resources, and its data.

Two consequences flow from defining data as sensitive and needing protection. First, those data must be made secure; second, access must be controlled. Access control can be operationalized by HDO planners and legislators in a form that this committee would term "information-use policy." It leads to policymaking about who may be allowed to use health-related information and how they may use it. It might also include consideration of whether some data should be collected at all.

In a study that focuses on the protection of health-related data about individuals, defining which items are health-related is more difficult than one might initially think. Any data element in medical records, and many data items from other records, *could* be considered either health-related or sensitive, or both. In considering the actions of HDOs, this committee proceeds from an assumption that *all* information concerning an individual and any transactions relating directly or indirectly to health care that HDOs access or maintain as databases must be regarded as potentially requiring privacy protections.

A National Identification System or Dossier

HDOs may be perceived as enabling the development of a national identification system or dossier. Privacy advocates can be expected to express acute concern about the potential for HDOs to be linked not only with one another, but, more importantly, with government databases and with other personal databases such as the financial, credit, and lifestyle databases maintained by consumer reporting agencies. The committee believes that HDO proponents should take every practicable step, including those recommended by the committee, to assure that HDOs will not contribute to the development of a national identification database.

Personal Identifiers and the Social Security Number

The personal identifier (ID) that is used in an HDO to "label" each of the individuals on whom it keeps data is a crucial issue. It not only is related to past practices, but it will also be strongly influenced, if not mandated, by the health care reform actions now under way in the nation.

An "Ideal" Identifier

The choice of a personal ID that is satisfactory for the operational needs of health care delivery but at the same time assures the confidentiality of medical data and the privacy of individuals is neither easy nor casual. An ideal identifier would meet the requirements described in detail in the report. Superficially, the choice would be the Social Security number (SSN), Medicare number, or something similar simply because people are accustomed to using them, systems are used to handling them, and the government would bear the burden of administering the enumeration system and the cost of assigning new numbers. The SSN has many faults, however, that are familiar to researchers and privacy experts. Perhaps the most salient of these is that if the SSN were to become the ID for health care delivery, linkage of medical records to all the other databases would become easy.

The most problematic objection to the SSN as a medical ID is that it has no legal protection, and because its use is so widespread, there is no chance of retroactively giving it such protection. As a data element, it is not characterized by law as confidential; hence, organizations holding it are under no legal requirement to protect it or to limit the ways in which it is used. Its use is for all practical purposes unconstrained, and this makes the risk of commingling health data with all other forms of personal data and an individual's actions extremely high. Major privacy risks arise when medical information is used in decisions unrelated to health care, such as employment, promotion, and eligibility for insurance or other benefits. Further, access by unauthorized users would be very much simpler because the SSN is so readily available.

Relevance to HDOs of Existing Laws
on Confidentiality and Privacy

The committee examined existing law—constitutional, statutory, and common law—for its relevance to HDOs and its adequacy for protecting patient privacy and confidentiality. The committee also examined the way these laws might affect the design, establishment, and operation of HDOs.

It concludes that most of this body of law is unlikely to apply to HDOs. With the exception of laws that regulate certain information considered sensitive, existing laws regulate recordkeepers and their recordkeeping practices; they do not regulate on the basis of either the content or the subject matter of a record.

Recommendations Regarding Protection of Patient and Person-identifiable Data

Given (1) the unprecedented comprehensiveness and inclusiveness of information expected to be in HDO databases, (2) the generally scanty and inconsistent legal protections across geopolitical jurisdictions, and (3) the current public interest in and concern about privacy protections, the committee believes that HDOs have both an obligation and an opportunity to fashion well-delineated privacy protection programs that will also foster the realization of HDO goals. Some of these protections, such as the establishment of data protection boards and organizational policies regarding security and access control, can be implemented in the short term. Others, such as passage of federal preemptive legislation, will likely require longer-term efforts.

Preemptive Legislation

The committee recommends that the U.S. Congress move to enact preemptive legislation that will:

* establish a uniform requirement for the assurance of confidentiality and protection of privacy rights for person-identifiable health data and specify a Code of Fair *Health* Information Practices that ensures a proper balance among required disclosures, use of data, and patient privacy;
* impose penalties for violations of the act, including civil damages, equitable remedies, and attorney's fees where appropriate;
* provide for enforcement by the government and permit private aggrieved parties to sue;
* establish that compliance with the act's requirements would be a defense to legal actions based on charges of improper disclosure; and
* exempt health database organizations from public health reporting laws and compulsory process with respect to person-identifiable health data except for compulsory process initiated by record subjects (Recommendation 4.1).

In the last item, the committee believes that both processes—public health reporting and responding to compulsory process such as subpoenas—should remain the responsibility of the provider, as is now the case.

The committee concludes that federal preemptive legislation is required to establish uniform requirements for the preservation of confidentiality and protection of privacy rights for health data about individuals. It further advises that Congress enact such legislation, including a Code of Fair *Health* Information Practices, as soon as possible. At a minimum, federal legislation should establish a floor and allow states or HDOs to implement more stringent standards so that state-imposed safeguards are not weakened.

Although current state protections often apply duties of confidentiality to the recordkeeper (e.g., the hospital), such protection is no longer in effect once the data have left the recordkeeper's control. This means that health data can be deprived of legal protection unless such protection is specified by another law; furthermore, such protection is likely to be left to the discretion of organizations or individuals who acquire such information as secondary data. That is little shelter indeed. Therefore, legislation should clearly establish that the confidentiality of person-identifiable data is a property afforded to the data elements themselves, regardless of who holds those data. Proper preemptive legislation should also provide for enforcement by government officials and aggrieved private parties. It should also impose penalties for violations of the act. It will be important that the legislation clarify whether individuals have standing to bring suit.

Federal legislation can be expected to encourage standard setting in such areas as connectivity and transmissions standards. Standard setting is a major obstacle to the development of automated medical records and will be no less a problem for HDOs. Thus, the committee sees the route of federal legislation as one more mechanism for addressing this problem for all computer-based systems that deal with health data.

Data Protection Units

HDOs will need clear and enforceable, written organizational policies and procedures in several areas: informing patients of their rights regarding their own data; protecting medical information and materials; ensuring the accuracy of data; and verifying compliance with their policies. Members of the public should be able to request and receive clearly written materials describing these policies. Although precise policies cannot be written to cover every eventuality, they must be broad enough to address the most common situations, such as types of data and potential requestors. Organizations should also make considerable efforts to educate (and reeducate) staff, the public, and potential requestors about these policies. Thus, the committee recommends that HDOs establish a responsible administrative unit or board to promulgate information policies concerning the acquisition and dissemination of information and to establish whatever administrative mechanism is required to implement these policies. Such an administrative unit or board specifically should:

- promulgate and implement policies concerning data protection and analyses based on such data;
- develop and implement policies that protect the confidentiality of all person-identifiable information, consistent with other policies of the organization and relevant state and federal law;
- develop and disseminate educational materials for the general public that will describe in understandable terms the analyses and their interpretation of the rights and responsibilities of individuals and the protections accorded their data by the organization;
- develop and implement security practices in the manual and automated data processing and storage systems of the organization; and
- develop and implement a comprehensive employee training program that includes instruction concerning the protection of person-identifiable data (Recommendation 4.2).

The commitment to protection of confidentiality of the governing body and executives of the HDO will be critical, and these objectives should be written into the organization's bylaws. The committee strongly advises that HDO policy boards include in their policies and procedures fair health information practices. Any HDO should consider these practices as the foundation of its privacy framework and depart from them only after careful consideration and explanation.

Legislation and organizational policies have sometimes distinguished among levels of sensitivity of various elements of health-related data, based on the belief that it is possible to identify categories of data that warrant special protection. Despite precedent for adopting such a stance, this committee has decided otherwise. It has concluded that a given data element cannot always be designated reliably as inherently sensitive; rather, the sensitivity of data depends on the kinds of harm to which individuals are or believe themselves to be vulnerable if the information were known to others. Such assessments could differ dramatically from one person to another, one circumstance to another, one place to another, and over time as cultural attitudes change. Rather than recommending special protections for certain categories of data, the committee prefers that all data accessed by HDOs be afforded stringent, and essentially equal, protection.

Release of Person-Identified Data

Policies Relating to Access and Disclosure

Clearly, the question of who *outside* the HDO has access to what data, and under what circumstances, is supremely important and is the essence of the privacy issue from the patient's point of view. The committee takes up these matters in a series of recommendations (presented below) that refer to person-identified or person-identifiable information only. As discussed earlier in this summary, the committee recommends release and disclosure of non-person-identifiable information that protects patient identity but that provides reliable, valid, timely, and useful descriptive and evaluative information on a full range of health care providers and clinicians.

The committee recognizes that there must be release of patient-identified data related to the processing of health insurance claims. The committee recommends, however, that a health database organization *not* release person-identifiable information in other circumstances *except* the following:

- to other HDOs whose missions are compatible with and whose confidentiality and security protections are at least as stringent as their own;
- to individuals for information about themselves;
- to parents for information about a minor child except when such release is prohibited by law;
- to legal representatives of incompetent patients for information about the patient;
- to researchers with approval from their institution's properly constituted Institutional Review Board;
- to licensed practitioners with a need to know when treating patients in life-threatening situations who are unable to consent at the time care is rendered; and
- to licensed practitioners when treating patients in all other (non-life-threatening) situations, *but only with the informed consent of the patient.*

Otherwise, the committee recommends that health database organizations not authorize access to, or release of, person-identifiable information with or without informed consent (Recommendation 4.3).

In the last item, the committee has specifically recommended that consent for access to the database be a necessary and sufficient condition in only one circumstance: when needed by the treating practitioner in non-life threatening situation. In such a situation it will be important that specific consent mechanisms be in place. Otherwise, the committee believes that informed consent should *not* be required for release of person-identifiable information in six situations as described below.

First, HDOs will need to acquire information about out-of-area care provided to persons in their databases and should be able to do so. Second, HDOs also ought to release person-identifiable data without requiring consent when individuals seek information about themselves. The third and fourth cases above reflect the need to care for minors and persons who are legally incompetent to give consent for themselves.

The fifth case concerns researchers with approval from relevant human subjects committees or institutional review boards (IRBs). In this case, person-identified information is not being sought *by* a patient or *for care of* a patient, but to conduct studies that are regarded as being in the public's interest. Such uses of the databases are considered by this committee to be central and vital to the effective implementation of HDOs.

The sixth case involves treatment of licensed practitioners with a need to know in life-threatening situations, whom the committee believes also ought to be able to access data about a patient. This requires that the patient be unable to consent at the time care is rendered.

The seventh case—the release of data to licensed practitioners when treating patients in all other (non-life-threatening) situations, but only with the informed consent *of the patient*—is the only case in which the committee has recommended the use of informed consent to release of person-identifiable information. Such a circumstance might occur when a treating physician wishes to access the HDO database in addition to the medical records he or she keeps. For example, information on medications prescribed by other practitioners might be pertinent. In such cases, the treating practitioner should obtain explicit consent of the patient. As discussed earlier, consent might be given electronically and might be time limited.

Finally, the committee recommends above that HDOs *not* authorize access to or release of health information on individuals *with or without the informed consent* of the individual in any situation or to any requestor other than those stated above. To ensure that individuals (i.e., patients, parents of minor children, or patients' legal representatives) are not placed in an untenable situation concerning release information, the committee has opted for a position that does not rely on consent procedures insofar as most uses or disclosures of data are concerned. It prefers to rely on stringent policies against disclosure or release of personal information on individuals. The consent procedures described in this recommendation are for release of information by the HDO. Patients will always be able to consent to release of information directly by each of their care providers.

Special circumstances exist in the health sector that are of particular concern to the committee. One involves the current practice of extensive exchange of medical information between employer and payer with little control by providers or patients. This practice has dramatic implications for patients whose information is accessed by an HDO if the employer and payer are readily able to tap into data in the network. Such exchanges of information could be especially harmful to patients because the information exchanged could cover all encounters the patient has with the health care system (not just those covered by insurance or by the employer's health plan). The committee acknowledges the danger and inappropriateness of these practices and regarded them as sufficiently worrisome that it recommends that employers not be permitted to require receipt of an individual's data from a health database organization as a condition of employment or for the receipt of benefits (Recommendation 4.4).

Universal Person-Identifiers

The committee believes that unique individual person-identifiers are essential to facilitate the efficient operation and data interchange of HDOs. The committee also recognizes that there are strong arguments against the SSN being used as the unique identifier. The great majority of the committee agreed on the need for a new unique identifier on the grounds that the SSN offers too many opportunities to breach confidentiality. The creation of a new number would (1) permit legislative protection of that number, (2) offer the possibility of providing greater protection for health information than is possible with the SSN, and (3) likely occur at the time of implementation of universal health care coverage, which will, if enacted, require some scheme for unique identification.

THE FUTURE

Little is yet known about how HDOs will function, what their likely benefits will be, or how they will evolve over time. In emphasizing the use of aggregated health information, the Clinton Administration's health reform proposal has put the issue of confidentiality squarely on the agenda. What is not known is which uses of health care information will be acceptable and will wisely serve the needs of society. Moreover, new uses for and users of data will emerge, some raising new threats to privacy. Accordingly, the privacy dimension of health care information is dynamic and should be revisited from time to time.

Regional HDOs hold tremendous promise for evaluating and improving health care and implementing effective new ways to protect health information. Although the great public benefit may be easily understood, the potential for harm or lack of fairness may create concern and fear in many. To gain public support for the vision advanced in this report—and to ensure the best public use of the health-related information that will be released—

HDOs, government agencies, and public- and private-sector institutions must implement carefully planned strategies for fairness and privacy protection and educate the public, health care providers, policymakers, and patients about these protections. This report is intended to be an early step in that educational and public policy-making process.

1

Introduction

The Bradys have recently moved to Capital City from a small town in another state. According to the family practitioner in their former residence, their young daughter needs heart surgery, and they want to identify a surgeon and hospital with considerable experience and good outcomes to do the surgery. They need to choose a health plan from among those offered by Mr. Brady's employer that covers services by these providers. Which plan should they choose?

Mike, a shy three-year-old, has been brought to the attention of the Montgomery County Protective Services unit because of concerns about his failure to thrive. He has been living on and off with an aunt. She has no records of any previous medical care and no special knowledge of any illnesses. How can the county caseworker acquire health-related information as part of her responsibilities to manage this case and make recommendations for appropriate referrals?

Alice Johns, an elderly woman who rarely visits any physicians, appears in Dr. Mark's office with fever and other flu-like symptoms. Dr. Mark needs to know what infectious organisms have been appearing in their community lately as a guide to treating Mrs. Johns appropriately on this one examination. How can he quickly get this information?

Gerry Middlemarch, a health services researcher at State University, leads a team that is studying treatments for low back pain. They want to know: What are the outcomes for patients who have surgery, who attend pain control clinics, or receive chiropractic services? How well are these patients functioning? How satisfied are they with their treatment? What have been the relative costs of care?

A man in jogging clothes arrives unconscious at the emergency department of Santa Teresa Memorial Hospital, having been found collapsed at an intersection nearby. Who is he? What medications is he taking? Is he diabetic? Does he have a history of heart disease? Is he allergic to any medications?

Officials in the Columbia County Department of Health must begin to plan for long-term development of health facilities in the area, making the best use of local resources, tax revenues, and bonds. In particular, they need to decide: whether to renovate the only community hospital to expand traditional inpatient care services; whether to shift inpatient beds to rehabilitation and skilled nursing beds or to authorize construction of a new nursing home; and whether to establish additional neighborhood clinics for maternal and child care, to upgrade the emergency medical services system for both adults and children, or to add staff for substance abuse facilities. How can they determine the community's greatest needs now and five to ten years from now, and how can they calculate the most cost-effective use of the county's limited health budget?

The Tectonic Plate Manufacturing Company, a large employer in Ironweed City, is facing soaring costs for its health benefit plan. The company is a somewhat paternalistic one, with a generous health plan, and it does not want simply to direct its employees to the "cheapest" hospitals in the area. As the metropolitan area has many hospitals, which range widely in size, services offered, and reputation, how can the company determine which ones will likely have good outcomes with only moderate charges?

The local chapter of the National Paralysis Foundation has a young and energetic executive vice president who wants to move the organization more in the direction of outreach and case management and away from simple fund raising. She wants to find better ways to identify children and families to whom a greater range of services might be offered. How can she best target these efforts in this city of 800,000 as well as in the larger suburban counties surrounding the city?

These vignettes are fiction. Yet, every day, across the nation, these and similar scenarios play out and each describes a valid and legitimate need for medical information. Sometimes the questions are answered quickly and correctly. Sometimes they are not, especially when no central repository of information or network of data sources exists or can be queried easily. In response to this situation, many experts in the health care field share an exciting vision: a community-oriented database or group of linked databases that can address all kinds of inquiries about health care matters in a timely and satisfactory manner.

This report from an Institute of Medicine (IOM) study committee examines the potential that existing and emerging health databases offer for fulfilling this vision. It gives special attention to appropriate uses of data in such repositories and to adequate protections for the privacy and confidentiality of individually identifiable information. It concludes that "health database organizations" can play a pivotal role in health care delivery and research but that they, or other interested parties, will have to take significant steps to ensure that private information remains private. To promote these ends, the committee advances recommendations that are detailed in subsequent chapters. Taken together, the committee's findings, conclusions, and recommendations underscore the extreme importance of the ways in which health care information is to be controlled and used in the future.

ADVANCING THE PROSPECTS FOR COMPREHENSIVE HEALTH DATABASES AND NETWORKS

The Problem

The desire to understand and improve the performance of the health care system begets a need for data to answer the questions that opened this report. This, in turn, motivates proposals for the creation and maintenance of comprehensive, population-based health care databases that can provide such information with ease and reliability. The past quarter-century has already seen an exponential rise in the number, complexity, and sophistication of health databases, yet they do not approach in extent, inclusiveness, or quality the vision offered above.

What is the state of health databases today? The databases briefly noted here illustrate the range of existing databases; Chapter 2 discusses selected databases in more detail. Among the oldest and best known of the so-called administrative data sets are those associated with the Medicare program, particularly the Part A and Part B files (for, respectively, inpatient and outpatient services) and more recent compilations such as the National Claims History system. All states maintain some form of database for their Medicaid programs; more than two-thirds maintain databases on hospital discharges, such as the Statewide Planning and Research Cooperative System (SPARCS) database in New York State; a similar proportion collect information on emergency medical services (chiefly for prehospital emergency vehicle runs); and more and more states are establishing state databases to support research, policy analysis, and performance of the health care delivery system. As something of a counterpoint to existing databases in the United States, Canadian provincial databases, such as those in Manitoba, contain information on virtually all health encounters (inpatient and outpatient) for all persons in the province, permitting the analyses contemplated for state databases and by this committee.

Other databases are maintained by insurers in the private sector; they are derived from insurance claim forms and include groups covered by service benefit, indemnity, or employer-based health insurance plans. In the past, such databases served chiefly to adjudicate claims for reimbursement; today, they also support research applications. Some health maintenance organizations (HMOs), particularly group and staff model HMOs maintain patient health records that can be used both for patient care and research. Other major databases (and public use files) have been specially constructed for research studies, such as the RAND Health Insurance Experiment, and for national surveys, such as the National Medical Expenditures Survey and the National Health and Nutrition Examination Survey and its various supplements.

Despite this activity and progress, many difficulties obstruct the realization of this committee's vision. Some problems relate to the content and structure of current health databases; others pertain more to the difficulties of creating and maintaining comprehensive databases. One major drawback is that most information gathered today reflects independent events and a single setting (almost always hospital admissions). In the absence of computer-based patient records, even hospital databases are often limited in the quality and quantity of the patient data they contain. Correspondingly, databases often have little or no information about ambulatory and other nonhospital services; thus, they lack facts about primary care, despite the major impact that primary care has on the public's health. Another, related challenge is that episodes of care—longitudinal records that tell how patients fare "in the system as a whole"—cannot easily be constructed. In addition, currently available information is not (or cannot easily be) adjusted for important characteristics about patients' sociodemographic circumstances or health status, and this makes it difficult to compare the performance of providers and practitioners or to set insurance premiums or capitated payments correctly and without bias.

Databases created from information generated by the use of health care services, such as those assembled from insurance claim forms, reflect information only on users of the health care system; missing is information on those who never seek or obtain care. As a consequence, planners and others usually cannot use today's databases to learn much about the population as a whole or to assess unmet needs in a community. Moreover, many contemporary databases are essentially archives of information collected at some time in the (possibly remote) past; this retrospective aspect of the information may give little if any support for real-time patient care. Furthermore, much more information will be available on what was done to patients (the processes of care) than on the end results (the outcomes) of that care, yet those wishing to make decisions about treatments or providers prefer, indeed require, outcome-related information. Even the clinical information, if gathered through insurance claims or encounter forms, may be quite limited and of questionable reliability and validity; if obtained from paper-based medical records, then considerable manual abstraction and computer data entry are required (all tasks that introduce their own inaccuracies and biases). The cleanest and most comprehensive data on some topics may come from research projects, but such databases have their own limitations in populations covered, timeliness, and access by individuals or organizations not involved in research.

Other issues may be more prosaic, albeit no less difficult. Chief among these is cost. Creating and maintaining databases, whatever the original source(s) of information, can be expensive. When private entities bear the costs, they may see little reason to share information with others who have not helped to shoulder the monetary burden; when the public sector bears the costs, other claims on the public treasury may take precedence.

Another obstacle is competition in the health field. Rival health care providers or insurers have not been (and are not likely to be) willing to share what they may regard as sensitive, proprietary information. Antitrust considerations may also play a role in the reluctance of possible or actual competitors to share data; health care reform may prompt reinterpretation of antitrust rules, but this area was well beyond the committee's charge or expertise. Even organizations that do not directly compete may see little or no incentive to make their databases available to others. In any case, such groups may not wish to participate in collective actions to set standards for terminology, definitions of data elements, or electronic transmission of information; this has been especially true for organizations whose long-established internal systems would be expensive to change or upgrade.

Finally, as reasons accumulate for creating large health databases, so do the possibilities that such databases (or, more correctly, their users) will do harm to patients, to providers (institutions, physicians, and others), to payers (government, private insurers, and corporations), and to the public at large. The balance between the advantages of such databases and their potential for harm, or at least unfairness, to some groups is not yet clear, and the question of whether and how such entities ought to evolve has been incompletely explored. This perception of potential harm from the proliferation of large databases is itself a barrier to their development.

The Opportunity

In the past few years, diverse groups of researchers, business leaders, and policymakers at state and regional levels have begun to design and develop an array of databases, networks, repositories, and the like. These are intended to overcome some of the above problems and to permit far more sophisticated analyses of community health needs, practice patterns, and costs and quality of care than has been possible to date. The interests that have prompted such action cover a broad range: controlling business costs attributable to health benefits; applying computer technologies to decrease costs of processing insurance claims; evaluating and improving health care; conducting technology assessments; planning the expansion and contraction of health care facilities and services across the nation; and transmitting medical history information for an increasingly mobile population. The success of health care reform—as well as the ability to assess the effect of a reformed system on the health of the public—depends on access to the kinds of data that too often are unavailable.

Coincident with this conjunction of needs, interests, and enthusiasm are greatly enhanced electronic capabilities for data management in many aspects of daily life. Comprehensive, computer-based health data files can easily be linked, and information from those files can be moved essentially instantaneously. Thus, an unparalleled opportunity exists to apply computer technologies creatively to address many of the informational needs and data problems noted above. This report focuses on the actions that might be taken to foster such action and progress by what the IOM committee terms *health database organizations*.

HEALTH DATABASE ORGANIZATIONS

Many kinds of health databases, networks, and repositories exist today, although they differ in many characteristics. They may be created by business coalitions, built by entities supported with private funds, mandated by state health legislation, or established by federal action. For purposes of this report, these entities are collectively termed *health database organizations* (HDOs).

As ideally conceptualized by the committee, and discussed more fully in Chapter 2, HDOs have several important characteristics in common. They:

- operate under a single, common authority;
- acquire and maintain information from a wide variety of sources and put their databases to multiple uses;
- have files containing person-identified and person-identifiable data;[1]
- serve a specific, defined geographic area;
- have inclusive population files;
- have comprehensive data with elements that include administrative, clinical, health status, and satisfaction information;
- manipulate data electronically; and
- support electronic access for real-time use.

The prospect of creating these entities has raised numerous issues. Among the more conspicuous are: (1) worries on the part of health care providers and clinicians about use or misuse of the information that HDOs will compile and release and (2) alarm on the part of consumers, patients, and their physicians about how well the privacy and confidentiality of personal health information will be guarded. Addressing these two concerns was the chief focus of the IOM committee appointed to conduct this study. A third issue—the technical and political feasibility of building such repositories of health information and assuring that the expected benefits are achieved—is often voiced, but addressing it was beyond the scope of the study.

THE INSTITUTE OF MEDICINE STUDY

The direct impetus for this study came from discussions between staff of the John A. Hartford Foundation and the IOM in the early 1990s. The Hartford Foundation has a long-standing interest in issues relating to the generation and application of information to improve health care delivery and to increase the value of health care spending. Its interests have intensified in the present context of vastly greater computer capabilities in the health care sector, increasing attention to health matters in the business community, rising interest among health professionals in understanding the effectiveness and appropriateness of the health care services they deliver, and growing sophistication among consumers about health care matters. In

---

[1]*Person-identified* means that the record contains an obvious individual-related identifier such as name or Social Security number. *Person-identifiable* means that the record contains a variety of facts that collectively can be used to infer the identity of the individual. That is, person-identified is a subset of person-identifiable data. These two related terms are discussed more fully in Chapter 2.

this framework, the foundation had supported earlier IOM studies on computer-based patient records (IOM, 1991a) and clinical practice guidelines (IOM, 1992a). It now had specific questions concerning potential obstacles to the successful implementation of regional health data networks or repositories—known as Community Health Management Information Systems (CHMISs)—whose creation it was supporting in several areas of the country.[2]

The Study Committee and Its Charge

In early 1992 the IOM appointed a study committee that conducted the major part of its work between March 1992 and December 1993.[3]   The study committee, chaired by Roger Bulger, M.D., consisted of 16 individuals (see roster) with expertise in the administration of medical centers and academic health centers, the practice of medicine, health insurance, utilization management, use of large administrative and research databases for research purposes, administration of large (nonhealth) corporations, consumer services, health and privacy law, ethics, data security, informatics, and state health data organizations.

During meetings and other study activities, the committee addressed the charge given below, which incorporated both the concerns of the Hartford Foundation (about what was then termed regional health data networks) and a somewhat wider set of issues and concepts that committee members themselves believed significant:

> The study committee will examine regional health data networks and possible impediments to their effective implementation. The focus will be on ways to facilitate cooperative regional efforts among payers, employers, insurers, health care providers, and other parties that will be practical, useful, and acceptable to a wide array of community interests and mem-

---

[2]Apart from the major support for this project from the Hartford Foundation, additional funding was made available by the American Health Information Management Association, Electronic Data Systems Corporation (EDS), and Science Applications International Corporation. The interests of these groups varied widely and are reflected in the committee charge; the particular concern with ethical problems of privacy and confidentiality expressed by EDS were addressed not only by committee discussions but also by reliance on IOM reports being prepared at the same time that dealt directly or indirectly with these matters (IOM, 1993b; IOM, 1993e).

[3]The IOM committee conducted this project chiefly during the 18 months before the Clinton administration introduced its Health Security Act in the fall of 1993. Therefore, the study was neither designed nor intended to reflect specifics of that or any of the other health care reform proposals that were being debated as this report was being released. Although the committee takes no stance on the desirability or feasibility of elements of the various contending proposals, it does note throughout its report the features of the administration's proposals most germane to its formal charge.

bers. The study will address privacy, confidentiality, security, and other concerns about health-related information in several kinds of regional data repositories and files in the broad context of the uses to which these databases might be put. Specifically, the committee will seek to understand more about databases now in existence and those now under development and will consider how current impediments to their successful implementation might be addressed in the context of public and private decision making about the costs, quality, appropriateness, effectiveness, and cost-effectiveness of health care services and care providers. The committee will seek information from many sources (e.g., site visits, expert panels or workshops, focus groups, commissioned papers) and will produce an NRC-reviewed report.[4]

Questions Confronting the Study Committee

The IOM committee took as a given that, even as it conducted its investigations, a variety of HDOs were being created and moving into operational phases. It thus initially addressed itself to two critical "downstream" questions: (1) What current dangers arising from electronic data interchange and the widespread sharing of personal health data might continue, be exacerbated, be ameliorated, or be prevented by such entities? (2) What new harms might be anticipated and minimized or avoided by design? Within the broad sweep of these questions, several more specific issues surfaced during the study.

First, how will HDOs be governed? Developers, providers, consumer representatives, and others ask who will and should own these organizations, what sorts of organizations they will be, and how they should be governed. The different legal mandates that might give rise to such entities and contribute to their effectiveness also come into play. For instance, HDOs might emerge in the private sector as the result of the interests of a business coalition or provider association. Conversely, state legislation might prompt and direct their development. Yet other data repositories might come about through a combination of public- and private-sector interests, data sources, and governing structures.[5]

---

[4] Procedures of the National Research Council (NRC)—the administrative arm of the National Academy of Sciences, the National Academy of Engineering, and the Institute of Medicine—establish rigorous requirements for expert peer review of all committee reports resulting from the activities of those organizations. Reports such as this one are not released to the public or the sponsoring agencies or institutions until that review is successfully completed.

[5] The logistics and costs of HDO implementation and operation arise naturally in this context. The committee did not explore these matters directly, however, because little if any empirical information was available to the study and because the committee felt that these issues would be highly idiosyncratic to locales.

Second, what is the scope of an HDO? One factor is whether such databases can be designed and implemented to ensure that they encompass a given region's population, not just the users of health care in the area. The more inclusive and comprehensive the database, the more likely it is to have value for a broad range of users and uses, such as research into the epidemiology of disease or the effectiveness of medical treatments, health care planning, and quality assurance and improvement. Clearly, however, the more expansive the database, the more difficult and more expensive it is to create and to maintain. The arguments concerning the breadth of the population covered relate equally to health care providers; that is, databases that include *all* independent practitioners and types of facilities are certain to be more useful than those that, for example, cover only physicians with hospital admitting privileges.

Third, how good will the data be? Many of the experts contributing to the IOM committee's fact-finding efforts raised questions about data accuracy, quality, comprehensiveness, reliability, and validity. This led many committee members to wonder how the public, policymakers, providers, and others can determine whether data are factual, sufficiently complete, and appropriate for the analyses in which they are used. Even when data for a given purpose appear to be adequate in these respects, many observers worry about using data for aims other than those originally intended; a case in point is the use of information originally intended for administrative functions to support patient care or quality assessment applications.

Fourth, what about the "safety" of personal health data? Many individuals question whether private information about an individual (however "private" is construed by the individual in question) can be kept private and confidential in these databases, especially when such information is accessible over electronic networks. Aggregation of personal health data in data repositories greatly increases the possible benefits as well as the potential for harm. Thus, many wonder whether it will be possible to assure the public that very sensitive personal health data will be protected, and they ponder the circumstances under which various users should gain access to person-identifiable data.

Fifth, how "secure" will these HDOs be? Apart from protecting privacy and confidentiality through rules about access to data files that contain person-identified information or about release of person-identified information to others, what security measures for the system as a whole can and should be put in place? Many experts state that the threats of breaches of security are myriad and sometimes difficult to detect; although less technologically oriented, lay persons worry as well about unauthorized access to their personal information. All consider that finding ways to prevent, or alternatively to detect and mitigate, such security problems is a significant challenge.

Sixth, who will see and use whose data?   The rules that now govern access to patient-, provider-, employer-, and payer-specific data, and should continue to do so in the future, all occasion concern. The reasons for and levels of apprehension differ widely depending on the potential users—patients (including their families and proxies); health care providers (and their employees); insurers and third-party administrators; employers (including those who self-insure medical care for employees); researchers; local health care planners; clinical and health services researchers; community and consumer interest groups; attorneys (including patients' attorneys); law enforcement officials; and other interested parties. For health care providers, employers, and insurers, data on competitors may be of intense interest; similarly, plaintiffs' lawyers in malpractice suits will seek to acquire information from HDOs concerning other patients cared for by the defendants. Many observers question whether access to such information should be permitted.

As another case in point: even if access to or use of person-identified information is severely restricted, one can still inquire about the proper uses of data on defined populations. For instance, should analyses be done and made public (even if individuals are never identified) on groups characterized by having certain diseases or belonging to a given socioeconomic or ethnic group?

One significant issue relating to health care providers is whether different rules should govern access to and public disclosure of data on specific institutions *versus* named practitioners. One can also ask about the propriety of releasing information on groups or categories of providers and practitioners. A principle of fairness in the use of data lay behind much of the committee's thinking on these matters.

Seventh, how should information be made public? Given that HDOs meet conditions for adequate data as well as those relating to security and to privacy and confidentiality of person- or patient-specific information, a further question is how to ensure that they release and disseminate useful knowledge and information in ways that can be understood by the public at large.

Eighth, where do current laws and statutes fit in? Present-day laws and regulations at both the national and state levels may pose constraints for regional HDOs, or they may not affect them at all. The impact of current statutes will depend on the issue at hand, the jurisdiction under consideration, and the reach of existing laws to secondary records. Among the issues are barriers to accessing certain categories of data, such as information on mental health or substance abuse treatment, and statutes establishing time limitations on keeping (or destroying) data.

STUDY ACTIVITIES

The committee met five times between March 1992 and August 1993 to debate these matters. Several outside experts (see Appendix A to this volume) were invited to three of these meetings. They described analogs of regional HDOs and other databases and discussed several specific problems with the committee, such as the range of organizations, agencies, and individuals who now seek access to patient health records and possible approaches for addressing misuse of patient data.

To avail itself of expert and detailed legal analysis of issues beyond the time resources of its members, the committee commissioned a paper from an expert in privacy and confidentiality matters (Belair, 1993). The paper identified privacy interests relevant to HDOs (chiefly of the CHMIS variety); examined the impact of existing law on these organizations; advanced some short- and long-term options and strategies for privacy protection of patient-identified information; and gave particular consideration to the status and protection of clinical and other patient-identified data once they move beyond legal or other protections afforded to primary medical records.

When IOM studies with national significance involve activities initiated at the grassroots, state, and local levels, the IOM often makes a concerted effort to reach out to a wide range of people in those locales. The aims are to learn about the activities and to understand the views of interested parties about issues pertinent to the local efforts, and then to apply those lessons, as appropriate, to broad national, professional, and policy-related issues. The IOM takes care, in these circumstances, not to evaluate or draw public judgments about local efforts.

During the summer and fall of 1992, the committee conducted five major site visits to the following cities (and nearby locales): Memphis, Tennessee; Cleveland, Ohio; Des Moines, Iowa; Seattle, Washington; and Albany and Rochester, New York. During these site visits two or three committee members and IOM staff met with groups developing HDOs in business coalitions and other organizations, practicing physicians and representatives of local medical societies, insurers and third-party claims administrators, health maintenance organizations, consumers, hospital administrators and hospital associations, researchers, state and county health officials, employers, and computer system developers. (Sites and organizations visited are listed in Appendix A.)

ORGANIZATION OF THE REPORT

The committee considered all the questions raised earlier but focused on two primary issues. The first is the public release of descriptive and evaluative data on the costs, quality, and other attributes of health care institutions, practitioners, and other providers, which the committee assumed would be a major function if not a hallmark of HDOs. The second involves the opportunities, risks, and remedies for protecting the privacy and confidentiality of data that do (or may) identify individuals in their role as patients or consumers, not as clinicians or providers. These topics are taken up, respectively, in Chapters 3 and 4. Before that, Chapter 2 describes health databases and HDOs in more detail, discusses their ostensible benefits in general and with respect to a wide range of potential users, and introduces some caveats about how their intrinsic limitations (e.g., poor or incomplete data) must be recognized and overcome.

COMMENT

This report reviews the tremendous promise of regional health data networks for evaluating and improving health care and controlling its administrative costs. While the potential for great benefit to the public may be understood by those in the relevant fields, the potential for harm or lack of fairness in their use may create doubt and fear in many.

Powerful technologies (and electronic technologies are increasingly powerful) can be deliberately or inadvertently misused and cause great harm, in this case primarily in the loss of privacy and confidentiality and the resultant harms this may engender. To gain public support for the vision in this report, and for the public to make best use of the health-related information that will be released, carefully planned strategies must be developed for education about the data networks, about how the data can be used to help the public access and obtain better care, and about what each individual needs to know about the right to privacy and confidentiality and the steps being taken to protect their rights. The responsibility for providing usable public information should be assumed by those who undertake to make the vision of regional data networks become reality.

2
Health Databases and
Health Database Organizations:
Uses, Benefits, and Concerns

No one engaged in any part of health care delivery or planning today can fail to sense the immense changes on the horizon, even if the silhouettes of those changes, let alone the details, are in dispute.[1] Beyond debate,

---

[1] The Clinton administration's proposed Health Security Act (HSA, 1993) gives appreciable attention to information systems and related matters. It calls for the establishment of a National Health Board to oversee the creation of an electronic data network consisting of regional centers that collect, compile, and transmit information (Sec. 5103). The board will, among other duties, provide technical assistance on (1) the promotion of community-based health information systems and (2) the promotion of patient care information systems that collect data at the point of care or as a by-product of the delivery of care (Sec. 5106).

The types of information collected would include: enrollment and disenrollment in health plans; clinical encounters and other items and services provided by health care providers; administrative and financial transactions and activities of participating states, regional alliances, corporate alliances, health plans, health care providers, employers, and individuals; number and demographic characteristics of eligible individuals residing in each alliance area; payment of benefits; utilization management; quality management; grievances, and fraud or misrepresentation in claims or benefits (Sec. 5101).

The HSA further specifies the use of (1) uniform paper forms containing standard data elements, definitions, and instructions for completion; (2) requirements for use of uniform health data sets with common definitions to standardize the collection and transmission of data in electronic form; (3) uniform presentation requirements for data in electronic form; and (4) electronic data interchange requirements for the exchange of data among automated health information systems (Sec. 5002). It also calls for a national health security card that will permit access to information about health coverage although it will contain only a minimum amount of information (Sec. 5105) (Health Security Act. Title V. Quality and Consumer Protection. Part 1. Health Information Systems).

however, is the need for much more and much better information on use of health care services and on the outcomes of that care. The needs are quite broad: health care reform; evaluation of clinical care and health care delivery; administration of health plans, groups, and facilities; and public health planning.

Policymakers, researchers, health professionals, purchasers, patients, and others continue to be frustrated in their attempts to acquire health information. They may not be able to determine with confidence the outcomes, quality, effectiveness, appropriateness, and costs of care for different segments of the population, for different settings, services, and providers, and for different mechanisms of health care delivery and reimbursement. When this is so, they can say little, with confidence, about the value of the investment in health care for population subgroups, regions, or the nation as a whole.

In principle, this information can be acquired through numerous avenues, such as surveys, electronic financial transactions for health insurance claims, computer-based patient records (CPRs), and disease registries. In practice, no one system will suit every need or produce information appropriate for every question. As introduced in Chapter 1, however, *health database organizations* (HDOs) hold considerable promise as a reasonably comprehensive source of the information needed to:

- assess the health of the public and patterns of illness and injury;
- identify unmet regional health needs;
- document patterns of health care expenditures on inappropriate, wasteful, or potentially harmful services;
- find cost-effective care providers; and
- improve the quality of care in hospitals, practitioners' offices, clinics, and various other health care settings.

The latter half of this chapter outlines these and other benefits of HDOs, the databases they access or control, and the analytic and information dissemination activities they undertake. It also discusses the applications that user groups might have for different types of databases. The committee advances some views on how major concerns about these databases, chiefly relating to the quality of their data, might be addressed, and it makes two recommendations. In preparation for those sections, the chapter next offers some definitions of key concepts and terms, explores the basic construct of HDOs (which the committee sees as the administrative and operational structure for regional health databases), and provides some examples of the variety of entities that now exist, are being implemented as this report was written, or are envisioned for the future.

DEFINITIONS

Even among experts, terms such as database and network are not used in the same manner. For this report, the committee advances the following working definitions for certain major concepts, building to its view of an HDO.

Database

The term *database* embraces many different concepts: from paper records maintained by a single practitioner to the vast computerized collections of insurance claims for Medicare beneficiaries; from files of computerized patient encounter forms maintained by health plans to discharge abstract databases of all hospitals in a given state; from cancer and trauma registries maintained by health institutions and researchers to major national health survey data of federal agencies. As commonly used and meant in this report, a database (or, sometimes, data bank, data set, or data file) is "a large collection of data in a computer, organized so that it can be expanded, updated, and retrieved rapidly for various uses" (*Webster's New World Dictionary*, 2nd ed.).

Although databases may eventually be linked (or linkable) to primary medical records held by health care practitioners, this report addresses databases composed of secondary records.[2] Secondary files are generated from primary records or are separate from any patient encounter (as in the case of eligibility or enrollment files for health plans and public programs). They are not under the control of a practitioner or anyone designated by the practitioner, nor are they under the management of any health institution (e.g., the medical records department of a hospital). Furthermore, they are not intended to be *the* major source of information about specific patients for the treating physician. Secondary databases facilitate *reuse* of data that have been gathered for another purpose (e.g., patient care, billing, or research) but that, in new applications, may generate new knowledge.

---

[2] According to the IOM (1991a, p. 11): "A *primary patient record* is used by health care professionals while providing patient care services to review patient data or document their own observations, actions, or instructions. A *secondary patient record* is derived from the primary record and contains selected data elements to aid nonclinical users (i.e., persons not involved in direct patient care) in supporting, evaluation, or advancing patient care." At present, most medical records are maintained on paper, not in computers, and the U.S. General Accounting Office provides the following startling figures on the equivalent volume of paper: "We estimate that the 34 million annual U.S. hospital admissions and 1.2 billion physician visits could generate the equivalent of 10 billion pages of medical records" (GAO, 1993a, p. 2).

The committee distinguishes between databases composed of secondary records and CPRs or CPR systems (IOM, 1991a; Ball and Collen, 1992), but its broader vision of computer-based health information systems includes direct ties to CPR systems. Many experts argue that until CPR systems are linked in some fashion to such data repositories or networks, neither will be complete or reach their full health care, research, or policymaking potential.[3]

This chapter cites several examples of health databases used today for many purposes, but the ones noted are highly selective and intended to illustrate particular applications or kinds of data maintained. To understand the range of databases that HDOs might access and why there might be concern about protection of personal data, readers are referred to the many inventories of health databases. Publications from the National Association of Health Data Organizations (NAHDO) describe state and insurance databases (NAHDO, 1988, 1993). For databases related to federal programs supported by the Department of Health and Human Services (DHHS), readers can consult publications and manuals from the Health Care Financing Administration (HCFA, for Medicare and Medicaid), the Public Health Service (PHS, for surveys conducted by the National Center for Health Statistics; see also Gable, 1990; IOM/CBASSE, 1992; NCHS, 1993; Smith, 1993), and the Agency for Health Care Policy and Research (AHCPR, for the National Medical Expenditure Surveys and Patient Outcome Research Teams [PORTs]; AHCPR, 1990a). Major research databases include those developed for the RAND Corporation's Health Insurance Experiment (a large-scale social experiment conducted in the late 1970s and early 1980s on the utilization, expenditures, and outcomes effects of different levels of cost sharing [Newhouse and Insurance Experiment Group, 1993]), which were turned into a large number of carefully documented public-use tapes.

Key Attributes of Databases

In reviewing the considerable variation in databases that might be accessed, controlled, or acquired by HDOs, the committee sought a simple way to characterize them by key attributes. It decided on two critical

---

[3] One major hurdle to the development of CPRs involves standards for vocabulary, structure and content, messaging, and security, according to GAO reports (1991, 1993a); without standards for uniform electronic recording and transmission of medical data, effective automated medical record systems will be delayed. This committee did not examine these technical issues, although they pertain as well to large-scale regional HDOs; arguably, the government and the private sector will need to move more forcefully on development of such standards—perhaps moving beyond near-total reliance on voluntary efforts—if CPRs, CPR systems, and regional health databases and networks are to succeed.

dimensions of databases: *comprehensiveness* and *inclusiveness*. (Because these terms are used with distinct meanings in this report, they are italicized whenever used.)

Comprehensiveness. Comprehensiveness describes the completeness of records of patient care events and information relevant to an individual patient (Table 2-1).[4] It refers to the amount of information one has on an individual both for each patient encounter with the health care system and for all of a patient's encounters over time (USDHHS, 1991, refers to this as completeness). A record that is *comprehensive* contains: demographic data, administrative data, health risks and health status, patient medical history, current management of health conditions, and outcomes data. Each category is described briefly below.

• *Demographic data* consist of facts such as age (or date of birth), gender, race and ethnic origin, marital status, address of residence, names of and other information about immediate family members, and emergency information. Information about employment status (and employer), schooling and education, and some indicator of socioeconomic class might also appear.

• *Administrative data* include facts about health insurance such as eligibility and membership, dual coverage (when relevant), and required copayments and deductibles for a given benefit package. With respect to services provided (e.g., diagnostic tests or outpatient procedures), such data also typically include charges and perhaps amounts paid. Administrative data commonly identify providers with a unique identifier and possibly give additional provider-specific facts; the latter might include kind of practitioner (physician, podiatrist, psychologist), physician specialty, and nature of institution (general or specialty hospital, physician office or clinic, home care agency, nursing home, and so forth).

• *Health risks and health status* Health risk information reflects behavior and lifestyle (e.g., whether an individual uses tobacco products or engages regularly in strenuous exercise) and facts about family history and genetic factors (e.g., whether an individual has first-degree family members with a specific type of cancer or a propensity for musculoskeletal disease).

---

[4] The discussion of *comprehensiveness* and *inclusiveness* of databases is couched in terms of what might be regarded as the traditional domain of medical care, including mental health care. Clearly, more advanced databases could include information on dental care and care provided by health professionals that practice independently, such as nurse-practitioners and nurse-midwives, acupuncturists, or alternative healers of various sorts. Even more far-reaching databases might contain information on sociomedical services provided through, for instance, day care and home care for adults or children.

TABLE 2-1 Comprehensiveness: Data Elements as a Critical Dimension of Health Care Databases

Data Elements	Examples of Data Elements that Might Be Included in HDO Databases
Demographic	Name Address of residence Names and other information on immediate family members and emergency information Age (or date of birth) Gender Race and ethnic origin Employment status (and employer) Schooling and education Indicator of socioeconomic class
Administrative	Unique identifier Health insurance eligibility and membership Dual coverage when appropriate Required copayments and deductibles "Insurance claim" information, e.g., charges for diagnostic tests and procedures and amounts paid Provider and provider identification number Type of practitioner Physician specialty Type of institution Provider-specific authorization and date for informed consent
Health risks	Health-related behavior, e.g., use of tobacco products and seat belts, exercise Genetic predisposition
Health status (or health-related quality of life)	Physical functioning Mental and emotional well-being Cognitive functioning Social and role functioning Perceptions of health
Medical history	Past medical problems, injuries, hospital admissions, pregnancies, births Family history or events (e.g., alcoholism or parental divorce)
Current management of health conditions	Current problems and diagnoses Medications prescribed Allergies Health screening Diagnostic or therapeutic procedures performed Counseling
Outcomes	General and/or condition-specific states, e.g., functional status, readmission to hospital, and unexpected medical or surgical complications of care Satisfaction

Health status (or health-related quality of life), generally reported by individuals themselves, reflects domains of health such as physical functioning, mental and emotional well-being, cognitive functioning, social and role functioning, and perceptions of one's health in the past, present, and future and compared with that of one's peers. Health status and quality-of-life measures are commonly considered outcomes of health care, but evaluators and researchers also need such information to take account in their analyses of the mix of patients and the range of severity of health conditions.

•   *Patient medical history* involves data on previous medical encounters such as hospital admissions, surgical procedures, pregnancies and live births, and the like; it also includes information on past medical problems and possibly family history or events (e.g., alcoholism or parental divorce). Again, although such facts are significant for good patient care, they may also be important for case-mix and severity adjustment.

•   *Current medical management* includes the content of encounter forms or parts of the patient record. Such information might reflect health screening, current health problems and diagnoses, allergies (especially those to medications), diagnostic or therapeutic procedures performed, laboratory tests carried out, medications prescribed, and counseling provided.

•   *Outcomes data* encompass a wide choice of measures of the effects of health care and the aftermath of various health problems across a spectrum from death to high levels of functioning and well-being; they can also reflect health care events such as readmission to hospital or unexpected complications or side effects of care. Finally, they often include measures of satisfaction with care. Outcomes assessed weeks or months after health care events, and by means of reports directly from individuals (or family members), are desirable, although these are likely to be the least commonly found in the secondary databases under consideration here.

The more *comprehensive* the database is, the more current and possibly more sensitive information about individuals is likely to be. This suggests that *comprehensiveness* as envisioned here will have a direct correlation with concerns about privacy and confidentiality. By analogy, the Department of Defense treats information with increasingly higher levels of security as it becomes more *comprehensive*, even when the aggregated information is not considered sensitive (Ware, 1993).

Some patient events are unlikely to appear in databases (depending on how they originate); missing from the databases considered here are services that may have been advised but neither sought nor rendered—screening examinations not given, physician follow-up visits not advised or kept, and prescriptions given but not filled. Other reasons for missing data involve out-of-area care for an individual who is otherwise in the database; an example is medical services provided in Florida to New York residents when they are on vacation or living part of the year out of state. Yet another is when patients do not make claims against health insurance policies (regardless of where they are rendered); this transaction may not be recorded through any of the usual claims processing mechanisms used to generate the database.

Furthermore, databases may never be sufficiently *comprehensive* for research or outcomes analysis, especially if the choice of core data elements is parsimonious. Thus, when the question at hand is health status and outcomes long after health care has been rendered, HDO staff or outside researchers may need the capability and authority to contact individuals (providers and possibly patients) for information about outcomes and satisfaction with care. Such outreach activities would require some adequate funding mechanism.

Inclusiveness. *Inclusiveness* refers to which populations in a geographic area are included in a database. The more *inclusive* a database, the more it approaches coverage of 100 percent of the population that its developers intend to include. Databases that aim to provide information on the health of the community ought to include an enumeration of all residents of the community (e.g., metropolitan area, state) so that the information accurately reflects the entire population of the region, regardless of insurance category. Conversely, *inclusiveness* is reduced when membership is restricted to certain subgroups or when individuals expected to be in the database are missing (Table 2-2). For instance, a database that is intended to include all residents in a local area may include only those who are insured and file claims for services; it misses those not insured and those who, although insured, do not use health services. An insurance claims database that does not include members of a health maintenance organization (HMO) because no claims are filed will also not be *inclusive* for the geographic area.

Databases may be (and often are) designed to include only subsets of the entire population of a geographic area: those eligible for certain kinds of insurance, such as enrollees (subscribers, their spouses and dependents) in commercial insurance plans; persons receiving care from specific kinds of providers or in certain settings (e.g., prehospital emergency care from emergency medical services and hospital emergency departments); persons with a given set of conditions (e.g., a cancer or trauma registry); an age group such as those age 65 and older (e.g., Medicare beneficiary files);[5] residents of a defined geographic area or political jurisdiction or scientifically selected samples of individuals, as in major health surveys. Clearly these categories are not mutually exclusive—individuals (as well as providers)

---

[5] This is illustrative only because Medicare files also include younger but disabled beneficiaries and persons with end-stage renal disease.

TABLE 2-2 *Inclusiveness*: Populations Covered as a Critical Dimension
of Health Care Databases

Defined Populations	Examples
National	All persons physically resident in the 50 states, District of Columbia, Puerto Rico, and the Trust Territories
Geographic area	All persons resident in a defined geopolitical or other describable area, such as an MSA
Insurance type	HMO, indemnity, Medicaid, none
Site and care setting	Hospital, nursing home, clinic
Disease, injury type	Cancer, trauma registry
Age or other demographic characteristic	Age 65 or older, belonging to a defined ethnic or racial group

NOTE: MSA = Metropolitan statistical area.

can and do appear in more than one such database. The potential benefits
of the database, however, will increase as the database moves toward being
inclusive of the entire population of a defined geographic area.

HDOs will have to be clear about what groups are missing when describing their databases and the results of their analyses. Perhaps more
important, HDOs should seek ways to ensure that all relevant populations
are included, so that their analyses accurately reflect the population of the
region and, thereby, yield estimates of the levels of underuse of health care
in their respective regions.

Table 2-3 summarizes these two attributes.[6] The dummy matrix, al-

---

[6] The congressional Physician Payment Review Commission (PPRC) has been in the fore-
front of advocates for a national data system (PPRC, 1992, 1993). In its 1992 annual report,
PPRC described an *"all-patient database"* [emphasis in the original], conceptualized as a
"network of local or regional data processing centers . . . to streamline the transfer of administrative information for payment and service-use tracking purposes" (p. 269). The report goes
on to posit "parallel organizing entities . . . to coordinate the use of these data [and] the data
processing centers and the organizing entities would make up an *all-patient data network*" (p.
269). The commissioners also envisioned the network evolving into a "means to link and
assimilate more detailed clinical information." Although the general thrust of the PPRC idea is
consonant with the long-range views of this IOM committee, the specific understanding of
what a database or network is differs. In defining an all-patient database, the commissioners
appear to have in mind what this committee terms *inclusiveness*; what the PPRC report lays out
as "core data elements" in that database approaches what the IOM report calls *comprehensiveness*.

TABLE 2-3   Characteristics of Databases According
to Two Critical Dimensions

COMPREHENSIVENESS (Data Elements)	Inclusiveness (Population)	
	High	Low
High	a	b
Low	c	d

though empty, illustrates how databases can be described, evaluated, and differentiated from each other.   Cell *a* represents patient populations and data elements that are included in a database.   Cell *b* depicts the individuals who are missing from a database that is otherwise fairly *comprehensive.* Cell *c* represents patient nonevents and missing data in a database that is otherwise reasonably *inclusive.*   Cell *d* represents missing individuals and missing data.   To the extent cells *b, c,* and especially *d* are large, the database in question will be less able to provide extensive, or unbiased, information; the sizes of cells *b, c,* and *d* are, therefore, three determinants of database quality.

Other Characteristics of Databases

The more *comprehensive* and *inclusive* databases are, the more they facilitate detailed and sophisticated uses and, in turn, entail both greater anticipated benefits and possible harms.   The magnitude of either benefits or harms can depend on several other important properties of databases, however, as noted below.

Linkage over time.   The ability to analyze patterns, quality, and costs of care over a period of time may be very important to users.   They may want to construct episodes of care or develop other longitudinal profiles; cases in point (respectively) involve all the care provided to a specific patient for a discrete course of illness or injury, regardless of site or setting, and compilations of information on services provided by a local HMOs over rolling five-year periods.   Such studies require not only unique identifiers for patients and providers (see below) but also a record structure that permits analysts to link dates and times with patient care events, problems, and diagnoses.

Timeliness.   Facts based on patient-provider interactions and other relevant information (e.g., employment, health plan, health status, or outcomes) should be entered or updated frequently enough to permit their timely use and analysis. If databases are to be of assistance with direct patient care, then information must be sufficiently up to date that caregivers can rely on it in all clinical decision-making situations.

Accuracy and completeness. Data used for clinical care—decision making about a given individual—must be of far greater accuracy and completeness than those required for administrative uses. Databases used for clinical decision making must, in describing an individual, describe *only* that individual and do so accurately. For instance, missing or out-of-date data or files that commingle data for more than one individual under a single identifier have grave potential for harm. In addition, correcting errors found at a later time must be possible; ideally, alerting past users of the database to those errors and corrections ought to be possible as well.

Control, ownership, and governance. Whether a given database has been established by the public or the private sector (or is some hybrid) will have important implications for *inclusiveness* and access. For instance, databases addressed in this report may be publicly supported—especially at the state level—and may be operated and administered by a private entity. Some state hospital discharge databases—such as the Health Care Policy Corporation in Iowa and the Massachusetts Health Data Consortium—are of this kind. Alternatively, they may be developed, maintained, and financed wholly in the private sector, such as those developed by professional or health care organizations, insurers, or business coalitions. A database created by state or federal law can require participation; that is, it can demand that health professionals, institutions, and patients participate in providing data. For example, Washington state has passed legislation that mandates development of a statewide data system by a health services commission that will identify a set of health care data elements to be submitted by all providers (e.g., hospitals and physicians) (Engrossed Second Substitute Senate Bill 5304, 1993). To the extent databases are developed and maintained in the public sector or are networked with public-sector databases (especially at the federal level), they will be subject to regulations that differ from those affecting databases operated purely within the private sector for the benefit of private sponsors. Given the evolving nature of state and national health care reform plans and programs, movement toward electronic data interchange (EDI), progress toward CPRs, and emergence of various hybrid arrangements for financing and delivering health care, the development of HDOs is taking place in very different (and perhaps unpredictable) environments that will likely have disparate effects over time.

Origin of data. Databases can vary widely in the source(s) of their information. For example, data may come from hospital discharge abstracts, self-completed questionnaires from patients or survey respondents, insurance claims submissions, employer files, computer-based pharmacy files, CPRs, and other sources.

Hospital discharge abstracts are common sources of publicly held data: 36 states have mandates for the collection, analysis, and dissemination of hospital-level information for prudent purchasing, decision making, education of the public, and rate regulation. Such databases may be maintained by a variety of entities, including: the Department of Insurance (North Carolina), a freestanding health data commission (Iowa and Pennsylvania), a rate-setting commission (Massachusetts), or the Department of Health (Minnesota, New Jersey) (NAHDO, 1993). One well-known model is that of the New York Statewide Planning and Research Cooperative System, called SPARCS, which has been an influential source of information for research on hospital-specific mortality (Hannan et al., 1989b).

An example of a survey database is the Medicare Current Beneficiary Survey, a longitudinal panel survey that the HCFA Office of the Actuary launched in September 1991. Individuals sampled from the Medicare enrolled population are interviewed three times a year. The survey includes demographic and behavioral data, health status and functioning, insurance coverage, financial resources, family support, source of payment, use of Medicare and non-Medicare services, and access and satisfaction. Information from the survey can be linked to Medicare claims and other administrative data.

Person-identified and person-identifiable data. For purposes of this report, *person-identified data* contain pieces of information or facts that singly or collectively refer to one person and permit positive (or probable) identification of that individual. An obvious piece of identifying information is an individual's name. Other identifiers may be biometric, such as a fingerprint, a retinal print, or a DNA pattern.

The committee uses the term *person-identifiable* to characterize information that definitely or probably can be said to refer to a specific person. It includes items of information (e.g., the fact of a physician visit on a given day) that will allow identification of an individual when combined with other facts (e.g., zip code of residence, age, or gender). To render data non-person-identifiable, some data managers convert facts to a more general form before releasing those data to others. For instance, date of birth may be converted to age, date of admission to month of admission, or date of physician visit to intervals between visits.

Concerns about misuse or improper disclosure of person-identifiable data are likely to escalate as more health information is stored in computer files. Ultimately, protecting patient identity in the commonly understood sense may become very difficult given increasing computer capabilities, creative cross-linkages among data sets, and the usual curiosity of human beings.

Unique, universal person-identifiers. A unique identifier (1) applies to one and only one person and (2) does not change over time. It includes the biometric identifiers noted above as well as numeric or alphanumeric codes. Health insurers, plans, and entitlement programs assign identifiers; among them are the Social Security number (the basis of the health insurance claim numbers used by Medicare) and other alphanumeric codes typically used by Medicaid programs and commercial insurers. Such identifiers may be neither reliably unique nor universal in the sense of linking health databases. Providers also assign identifiers to patients—usually a medical record or account number—but they are not universal, as they are not used beyond that specific provider, and generally they cannot be matched to identifiers assigned by other providers, plans, or programs. The term universal as used here does *not* apply to identifiers that could link health and nonhealth (e.g., financial) databases.

The extent to which unique and universal identifiers are available for individuals in the database—for instance, all persons in a geographic area, or all users of the health system—may prove to be a critical factor in the utility of that database. They are a prerequisite for the construction of longitudinal records on individual patients that can reflect their health care events and outcomes across sites and time. Ideally, *inclusive* population-based databases will have unique universal identifiers for all members of the relevant population group, so that nonusers of the health care system can be taken into account in various analytic applications. The need for a universal identifier and the debate about the use of the Social Security number (or its derivatives) for this purpose are discussed in detail in Chapter 4.

Nonvolitional identifying information—for example, fingerprints or retinal prints—may also be important, particularly for HDOs that intend to contribute to direct patient care. These markers allow positive identification of individuals, such as trauma victims, who cannot identify themselves, presuming of course that the data about individuals are in the database. They may also help to ensure that a patient record corresponds to the presenting patient both in delivering patient care and in verifying eligibility for benefits.

Unique identifiers for health care providers and practitioners. This characteristic pertains to individual practitioners, particularly physicians; hospitals and other inpatient or residential facilities or institutions; HMOs as well as independent practice associations (IPAs), preferred provider organizations (PPOs) and similar organized, integrated health systems; and various other providers such as pharmacies (and pharmacy chains) and home health agencies. HCFA assigns a universal physician identification number, or UPIN, for records of care to Medicare patients. Because not all providers see Medicare patients (e.g., pediatricians do not), however, UPINs are not a means of identifying all practicing physicians in the country.

As with patient identifiers, unique identifiers for providers will ideally be consistent over time and used for one and only one individual institution or clinician. Failing that, HDOs will need to find ways to link multiple identifiers (e.g., when a physician belongs to more than one health plan or bills from different addresses with different tax numbers) and to assign individual identifiers to a group using a single number (e.g., when all physicians in an HMO use the HMO's identification number).

Data Network

A *data network* can be thought of as a set of databases that: (1) are hosted on several computer systems interconnected with one another and to terminals and (2) serve some community of users. Such a network will typically have a number of attributes. First, the databases are dispersed over several machines; each database or group of databases resides on one or more computer systems. Second, the computer systems are often, but not necessarily, physically distant from one another. Third, all the machines in the network are linked so that information can be transmitted from one machine to another. Finally, each machine has software to permit exchange of information among individual systems in the network and, in turn, to allow individual users of the network to query the many databases and to receive, analyze, and aggregate these data. This report focuses on networks in which one or more common data elements (e.g., patient name, provider identity, facility name) is a link parameter that relates records in one database to those in others.

Databases in data networks may be linked by various physical or other arrangements. These include telecommunications (e.g., microwave channels, local-area networks, the public-switched network, satellite circuits), physical transfer of magnetic tapes or disks, and dial-up connections. This report is intended to apply to any or all of these mechanisms for linking databases; that is, the term *network* does not imply here that an electrical connection between computers must be in place (in contrast to the common terminology of computer professionals, for whom *network* usually does include electrical linkage).

Hospitals, pharmacies, physicians' offices, insurance companies, public program offices, and employers all generate inputs to databases that are interconnected in such networks. This committee, however, is particularly interested in data networks with linked databases that have, at a minimum, two specific characteristics: (1) their linking implies or involves movement of health data outside the care setting in which they have been generated and (2) they include person-identified or person-identifiable data.

Health Database Organization

The Concept of HDOs

The committee chose the phrase *health database organization* (HDO) to refer to entities that have access to (and possibly control of) databases and that have as their chief mission the public release of data and of results of analyses done on the databases under their control. For purposes of this report, *prototypical* HDOs have the characteristics outlined in Chapter 1; these properties may not, however, be present to the same degree in existing or emerging HDOs today. As conceptualized by the committee, HDOs have a number of crucial characteristics.

- They *operate under a single, common authority.*
- They *acquire and maintain information from a wide variety of sources* in the health sector—for example, institutions and facilities, agencies and clinics, providers such as pharmacies, and physicians in private practice. They might also obtain information from other sources not directly connected with personal health care, such as the administrative files or databases on persons covered by a specific insurance plan or employed by a given company. In all these cases, HDOs might add and update information periodically (from hourly to annually) or on a case-specific basis (e.g., on all patients with a certain diagnosis or on all providers of a certain type). They put these *databases to multiple uses* (some of which may not yet be imagined), in contrast to administrative or research databases created to perform specific tasks or to answer only specific questions.
- Files accessible to HDOs will include *person-identified or person-identifiable data.*
- HDOs *will serve a specific geographic area* that is defined chiefly by geographic or political boundaries (e.g., metropolitan area, county, state) and will include those who reside in or receive services in that area, or both.
- HDO *population files will be inclusive*, meaning that they include all members of a defined population—for instance, in a region—so that denominators are known and population-based rates of service utilization and health outcomes can be calculated.
- The *data will be comprehensive* in the kinds of data included about individuals and will include not only administrative and clinical information, but also information about health status and satisfaction with care.

- HDOs will process, store, analyze, and otherwise *manipulate data electronically.*
- Files held by HDOs can be *designed for interactive access in real time* for assistance with patient care when primary records are unavailable to a treating physician. They are not, however, typically viewed as primary patient records (e.g., a computer-based patient record), and they are not meant to be simply passive archives or warehouses for health information.

For maximum accountability, security, protection, and control over access to data, HDOs should have an organizational structure, a corporate or legal existence, and a physical location; for example, they would have a governing board, a staff, a building, and a mailing address. They would conduct business, articulate a mission statement, promulgate policies, implement procedures, and carry out manipulations and analyses of data, and they could be held accountable for their actions. Assuming these characteristics exist, the committee targets most of its recommendations at such HDOs. Some organizations may develop the functions described above, but not as their *primary* mission. The committee intends its recommendations to apply to those HDO-like units as well. One might also imagine proprietary programs, systems, or entities with units that function as HDOs and that would be controlled by the same general principles.

Although the committee adopted the simplified construct offered above for its study, it was aware that more complex entities may arise. The variations that may emerge—for instance, bifurcated legal structures that include a network operator and a user organization—may result in consortia of legal entities. To the extent that this trend decentralizes authority and undermines common operating rules, the issues addressed in this report will become far more serious and possibly unresolvable.

The committee examined the repository function of an HDO. In this role, information collected at the level of the patient or about patients, providers, plans, and clinical encounters is accessed, stored, and made available for others, such as providers, researchers, insurers, and planners, to analyze. In some cases HDOs may have additional functions, such as claims transfer and adjudication, but these were not the subject of the committee's work or recommendations.

Throughout its discussions, the committee focused on *regional* databases and HDOs. In this context, the term *regional* is meant to suggest that HDOs and their constituent networks and databases pertain to a *defined population* of individuals living in, or receiving health care in, some *specifiable geographic area.* These may be city centered, such as the established metropolitan statistical areas that comprise cities and their surrounding counties or suburbs; they may be statewide (and not cross state borders). In some uses, *regional* conveys the idea of a multistate territory (e.g., the Mountain

States or the Mid-Atlantic region), but most of this committee's work has been directed at smaller regions. Far-thinking experts envision a time when regional entities will be linked across the nation, even if their governance and operations remain close to home. This creates the very long-range view of a national health data repository operated by a single organization or a federation of regional or state entities. Especially in the short term, however, HDOs may have overlapping geographic and population boundaries; that is, there might be several in a metropolitan area or within a state's boundaries that include different subpopulations.

The committee elucidated these concepts precisely because regional HDOs are only now emerging in the United States. Some have been legislated or are under consideration by several cities and states for legislative mandate, but none is in full operation. It believes, however, that such entities will become repositories of an immense array of health information—far more extensive in their holdings than any of today's data systems. Thus, the issues raised in Chapters 3 and 4 of this report are explored with an eye to the policies and procedures these emerging HDOs might establish today to realize their many potential benefits while protecting against or minimizing possible harms to individuals (whether patients or practitioners), institutions, or society in general.

HDOs Under Development

Described below are several HDOs currently under development that represent the kinds of entities the committee considered during this study. Only selected characteristics of these programs are given, as a means of illustrating specific points that reflect the attributes of prototypical HDOs as defined earlier in this chapter.

Hospital Consortium of Greater Rochester. In existence since the late 1970s, the Rochester Area Hospital Corporation (RAHC) was originally established to enhance cooperative links among the community hospitals and to put community resources to their best use. A recent initiative has led to its reorganization as the Hospital Consortium of Greater Rochester (HCGR) and to the continuing development of a community-wide health information network that has HDO characteristics. Recent community discussions have focused on the creation of a health care commission that will include representatives of the area's eight hospitals, physicians, employers, the two major third-party payers, and residents (Gates, 1993a; personal communication, Beverly Voos, President and CEO, RHI Group, November 1993). While the function of this commission is still being discussed, the initiative could include the use of a database maintained by the Rochester Healthcare Information Group (RHI Group), a wholly owned, for-profit subsidiary.

From 1980 to 1987, RAHC administered an experimental payment program with both state and federal funding. Under this program, it established a community-wide hospital data system and administered an annual global budget using a community database. That database contains demographic, clinical, and financial data on all acute-care discharges from RAHC hospitals from 1980 onward. It has approximately 100 data elements per patient record in the following categories: Social Security number, demographics, clinical information, patient classifications, provider identification, payer data, and resource use data. Reports are provided to HCGR and to member hospitals on an ad hoc basis. Regional and national comparisons can be made using statewide data and the National Hospital Discharge Survey.

Beginning with 1980, more than a million patient discharge records are recorded in this database. Reports can provide case-mix analyses (which compare lengths of stay by diagnosis, payer, age, and hospital); trend reports on mortality statistics and readmission statistics by year and by diagnosis; payer analysis (which uses cases by insurers by years to analyze age and length of stay); resource utilization analysis comparing routine daily care and ancillary care; severity-of-illness analysis; market share analysis using zip codes; and physician caseload and hospital case mix.

The RHI Group database now includes ambulatory surgery and will soon include outpatient clinic visits as well. Other database components include patients awaiting discharge from a hospital to a nursing home and a perinatal database that is under development. Eventually, it is expected that the database will include information from every clinical setting. RHI Group is able to track patient care over time because it has Social Security numbers in the database.

Henry Ford Health System. The Center for Clinical Effectiveness at the Henry Ford Health System in Detroit is developing systems to track patients' long-term functional status six months or more after treatment as well as costs of their care (Gates, 1993b). This focus has provided the impetus for the development of a uniform electronic data collection system. The developers plan to integrate the collection of data from many operational units of the hospitals and sites of care (e.g., ambulatory care physician visits, tumor registries, patient satisfaction surveys) to make data available for a variety of uses within Henry Ford's large integrated health care system, ranging from patient reminders and managed care activities to outcomes research that would be supported by a central data repository. From the standpoint of *inclusiveness*, such a system would include only patients at Henry Ford sites. That system includes over 400,000 HMO members of the Health Alliance Plan and 920 physicians. It owns four hospitals, operates two nursing homes, and has joint ventures to manage four other hospitals. The Henry Ford Health System is an independent, not-for-profit provider network (Anderson, 1993).

The New York Single-Payer Demonstration Program. New York State is implementing a three-year program to improve administrative efficiency of hospitals and other providers (some free-standing clinics and physicians) by coordinating, automating, and standardizing claims processing, billing, and payment systems. The initiative is not literally a single-payer effort but rather a single-claim demonstration to translate insurance claims and billing forms in whatever format they are submitted and forward them to payers. In terms of *inclusiveness*, the databases will be statewide and will include patients hospitalized in New York state; with respect to *comprehensiveness*, they will contain primarily hospital data with the addition of physician and clinic data from billing forms. The state does not plan to maintain a data repository, but the potential exists for it to direct data to such a repository in the future.

The Vermont Health Care Authority. The Vermont Health Care Authority (VHCA) is the creation of 1992 state legislation (Vermont Health Reform Act). It draws on earlier state efforts to share health care information, particularly the Vermont Program for Quality in Health Care, a project that has been under way since the late 1980s (Keller, 1993). The VHCA program will be *inclusive* (covering all Vermont residents) and *comprehensive* (all health care services that Vermont residents receive from providers both in state and out of state). The initiative will include a lifetime patient record—essentially a unified health care database—linked to an information repository.

The unified database is to be developed by a subsidiary group, Vermont Health Care Information Consortium, using files of all providers, a uniform insurance claims form, and electronic claims submission. The claims-driven health care database is intended to provide policy-related information such as aggregate levels of expenditures and utilization by sectors; it will include Medicare, Medicaid, Blue Cross and Blue Shield, and other provider or insurer groups (e.g., HMOs).

The information repository, when linked to the lifetime health record, is meant to be an integrated system that improves access, controls costs, gives consumers health care information, and improves quality of care. These outcomes are to be achieved through two proposed mechanisms that are similar to those examined in Chapter 3 of this report: (1) feedback programs to share data on quality and practice patterns with one-third of Vermont's practicing physicians and (2) public disclosure of information about providers.

As of late 1993, the role of state agencies was not yet clear, but governance of the not-for-profit consortium will include a public-private partnership, with representation of state government (the Department of Health and the governor's office), Vermont employers, the Vermont Business Roundtable, Blue Cross and Blue Shield, health care providers (hospitals, physicians, the state's medical school), and consumer and patient advocates. It will have an advisory committee and several subcommittees for activities focused on patient advocacy and confidentiality, a business plan, financial issues, technical concerns, and data elements.

Community Health Management Information System.   In the early 1990s the John A. Hartford Foundation launched a program of support for innovative, community-based development efforts to meet the shared information needs of all health system stakeholders at the local level: purchasers, consumers, providers, payers, and regulators.   The Hartford initiative has focused on several regions of the country; grantees are located now in the states (or cities) of Iowa, Minnesota, New York, Ohio, Tennessee (Memphis), Vermont, and Washington.   The program concept—generally known as the Community Health Management Information System (CHMIS)—has been described by Benton International (BI, 1991a, 1991b, 1992), which developed the CHMIS design and functional specifications that were being adapted by the local sites.[7]

The CHMIS is based on two components.   The first is a *transaction system.*   To facilitate point-of-service transactions for the patient and to speed claims processing, computer terminals at each provider site will be used to access patient information based on a *personal identification code* (PIC) and a magnetized card similar to those used by automatic teller machines.   At the time of service, patients or clerks will key in a PIC to allow access to eligibility, coverage, and billing information.   This approach is comparable to those followed by prescription medication plans that use terminals in pharmacies to confirm that a customer is eligible for plan coverage and to determine what charges should be paid.   Electronic *switches* or clearinghouses process bills and insurance forms from hospitals, physicians, laboratories, pharmacies, and other sites by electronically forwarding claims and encounter information to the insurance carrier, health plan, or third-party administrator.

The second component is a data *repository*, the main focus of this committee's interest.   Certain information about patients, providers, plans,

---

[7] Benton International is a consulting firm for the financial services industry, with expertise in credit card and ATM (automatic teller machine) transaction processing. All information about CHMIS in the BI specifications is in the public domain, and neither the John A. Hartford Foundation nor BI retains proprietary claims on this information.

and clinical encounters will be routed to and stored in a data repository (or made available through distributed databases); these data will then be available for use and analyses by providers, payers, purchasers, consumers, regulators, and researchers (see William M. Mercer, Inc., 1993). The repositories are intended to be *inclusive*—all individuals receiving care in a defined region or state. They are also designed to be *comprehensive*—including demographic, eligibility, clinical, health risk, and health status information.

As envisioned in the BI specifications for CHMISs, data sources are varied:

•   *Transaction-based information* In fee-for-service systems, encounter data typically associated with insurance claims, such as procedure and diagnostic codes, constitute much of the general data set and will be acquired directly from the provider as part of the claims transaction. In prepaid capitated systems (group and staff model HMOs) that do not normally produce insurance claims forms, special arrangements will be designed to obtain needed data. The system is intended to incorporate Medicare and Medicaid claims data at some point.

•   *Patient satisfaction surveys and health status questionnaires* This information will be obtained from the patient (or possibly a family member in the case of, e.g., minor children), on either a routine or a sample basis. Survey instruments and questionnaires might also contain inquiries about lifestyle and health habits.

•   *Special studies* The general data set will be augmented by specified clinical data acquired from providers to permit researchers and others to conduct special studies of specific health conditions or other topics. The subjects of special studies would likely change over time, but clearly could include matters related to quality of, satisfaction with, access to, and costs of health care in the relevant community or state.

Although not fully operational as this report was being prepared in 1993, the Hartford CHMISs were moving forcefully toward implementation. Two different operating models seem to predominate. One model is based on a state legislative requirement for all providers to send data to a public agency that contracts with the CHMIS operating entity; Washington State and Vermont fall into this group. A second model is voluntary, relying on recognition by providers and payers of the system's benefit to them. In such cases local business or health care purchasing coalitions may require that all providers with whom they contract submit data through the CHMIS; the Memphis Business Group on Health exemplifies this approach.

THE BENEFITS OF HEALTH DATABASES

The gains expected from imaginative but responsible uses of the information held by HDOs accrue not only to various interest groups but also to populations generally, whether in a metropolitan or substate region, a given state, or the nation as a whole. The size of the potential benefits, whether to the community at large or to specific users, is likely to be a function of the *comprehensiveness* and *inclusiveness* of the databases—the more *comprehensive* or *inclusive* (or both) the more powerful the information will be at every level and for every potential user and use.

Broad-based Benefits

The intent of many database and HDO efforts today is to give regions a way to monitor and improve the value of their health care services and the well-being of their residents. HDOs might achieve this by making available information on access to care, costs, appropriateness, effectiveness, and quality of health care services and providers. HDOs can also contribute to improvements in quality of care by making information available to institutions and groups of practitioners for their use in quality assurance and quality improvement (QA/QI) programs and for regional health planning.

Many HDOs (especially those developed with public funds and by legislative mandate) can be expected to be useful in addressing a wide range of policy questions and in this way they will contribute to the national debate related to health care reform.[8] Regardless of the path of reform efforts, the questions noted below are of special importance, as implied by the brief scenarios that opened Chapter 1. For example:

• *Access* Are people in a given region receiving appropriate care in a timely manner? Are services equitably available and affordable by all groups in that population? Do access barriers relating to social and cultural factors appear to persist? Does the use of particular types of providers or facilities differ by patient or consumer characteristics?

• *Costs* Can the rate of increase in aggregate health expenditures be

---

[8] In a recent report, the Institute of Medicine (IOM, 1993c) outlined the critical elements of health care reform that it believed sound reform proposals ought to address. The five main topics were access, containing costs, ensuring quality, financing care, and enhancing the infrastructure of health care. Individual IOM reports have dealt with specific topics related to certain aspects of health reform, such as access (IOM, 1993a), employment-based insurance (IOM, 1993e), quality of care (IOM, 1990), clinical practice guidelines (IOM, 1992a), and the information infrastructure (IOM, 1991a).

moderated? Can accurate estimates be made of the costs of care in given geographic areas? Can health care delivery and administration be made more efficient? Can administrative costs be reduced? Can cost shifting within the public sector (e.g., between states and the federal government, or from the private to the public sector) be minimized?

• *Quality of care* Can the provision of health services be organized so as to increase the likelihood of health outcomes that are desired by individual patients? Can information from these databases address three main quality problems: use of inappropriate and unnecessary services, underuse of appropriate and needed services, and poor technical and interpersonal performance? Can clinical and other information in HDO files contribute to more, and better, practice guidelines? Can credible information about more effective and appropriate health care services be made available to clinicians and institutions in a more timely, and less threatening, fashion? Can useful information about the quality and outcomes of care of different kinds of providers be assembled and made available in convenient and prompt ways to consumers and organizers of provider networks and plans (e.g., insurance companies)?[9]

• *Delivery of health services* What services are appropriate and effective for what health care problems? How does the provision of those services vary across geographic areas, population groups, types of providers, settings of care, and time? Can innovative approaches to health care delivery be designed so as to promote the goals of health reform?

• *Disease incidence and public health* What are the major causes of death, illness, and disability for different groups in the population? How are these patterns changing over time?

• *Health planning* How might the acquisition, location, operation, and financing of facilities, capital equipment, health personnel, and other resources be made more rational, more affordable, and more responsive to clear community and regional needs?

----

[9] At the time this study was conducted, the Hartford Foundation sponsored a separate study from researchers at the Harvard School of Public Health to examine questions related to the establishment of an "Institute for Health Care Assessment," which would have as a major goal the advancement of quality measurement and improvement. Services that such an institute might provide to HDOs might include project formulation, technical assistance (in quality measurement, data collection and management, and analysis), report design and profiling (e.g., of morbidity, patient satisfaction, provider adherence to guidelines, and variation in use of costly technologies), and project evaluation. A clearinghouse effort and dissemination might also be contemplated. For further information, see McNeil et al. (1992).

Differential Benefits as a Function of Users and Uses

Answers to the questions above benefit almost all members of a given population; in that sense, the gains are broad based. Other benefits of HDOs and their activities will depend on a specific user and use, which are explored more fully in the next section. One aspect of differential benefits should be underscored, however. In today's complicated U.S. health sector, what may profit one party may well work to the detriment of other parties. For example, information that encourages insurers or others to contract only with certain providers in a community, on grounds of either quality or cost, is doubtless of benefit to those insurers and providers, and it does give insurers the opportunity to direct patients toward high-quality providers. Such practices may, however, threaten the financial stability, livelihood, or professional standing of other, noncontracted providers—this is certainly not a benefit for them and may undermine the systems for the delivery of care to other, less-favored patient groups.

The next section briefly identifies users—groups that have a stake in the use of health-related data—and is followed by a discussion of potential uses of HDO databases. Some potential applications of data raise concerns that the report returns to in Chapters 3 and 4. In developing positions and recommendations about the actions that HDOs should take with respect to data (this chapter), public disclosure of health-related information on providers (Chapter 3), and with respect to privacy and confidentiality of person-identified data (Chapter 4), the committee tried to balance the broad-based benefits (and the narrower benefits sought by certain groups) against the possible harms that might be done to individuals or to broader health and social policy goals.

USERS OF INFORMATION IN HDOs

As noted, many stakeholders in the health care system will share the general uses and the derivative benefits described above for HDOs. The major users include:

• *Health care provider organizations and practitioners* Provider organizations include physicians in solo practice and large multispecialty groups; managed care groups such as HMOs, IPAs, and PPOs; free-standing surgery centers and other ambulatory care facilities; institutions such as hospitals and nursing homes; and enterprises such as pharmacies, clinical laboratories, and home health agencies.

• *Patients, families, and community residents in general* The information in HDO databases may also be valuable for active patients and their families; more generally, it will be useful for residents who, although not patients at a given time, seek information about health care.

   • *Academic and research organizations* Academic and research organizations take many forms: academic health or medical centers affiliated with the nation's public and private universities; schools of medicine, dentistry, nursing, and allied health professions; and schools of public health. Private research institutes also fall into this group. Most of the entities in this category have major patient care and educational responsibilities, but they also carry out much of the health research in this country on issues involving access, effectiveness, utilization, costs, quality, and acceptability of care.

   • *Payers and purchasers* This category of users includes health insurance firms and companies with self-insured health plans that pay for some or all of the health care of their beneficiaries or employees. It also includes managed care companies, third-party payers (TPPs), and third-party administrators (TPAs), who will look to HDOs for assistance in managing standard insurance tasks. Insurers and self-insured employers also administer a variety of retrospective and prospective utilization management and case management programs.

   • *Employers and business or purchaser coalitions* Typically, business coalitions comprise major employers in a given area, many of whom have self-insured health plans; some coalitions may have provider members, but many do not. These groups have been a driving force in developing data networks in several regions of the country. (For example, as the CHMIS models were evolving during the period of this study, they were motivated in large measure by the concerns and interests of business or purchaser coalitions.)

   • *Health agencies* At the federal level, at least three PHS agencies might find HDO databases of considerable value in their daily operations (beyond the clear contributions that such databases would make to outcomes and effectiveness research): the Food and Drug Administration, for postmarketing surveillance and monitoring responsibilities (USDHHS, 1991); the Centers for Disease Control and Prevention, for public health and prevention activities; and the Health Services and Resources Administration, for its Maternal and Child Health block grants and health work force training programs. Other DHHS agencies—such as HCFA, the Administration on Children and Families, and the Administration on Aging—might be added to this list of potential users for similar federal oversight tasks. At the state, county, and municipal level, analogous health departments are likely to be users of HDO information for corresponding purposes; they are also likely to be central to HDO development and operations.

   • *Other potential database users* Other users may well view HDO information as valuable. These include community and consumer organizations; charitable groups and volunteer groups concerned with various diseases; social service agencies; law enforcement agencies at the federal, state, and local level; attorneys; and commercial entities such as direct marketing firms, financial and credit institutions, and bill collection agencies, to list only a few. To the extent that these users seek person-identifiable information, however, the committee takes an extremely negative view toward providing access to HDO files.

USES OF DATABASES

Without a clear understanding of potential users and their reasons for wanting access to data, HDOs cannot frame or implement sensible policies about a range of operational activities. To provide a background for reaching conclusions about HDOs and for developing recommendations to address the major issues implied by the vignettes that opened Chapter 1, the committee explored the uses of HDO information. Those described below are seen as the most likely in the short term, but as the direction of health reform becomes clearer, new uses and users may arise (e.g., related to health purchasing alliances), and some described below (e.g., insurer roles) may become obsolete. In some cases, uses of HDO data are illustrated by reference to databases held by organizations or public agencies that approach the HDO concept (see Table 2-4).

Assessing Access to Care and Use of Services

Assessing access or lack of access to care is critical in evaluating the performance of systems of health care delivery and the rational planning of those systems. Understanding the economic, geographic, and transportation barriers to health services, variations in, and access to health services is essential in the evaluation of the effects of ongoing or changing health care delivery systems. Several recent studies have examined the relationship between insurance, socioeconomic status, and race, on the one hand, and access to and use of health services, on the other (Bravemen et al., 1989; Burstin et al., 1992; Patrick et al., 1992; Adler et al., 1993); racial and gender differences in disease incidence and survival have also been examined (Ayanian and Epstein, 1991; Hannan et al., 1991b; Ayanian, 1993; Becker et al., 1993; Whittle et al., 1993). At the level of regions of the country, unmet health needs may be especially significant for minorities or other groups such as pregnant women or poor children; users of HDO information may need to pay special attention to such groups.

Among the better-known work on patterns of utilization is that related to the phenomenon of geographic or small-area variations in the use of

TABLE 2-4   Examples of Databases in Current Use

Database	Description
The Department of Veterans Affairs (DVA)	Within the DVA, the Veterans Health Administration (VHA) operates the largest centrally-directed health care system in the United States. During 1993, these facilities supported 1.1 million inpatient and 23.9 million outpatient visits. Files include all inpatients and outpatients who use DVA health services; this population includes veterans, their dependents, active duty military personnel, DVA employees, and other emergency patients.
	VHA's goal is the development of a fully automated patient record. In 1982, VHA began implementation of a national automation program to integrate software for patient registration, admission/discharge/transfer, clinical scheduling, outpatient and inpatient pharmacy, and clinical laboratory. Implementation now centers on film and chart tracking, dietetics, radiology, mental health, medical center procurements, surgery, nursing, order entry and results reporting, patient-based cost accounting, and payroll administration.
	Applications under way for the clinical record module include capture of clinical information such as coded encounter information, tracking of consult requests, preparation of discharge summaries, maintenance of problem lists, and provision of a clinical lexicon for providers.
	VHA utilization data include inpatient episodes in DVA and non-DVA hospitals, extended care facilities, DVA and community nursing homes, outpatient visits and ambulatory surgery, prescriptions (and payments) for non-DVA sources, social work treatment and placement, and drug dependence treatment programs.
	VHA files are also used to produce fiscal statistics and estimates of total and average costs for various service categories (e.g., medical beds, nursing home care, and outpatient care) at each DVA medical center and to produce information for pension and compensation benefits, death rates, and county-level enumerations of veterans.

Minnesota Clinical Comparison and
Assessment Project (MCCAP)

This project has been operating for five years with 50 participating health care institutions. It represents a coalition of provider institutions, professional societies, and others coordinated by the Healthcare Education and Research Foundation, a nonprofit research foundation in St. Paul.

MCCAP includes data collection, analysis, and dissemination organized into a system that gives participants both comparative information for quality improvement and provider education and an analysis of changing practices and variations in practice.

The Greater Cleveland Health Quality Choice (GCHQC)

GCHQC is a joint effort of the local business coalition, the Greater Cleveland Hospital Association and 32 of Cleveland's hospitals, and the Academy of Medicine (the county medical society) to measure and disseminate information about the quality of care in Cleveland hospitals. Manually abstracted hospital records of patients in the metropolitan area provide information on (1) outcomes of certain medical and surgical admissions, (2) outcomes of intensive-care admissions, and (3) satisfaction data from hospitalized patients. Risk-adjusted quality data have been provided at an institutional level to employers for use in contracting decisions by employer members of the coalition.

The Manitoba Provincial Health Database

This is the best known and the most used of the provincial databases. It is both quite *comprehensive* and *inclusive*. In Manitoba, claims filed routinely with the Manitoba Health Services Commission (MHSC) from many settings of care (hospital, medical, outpatient, and nursing home) have been linked with the population registries and with each other to provide good longitudinal histories. The claims are generally complete and, when used appropriately, highly reliable. Nonparticipation in the Manitoba Health Plan is minimal as residents are not required to pay any premiums.

continued

TABLE 2-4 (Continued)

Database	Description
Cardiac Surgery Reporting System (CSRS)	For many years the New York State Department of Health has gathered information on all coronary bypass operations, valve operations, and heart transplants in the state; included are data on patient demographics; admission, discharge, and surgical procedure dates; pre-operative risk factors; complications; and discharge status. Surgeon and hospital identifiers are included. An advisory committee, composed of practicing New York State cardiac surgeons and cardiologists as well as advisors from other states, determined the clinical data needed and developed the report form used by the 30 hospitals certified to perform open-heart surgery in the state. A series of pre-operative surgical risk factors were identified by cardiac surgeons and cardiologists. The advisory committee uses the data to identify priorities for their state site visits and to feed information back to hospitals twice a year; in this exercise, they provide the hospital with two diskettes, one with the hospital's own information and the other that allows hospitals to predict mortality for patients. The work has documented wide differences over the years in the mortality rates of both hospitals and individual surgeons.
The National Trauma Registry of the American College of Surgeons (TRACS)	TRACS includes 152 standardized data elements on patients treated for trauma at 19 trauma centers. Data elements include: type of injury; diagnosis; treatment provided; days in the intensive care unit and hospital; hospital charges and reimbursement; medical complications, readmissions, reoperations, and indicators of delayed treatment; impairments in self-care, mobility, or verbal ability; and final disposition. Additional modules will be directed toward data on pediatric trauma, autopsy, burn care, head injury, quality assurance, orthopedic services, prehospital care, and outcomes research.

Integrated Medical Systems, Inc. (IMS)

IMS is a vendor that has developed a database designed to provide administrative information and to aid current medical management through provision of information such as claims data, eligibility, benefits information, and utilization review. IMS owns (in most cases) and operates 23 information networks in 20 states with 90 hospitals and 5,000 participating physicians. A Colorado network involves 40 percent of the state's acute-care hospitals, 800 physicians, 5 pharmacies, a clinical laboratory, an insurance company, a diagnostic center, and an imaging center.

These information networks are what some term virtual databases in that no data to which they provide access are stored in a central computer. IMS uses telephone lines and modems to transfer text, voice, image, and graphics information (e.g., electrocardiograms, magnetic resonance images) among network sponsors and users authorized by each sponsor. Sponsors are typically institutional providers; their authorized users are typically individual practitioners.

Medicare National Claims History and Beneficiary Health Status Registry

As of 1990, these files have included about 96 percent of the U.S. population who are age 65 and over (29 million people), disabled persons (about 10 million), and almost 150,000 patients with end-stage renal disease (ESRD). The main files resemble the typical insurance-claims-driven data files of private- and public-sector payers, but they are by far the best known (and most inclusive, but not necessarily the most comprehensive) of all health-related administrative databases. Between 1989 and 1991, HCFA completed implementation of the National Claims History system, which consolidates all beneficiary information by linking hospital and physician payment records. The agency believes this system will increase appreciably its ability to track access to and quality of care and to support research and demonstration projects; such public-use tapes have been and will continue to be, therefore, a rich source of data for health services research. In the early 1990s, HCFA also began work on the Medicare Beneficiary Health Status Registry, which will contain longitudinal information on 2 percent of beneficiaries from enrollment into the program until death; data collected is to include sociodemographic variables, risk factors, medical history, and health status and quality-of-life information.

SOURCES: For DVA, DVA, 1992, 1993. For MCCAP, Borbas et al., 1990; Darby, 1992; Kane and Lurie, 1992. For GCHQC, CHQC, 1993. For Manitoba, Roos et al., 1982, 1985, 1993, in press. For CSRS, Hannan et al., 1989a, 1989b, 1990, 1991a; Zinman, 1991; also see Appendix 3.A. For TRACS, ACS, 1992. For Medicare History and Registry, IOM, 1990; PPRC, 1993.

medical services, particularly invasive procedures.[10] Much of the landmark research in this area has relied on the administrative and other databases that HCFA maintains for the Medicare program (Table 2-4); these files have been extremely useful for research purposes for more than a decade. Other studies have employed data from state data organizations (e.g., Wennberg and Gittelsohn, 1982). For purposes of tracking use of services, conducting many different kinds of health services and health policy research, and otherwise administering a complex population-based health system, many experts regard the databases maintained by the individual provinces of Canada as models for uses of HDO information (see Table 2-4 for a description of the Manitoba files).

Some uses of HDO data to explore patterns of utilization could raise concerns, however. For example, information that permits third party payers to devise insurance packages attractive to (or affordable by) only certain groups in the population is clearly of competitive benefit to the companies and the populations they target, but such practices may operate to the disadvantage of the excluded groups. To the extent the latter overlap with the vulnerable populations noted above, many would regard this use of HDO data as undesirable.

Assessing Costs and Identifying Opportunities for Savings

Curbing health care expenditures includes placing global limits on spending and linking fees to changes in the volume of services. For such efforts to be effective and equitable, however, those directing them will have to understand better the geographic variations in services and the reasons for these variations (Welch et al., 1993). Equally significant will be documenting the true economic costs of delivering health care as a means of understanding patterns of health expenditures and, secondarily, the efficiency of different plans and systems of care. To the extent that HDOs acquire reliable and valid information on services rendered and on charges and payments for those services (however questionable the actual relationship between billed charges and true costs), they will be in a position to clarify cost and expenditure issues.

---

[10] The literature in this area is extensive. Well-known articles—beginning about a decade ago on small-area-variations analysis—include McPherson et al., 1981; Roos and Roos, 1981; Roos et al., 1982; Wennberg and Gittelsohn, 1982; Wennberg et al., 1982, 1984; Eddy, 1984; Roos, 1984; Wennberg, 1984; *Health Affairs,* 1984; Chassin et al., 1986a, 1987; Merrick et al., 1986; Winslow et al., 1988a, 1988b; Wennberg, 1990; Paul et al., 1993. For a recent review of this literature and a new interpretation of this body of empirical work that suggests that physician enthusiasm for particular services explains much of the geographic variation in utilization, see Chassin, 1993a.

Evaluating Quality and Outcomes of Care

Information about quality of care is important to everyone—for choosing a source of care, designing a health plan, building a malpractice case, or trying to improve care—and this committee gave quality assurance and improvement issues special attention in its deliberations. Physicians, institutions, and others who deliver direct patient care and insurers who establish their own provider networks will need to carry out QA/QI activities. It can be argued that the quality issues will have even greater visibility if certain approaches to health care reform gain prominence (those premised on managed competition) because of the heavy reliance that will be placed on the availability of credible quality-of-care information to consumers, purchasers, and regulators. As noted above with respect to access, the work that HDOs might do or support on quality of care must take disadvantaged, at-risk, vulnerable populations more directly into account (Lohr et al., 1993).

If information available from HDOs is reliable and amenable to diagnosis-specific analyses and if it can be aggregated by physician, institution, and the like, then it may prove more useful for these purposes than current regulatory approaches to quality assurance. Of special interest to insurers (and policymakers in implementing health reform) is the potential for HDOs to use aggregate data to provide clinical practice benchmarks or norms. Such norms allow insurers (or others) to compare the practices and outcomes of a given provider with those of similar providers.

Hospital-specific Mortality Rate Studies

Hospital-specific mortality rate studies have been an early focus of quality of care studies using large databases. Much of this work began with HCFA'S release of such information in the mid-1980s, and a steady stream of reports (produced annually until 1993 by HCFA) from numerous teams of investigators has appeared since that time.[11] Statewide databases have also been used for research projects on mortality rates following open heart surgery. One example comes from the New York State Cardiac Surgery Reporting System (Hannan et al., 1989b, 1990, 1991a; Zinman, 1991; see also Chapter 3 of this report) and another from the Pennsylvania Health

---

[11] The first major release of hospital-specific mortality rates dates to publications from HCFA (e.g., HCFA, 1991). Other illustrative research efforts include those reported by Chassin et al. (1989) on all Medicare hospitalizations, by Dubois et al. (1987a, 1987b) on admissions to institutions belonging to a single hospital chain, and by Luft and Romano (1993) on risk-adjusted death rates from coronary artery bypass and graft operations for hospitals in California.

Care Cost Containment Council, whose report listed hospital charges and risk-adjusted mortality rates for coronary artery bypass graft (CABG) surgery for 35 Pennsylvania hospitals and 170 cardiac surgeons (PHCCCC, 1992).

A painstaking evaluation of the impact of the Diagnosis-related Group Prospective Payment System (DRG-based PPS) in Medicare also relied on Medicare files for critical data on patient outcomes (Kahn et al., 1992; Keeler et al., 1992a). Because the thrust of this work relates to quality of care, this report returns to such studies in Chapter 3.

Effectiveness and Outcomes Research

Yet another critical research area involves the effectiveness and outcomes of health care—the clinical evaluative sciences as some call it. Understanding effectiveness involves evaluation of the utility and appropriateness of health care in everyday settings with so-called average patients and usual providers (Brook and Lohr, 1985). William Roper, M.D., the former HCFA administrator, coined the phrase "what works in the practice of medicine" to characterize the questions that researchers in medical effectiveness might address (Roper et al., 1988). At about the same time, the National Center for Health Services Research (now AHCPR) began an ambitious research program whose grantees are known as Patient Outcomes Research Teams (PORTs) (AHCPR, 1990a, 1990b; Raskin and Maklan, 1991). A dozen or more PORTs are under way at any one time in this country, and all of those concerned with health problems of the elderly rely heavily on Medicare files.

Although these studies often involve rigorous design and statistical methods, by intent they are usually not randomized trials that require massive primary data collection—hence the attractiveness of information on health care that already has been collected and stored in data files. Information in these databases can, nonetheless, contribute to classic randomized, controlled trials—for example, by providing indications of the epidemiology of disease or treatment patterns or, in some circumstances, serving as a means of designing a sampling frame for the study.[12] As a case in point: two articles that appeared as this report was being prepared examined the utility of

---

[12] Technology assessment overlaps with these research efforts insofar as it extends beyond reviews of the published literature or operations of expert panels to actual collection and analysis of data. Often, however, technology assessment is directed more at emerging technologies—for example, new drugs, devices, or (less often) procedures—than at established ones. To the extent this is true, databases of the sort described in this report, particularly those derived from financial transactions in health care, will not contain much relevant or useable

surgery for prostatic cancer (Fleming et al., 1993; Lu-Yao et al., 1993). One paper relied on Medicare's claims system to estimate the risk of radical prostatectomy; the other examined time trends and geographic variations in prostate cancer diagnosis. Both can be traced to earlier analyses on variations in the use of transurethral prostatectomy for benign prostatic hypertrophy, which had been based on data contained in large-scale databases (see the citations in footnote 10). The committee thus placed great emphasis on the need to expand such uses of health databases—including those expected to be assembled by HDOs—to address the myriad health services research questions that now confront this nation. A recent report from AHCPR provides a useful compilation of automated data sources and a literature review for ambulatory care effectiveness research as well as a description of automated ambulatory record systems (USDHHS, 1993a).

Quality Assurance and Quality Improvement Programs

Providers will find information in HDO databases of particular value for QA/QI programs. In a health care environment emphasizing competition—one that may heavily regulate prices and other economic factors and disallow preexisting condition clauses, biased risk selection by insurers, and similar cost-shifting tactics—competition on the basis of quality of care may become far more prominent (AMPRA, 1993; IOM, 1993c; Palmer and Adams, 1993; Tillmann and Sullivan, 1993). Provider groups have a clear incentive to implement meaningful QA/QI efforts as a means of doing as well as possible in comparative analyses. Some internal efforts may involve recruiting high-quality staff or dismissing poorly performing staff; other elements involve improving performance across the board. Thus, these databases may offer provider groups help for strategic planning, marketing, and competing in local health markets; these benefits presuppose that providers choose to act on the information that they can glean directly from the database or that they are furnished as part of an external quality-review program.

In California, for example, all nonfederal acute-care hospitals submit discharge abstracts to the state's Office of Statewide Health Planning and Development. Among the data elements available for analysis are age, sex, presence of chronic conditions, dates of admission, surgery, and procedures

---

data on those newer technologies. They will, however, contain valuable information for the comparison of these new technologies with existing approaches (which always include watchful waiting). When the focus of technology assessment is on established technologies, databases are useful not only for such evaluation activities, but also for setting priorities for assessment (IOM, 1992b).

in addition to a primary operation; information dates back to at least 1983. Using data from this file, Luft and Romano (1993) reported on two sets of CABG-related analyses: (1) describing general patterns of CABG use and risk-adjusted outcomes over a seven-year period and (2) identifying hospitals with significantly or consistently higher or lower death rates after CABG than would be expected. These kinds of analyses are commonly done with hospital discharge abstract databases; often, however, they are subject to considerable criticism, especially because of the inadequacy of information to permit adjustment for patient risk factors, such as ejection fraction or previous CABG. Given the constraints of the database that Luft and Romano used, their study was considered exemplary because of their sophisticated approach to measuring outcome and performing statistical analyses (Chassin, 1993b).

Another example of quality-of-care applications of databases is the quantitative and qualitative work done for the IOM report on the end-stage renal disease (ESRD) program (IOM, 1991b). These analyses drew on information in one or more of three major ESRD data systems: the ESRD Program Management and Medical Information System, administered by HCFA; the United States Renal Data System, administered by the National Institute of Diabetes and Digestive and Kidney Diseases; and the United Network for Organ Sharing data system, a part of the Southeast Organ Procurement Foundation.

In short, for well more than a decade researchers have employed large databases, particularly those of the Medicare program, for studies that today have significant bearing on our understanding of the quality of health services in terms of both processes and outcomes of care. Apart from their intrinsic worth and findings, such studies have generated important hypotheses, the exploration of which promises to yield further, and considerable, social benefit.

Planning and Monitoring Patient Care

Health care practitioners will be able to use the information in HDO databases in many patient care responsibilities. Examples of such applications include: checking patients' allergies to medication, obtaining patient histories at the time of patient-practitioner encounters, planning the management of complex cases, and fostering better communication among all providers rendering care to an individual patient and between clinicians and ancillary personnel.

Descriptive information derived from such databases may enable primary care physicians (and their support staffs) to conduct outreach and health promotion activities; such tasks might involve identifying individuals who should receive periodic screening tests and providing up-to-date immunization records for school enrollment. Chronically ill patients and their families could use HDO data files to help maintain family health records (e.g., logs of visits to a specialist or admissions to a hospital) or to create a running sum of out-of-pocket expenses for office-based care, medications, or hospitalizations.

HDOs with prescription databases might enable physicians, pharmacists, and others to track prescribed medications and to report adverse drug reactions more readily. Their databases might also be used to identify medication abuse by patients who obtain a pharmaceutical agent from multiple providers or to detect medications prescribed by different providers whose interactions could cause adverse reactions or reduce their effectiveness.

Even for those who are not patients or relatives of patients at any given time, HDO databases may be of value. Descriptive information on primary care physicians, specialists, other caregivers, and health plans (e.g., location, special aspects of a practice or facility, or usual charges) may be of great help when individuals plan to seek care for new problems or in new locales. Health education materials that could be developed as an adjunct to HDO activity, such as guidelines for preventive care, nutrition, or available community resources, can be a valuable resource for residents as well.

Many large employers have become deeply involved in managed care, case management of high-risk or high-cost patients, and in workplace health promotion efforts. They are likely to use HDO information in all these kinds of programs for their employees, employees' dependents, and (possibly) retirees. Government is a significant employer at the federal, state, and local levels, and it has as much interest in good health and good decision making among civil servants, as does the private sector for its work force. Thus, the uses that corporate (or small) employers might have for HDO information apply equally to the public sector.

Less obvious reasons for seeking access to health databases can be imagined. For example, adopted children may wish to obtain information on certain health or genetic characteristics of their birth (natural) parents, as a means of making health-related decisions of their own; such requests might be brought through third parties as a way of protecting the privacy of the parents or the adopted child, or both. Although this example may seem remote today, uncommon uses of these databases—and the considerable ethical, psychological, political, and practical ramifications they may have— ought to be contemplated in advance as policies about access, privacy, and disclosure are set in motion.

Enhancing Administrative Efficiency

One major goal of health care reform is to make health insurance claims processing and financial transactions more efficient. All health insurers have databases derived from several sources. These databases have traditionally served as mechanisms for eligibility verification, provider reporting (for tax purposes), and claims adjudication. When their data flow in an electronic transaction (i.e., EDI) system, the efficiency related to billing, reimbursement, claims tracking, remittance reconciliation, and similar business matters can be very high; the Workgroup for Electronic Data Interchange, in its report to the Secretary of DHHS (WEDI, 1992), estimated benefits, savings, and strategies for implementing EDI in the coming years.

Analogously, when HDOs build their repositories through such electronic systems, they may be able to support nearly instantaneous verification of insurance plan eligibility and covered benefits,[13] facilitate claims submission, and eliminate time-consuming, costly paperwork. The closer that these databases approximate the medical record, the more exact reimbursement strategies will become and the less time can be spent on record requests and appeals.

Operating Managed Care Programs

Providers or others may find HDO databases helpful in identifying likely high-cost patients who would benefit from case management and in streamlining precertification tasks. Case management and precertification customarily call for case-by-case decision making—whether an individual's care for severe mental illness will be reimbursed if given in the inpatient setting or whether services for a high-risk pregnancy will be organized through a case manager.

TPPs and TPAs have begun to apply medical logic programs to augment their precertification programs with what might be called intelligent adjudication—that is, decision making that takes into account historical medical information. Given appropriate and consistent use of standardized coding rules, electronic (as opposed to telephone- or paper-based) precertification systems can simplify and speed decision making for patients, physicians, TPPs, and TPAs. HDO data may be useful for profiling services received

---

[13] The term "benefits," as used in this report, has two distinct meanings, depending on the context. One reflects the general notion of positive advantages, gains, and useful aids in the conduct of some activity. The other is the narrower insurance-related concept of a benefit package or contract, in which a set of services (typically characterized as "medically necessary") is specified as covered (and in which other services may be specifically identified as not covered). This committee assumes that major health care reform will likely bring about a standardized class of covered benefits, at least in a "basic" package mandated nationally; this would reduce the need for verification of covered benefits by providers and insurers. To the extent that reform initiatives permit differential types of supplemental insurance plans to be offered, however, such verification may still be needed and the desirability of doing that instantaneously remains high.

by patients who are subject to precertification programs and for portraying prevailing practices in a locale, thereby contributing to the construction of such logic programs.

In these ways, HDO data could be brought to bear to improve patient care and to minimize the frustrating, inequitable, or idiosyncratic features of present-day utilization review and case management. Looking well into the future, some experts hypothesize that information in large-scale databases will significantly change utilization management processes and, indeed, even obviate the need for utilization management as it is conducted today. This might happen as better epidemiologic data and the methods of artificial intelligence make it possible to create case-management protocols based on complex logic trees that take account of far more patient, clinical, and other variables than is possible today.

Strategic Planning and Selective Contracting

HDO data can facilitate a range of long-term planning, business, and financial management tasks that insurers, employers, and providers face. Such information can also be applied in the selective contracting activities that are becoming increasingly common.

Strategic Planning

With respect to long-range strategies, TPPs and TPAs might be able to improve their underwriting and benefits design through analysis of HDO data; for instance, such analyses might enable them to set premiums more accurately or to establish benefit packages. However, the committee hopes that TPPs and TPAs would not use HDO databases for selective underwriting that further fragments the risk pool. More broadly, payers and purchasers might be able to determine the risks they face with respect to future demand for health care more accurately from such databases than they could in the past. If HDO databases are reasonably *inclusive*, TPPs and TPAs might then be able to understand better how such demand might vary by geographic area or population group and how it might change over time.

Payers are likely to use HDO information in strategic planning for more than just the health insurance portion of their business. For instance, some health insurers may be part of conglomerates that offer life, disability, workers' compensation, and other forms of insurance. In theory, HDOs might provide information on individuals, or groups in a geographic area, that would be of considerable interest to those managing other activities of an insurance company. Such data might be helpful in devising nonhealth insurance packages that are attractive (or not attractive, as the case may be) to certain individuals or populations in those locales.

Providers may seek to use HDO databases for many reasons: to project market share when considering mergers with other facilities, to select sites for satellite clinics, to establish ambulatory surgery centers, to acquire group practices, and in other ways to plan future activities with financial implications. Some groups may wish to acquire competitive intelligence in order to set charges for their services, so that they can consider whether to lower or raise their charges for some or all purchasers or patients. Although such activities might well raise antitrust issues, addressing such questions was beyond the expertise of the committee or the scope of the study.

Selective Contracting

To develop provider networks—systems of practitioners (including physicians, dentists, optometrists, and psychologists), ancillary facilities (e.g., clinical laboratories or short-term substance abuse programs), hospitals and nursing homes, and agencies that deliver home health or home-based hospice care—that can compete effectively in the health sector today, insurers need more specific, accurate, and detailed data that will permit them to contract selectively with such providers. Selective contracting in this context means not only identifying practitioners and providers that can deliver high-quality care within some acceptable cost norms, but also recognizing those that cannot; in either case, it implies that providers will perform in accordance with responsible practice guidelines and protocols. In addition, providers might use measures of normative behavior to determine the standards of quality each provider or plan might expect of its practitioners.

Thus, HDO information might be applied in retrospective profiling of provider-related information as a means of identifying providers that might be brought into (or kept out of) selective contracting arrangements; it can also be employed to monitor performance over time. One of the chief aims of HDOs emerging today is, in fact, to aid payer or other groups in this process by enabling them to develop (or acquire) analyses of practice patterns, outcomes, costs, and similar variables that will permit them to make decisions about the providers their systems will include or exclude.

Other Business-related Uses

Nearly three-quarters of employers with 1,000 or more employees manage self-insured health plans (Foster Higgins, 1991, in IOM, 1993e). These firms can, for all practical purposes, be regarded as conducting (or being responsible for) the same tasks as insurers, as discussed above.[14] Health

---

[14] The technicalities—not trivial matters—relating to Employment Retirement Income Security Act (ERISA) preemptions with respect to self-insured employer plans were not directly

databases or HDOs based chiefly on the sponsorship of employers will thus, in theory, offer considerable advantages in benefits planning, selective contracting, monitoring provider network performance, and similar activities relating to management of employment-based health insurance coverage. For example, employers may want to create case-management plans that are increasingly directive and oriented toward exclusive provider organization (EPO) arrangements, like those that are common today for high-technology therapies such as transplantation and cardiac surgery.

Employers might also wish to use the information in some databases for personnel actions—promotions, relocations, dismissals, and the like.[15] As will be noted later in this report, serious concerns must be addressed about misuse of data in general and with respect to possible violation of the Americans with Disabilities Act (ADA), for instance. Nevertheless, the connections between workplace wellness and personnel actions are clear.

Tracking Injury and Illness, Preventive Care, and Health Behaviors

Those studying and having responsibility for public health efforts can be expected to use HDO databases for a broad set of applications. These include analyses of the incidence of injury and disease and studies of the prevalence of trauma-related health problems and chronic illness. Today, disease and injury registries provide information on traumatic events, episodes of illness, and the processes and outcomes of care that exemplify what might be done with HDO data in the future. For instance, cancer registry data from two states, Illinois and Washington, have been used to address a range of questions (Hand et al., 1991; Lasovich et al., 1991) including underuse of services in the hospitals studied. One study focused analyses on the percentage of early-stage breast cancer patients who do not

---

addressed by this IOM committee. Many observers believe, however, that meaningful health care reform will require modification, if not outright repeal, of ERISA insofar as health insurance is concerned (IOM, 1993e, 1993c). Federal preemptive legislation would override existing state statutes and regulations and effectively take some aspects of insurance regulation out of the hands of state insurance commissioners; if that occurs, distinctions between self-insured corporations and insurers subject to state insurance regulation will decrease if not disappear altogether. The ramifications of ERISA extend beyond insurance regulation to rules for protecting the privacy and confidentiality of personal health data, including those held by HDOs; informational privacy issues are addressed in Chapter 4.

[15] For purposes of making hiring decisions about individuals, *potential* employers may wish to obtain information on such persons. This committee will (in Chapter 4) take a very strong position against person-identifiable information being made available for this purpose and thus does not examine that possible use of health databases further.

receive indicated axillary lymph node dissection or assays for hormone receptors; in another, the study question was the percentage of women receiving breast-conserving surgery who did not receive indicated radiation therapy. In commenting on these studies, Chassin (1991) notes that they suggest problems "in the extent to which physicians fail to communicate options and outcomes data objectively" (p. 3473) and advocates routine feedback of these kinds of data to hospitals. With respect to injury, the American College of Surgeons National Trauma Registry is another example of a database that provides information on patterns of injury and their outcomes (see Table 2-4); for those concerned with emergency medical services, such sources of epidemiologic and clinical information are critical (IOM, 1993d).

Other public health applications of HDO databases relate to preventive care and health behaviors. For some industries, for instance, epidemiologic information from large databases may enable analysts to identify potential safety or health-related problems in workplace environments and to suggest corrective steps. Immunization tracking systems, currently under development regionally and nationally, might be incorporated into HDO databases to simplify monitoring and recording of children's immunization status both in aggregate and individually. HDOs might also maintain information about blood type, organ donors, and tissue matching in their databases, as a means of fostering improved blood banking and organ procurement and transplant services.

Promoting Regional and Community Health Planning, Education, and Outreach

Health Planning and Education

When HDO databases are statewide, or sponsored by state health departments, the potential uses by states and all subordinate levels of government for health planning, health care delivery, public health, and administrative responsibilities become quite extensive; they can involve the health departments and social services agencies of states, counties, and municipalities in many overlapping efforts. Planning and educational activities that could employ HDO data might be focused on improving access to, reducing costs of, and enhancing quality of care; on organizing provider systems of care; or on investigating epidemiologic patterns of injury or illness. For example, community-specific studies conducted using HDO data might examine the kinds of cases treated by local hospital emergency departments, whether use differs by hospital or patient characteristics, and whether patient outcomes differ accordingly. Such information might enable public agencies to target public funds or other resources in new ways to meet previously undetected problems or needs.

Integrating data on vital statistics, epidemiologic surveillance, and local and regional public health programs with those in the personal-health-care files of HDOs raises the possibility of more effective public health activities for monitoring health, attaining public health objectives at a population level, and targeting efforts for hard-to-reach individuals. For example, researchers in Boston have developed and operationalized a distributed health record system for a homeless population seen at many sites by many different providers (Chueh and Barnett, 1994).

Community Outreach

In addition to whatever public-sector agencies might do to monitor the public health of communities, community and consumer organizations may wish also to carry out population-based studies as a means of learning where significant health problems exist and of making elected officials and others more accountable for solving those problems. Another significant way that information held by HDOs may contribute to the work of community, voluntary, and consumer groups is in their public education and outreach programs. Here the data may suggest emerging problems that warrant increased attention (or waning problems that need reduced effort); data may also indicate where (in geographic areas or population subgroups) education initiatives might best be targeted. For example, recognition that bicycle accidents are a major source of children's head injuries could lead to community education programs in schools and neighborhood associations. Public-sector agencies, academic centers, or consumer groups might pursue such public health efforts by analyzing HDO data and developing community-specific informational materials (e.g., public information brochures on sources of care for special problems).

Charitable groups and voluntary organizations concerned with particular diseases and conditions have many roles: providing information to and support for patients with particular illnesses and for their families; sponsoring research; and lobbying for more policy attention, social acceptance, and research support for the problem. Because they are likely to be private organizations that secure their funds through donations from individuals and corporations, most must engage in aggressive fund-raising campaigns. Information from health data banks might enable them to increase their efficiency in amassing epidemiologic information and perhaps in targeting fund-raising efforts.

Other Uses for HDO Databases

The IOM committee identified a great many other potential users and uses of HDO databases, including agencies engaged in law enforcement at the federal, state, and local levels; law firms and attorneys; and various commercial entities. The more plausible are briefly described here.

Law enforcement officials can be expected to find many uses for the information held in HDO files. They may wish to trace individuals (for instance, to locate parents not paying child support). They may also need to investigate alleged illegal acts; in the health context, this might extend to abuse of illegal substances or cases of possible child abuse. Conceivably, law enforcement agencies might want genetic information to assist them in identification of a suspect. Finally, such agencies may be expected to monitor providers and patients for possible fraud.

Arguably attorneys and law firms might identify many uses for HDO data, including malpractice litigation. Plaintiffs' lawyers, for instance, might try to access information from HDOs concerning previous quality-of-care deficiencies of a physician or hospital; defendants' counsel might seek to demonstrate, through analysis of HDO data, that the provider acted well within community standards. One important application occurs in cases where the past or current health condition of the patient is relevant to the case or is at issue in the case. Product safety litigation may also call forth requests for data from the network, especially when a medical device is in question. Finally, attorneys representing health plans, insurers, medical groups, hospitals, and other providers in their business (e.g., financial) concerns may find information contained in the databases of use in advising their clients about risk management, taxes, financing, and similar matters.

A wide array of other kinds of companies, organizations, and services might well have an interest in the information available through HDOs. Among them are direct marketing firms, financial and credit institutions, and bill collection agencies. Such entities (especially the last named) might wish to have person-identified information, but in general many applications of the information might not be directed at patients but rather at providers or at groupings such as zip codes. Financial and credit institutions might be interested in health plan and hospital data to determine market share or estimate solvency for a given group practice or facility. In general, this committee takes an extremely negative view toward giving these groups access to HDO files, particularly any data that might conceivably identify individual persons, and thus these uses are not explored further here.

Comment

The committee emphasizes that its roster of users includes examples of current as well as potential HDO database users;[16] it does not believe that HDOs necessarily ought to satisfy all such claimants. It does acknowledge, however, that the mere existence of a database creates new demands for access and new users and uses. Consequently, those who establish health databases and HDOs may be creating something for which the end uses cannot always be anticipated.

Because this study took place at a time of change in both health care infrastructure and information systems, the committee tried to anticipate the probable sources of the tension that will exist between those who create databases and wish to protect the information and those who might argue for access to those databases on grounds of anticipated benefits. Historically, the creation of large databases, such as those to administer the Social Security program and the National Crime Information Network, has been followed by modifications in the databases themselves and in the policies and legislation that regulate access to them—which results more often than not in relaxing prohibitions or barriers to access. Realism dictates that large databases such as those maintained by HDOs will be dynamic. In the committee's view, policies regarding access to these databases should, therefore, be based on firm principles but flexible enough to accommodate unavoidable changes and unanticipated uses.

The benefits of electronic patient records should not be overlooked, however. These benefits include the availability of much more powerful databases, elimination of the need for repeated requests to record subjects for the same information, and assurance that information is available when needed. Despite the privacy concerns described, it should be possible to improve privacy protection and safeguard the confidentiality of health information in HDOs through a variety of methods described in later chapters.

Moreover, information must be acted on by individuals in a position to

---

[16] In *The Computer-Based Patient Record: An Essential Technology for Health Care,* the IOM examined in some depth the array of users of computer-based patient records (CPRs) and CPR systems, indicating that an "exhaustive list . . . would essentially parallel a list of the individuals and organizations associated directly or indirectly with the provision of health care. Patient record users provide, manage, review, or reimburse patient care services; conduct clinical or health services research; educate health care professionals or patients; develop or regulate health care technologies; accredit health care professionals or provider institutions; and make health care policy decisions" (IOM, 1991a, p. 31). It is difficult to improve on that enumeration in the present context, even though the nature of the databases themselves (CPRs versus networks based on, e.g., insurance billing transactions or surveys) is quite different and the emphasis (e.g., patient care delivery versus health plan management) differently placed.

change their own, and others', behaviors and performance. Most experts agree that getting information to people and organizations is just the first, and perhaps not the most important, step in the change process. Although this committee (in Chapter 3) places great store on information dissemination efforts by HDOs, HDOs will not be well placed to follow up the actions taken (or not taken) by recipients of that information.

Many of the challenges faced by the health care sector are essentially exogenous—for instance, the changing demographics of the U.S. population, problems of international competition in the manufacturing and information-services sectors, and increasing disintegration of social and familial structures. No amount of radical change in health care, let alone tinkering, will demonstrably affect those problems, and HDOs similarly cannot influence them.

Further, despite the promise that HDOs hold for addressing certain health policy issues, this committee emphasizes that information derived from the files of HDOs and similar entities will not be *the* solution to all the ills of the health care system. Information may be incomplete or untimely, lack critical variables such as health status, or otherwise be imperfect. In addition, such data may be observational, meaning that they lend themselves more to description than to causal or inferential analysis, and more to retrospective commentary than to prediction. In the terminology used earlier, HDOs and their constituent databases may be neither acceptably *comprehensive* nor *inclusive*.

Commentary on a related information activity is instructive. In 1992 the IOM, in conjunction with the Commission on Behavioral and Social Sciences and Education (CBASSE) reviewed the plans of the National Center for Health Statistics for a new National Health Care Survey. The survey is described as having the following objective: "to produce annual data on the use of health care and the outcomes of care for the major sectors of the health care delivery system. These data will describe the patient populations, medical care provided, financing, and provider characteristics" (IOM/CBASSE, 1992, p. 6). The IOM/CBASSE report commented at some length on the ability of existing data sources (e.g., current NCHS surveys) to provide these kinds of information and noted (p. 38):

> [They] are rapidly becoming outdated and less comprehensive than is desirable. Often they do not cover the universe of providers and sites of health care [or] patients or potential users of health care. They lack sufficient information on exactly what services are provided and what the outcomes of those services are . . . are inexact with respect to financial data . . . are not timely; and . . . are inaccurate, incomplete and unreliable.

These faults may well affect the data repositories and networks considered by this IOM committee; they are discussed in greater detail below.

ENSURING THE QUALITY OF DATA

The above discussion has outlined the many potential users, uses, and benefits of HDOs. Ultimately, however, the real rewards of developing and operating HDOs will depend heavily on the quality of the data that they acquire and maintain. The committee considers this subject of sufficient importance that it elected to comment on it directly.

The absolute prerequisites to successful implementation of any type of database or HDO with the expansive goals implied by the foregoing discussion are reliable and valid data. Developers must ensure that the data in their systems are of high enough quality that the descriptive compilations, the effectiveness research, and the comparative analyses envisioned can be done in a credible, defensible manner. (McNeil et al., 1992, describe limitations of current data systems for profiling quality of care, especially at the individual provider level.) Mistakes, qualifications and caveats, retractions, and similar problems must be minimized, and precision about what data are actually being sought must be maximized. All this must be done from the outset so that the long-term integrity and believability of the database and work based on its information will not be undermined irretrievably.

The committee did not wish to prescribe methods that HDOs might employ for ensuring data quality, judging that approaches might differ by type of database and HDO. It did, however, consider that success in meeting this responsibility will call for attention on several fronts.

First, the committee held the view that information becomes more useful when it is used. Although the characteristic of *comprehensiveness* is clearly of primary importance in considering the value of a database, HDOs need to avoid the trap of collecting everything that it is possible to collect, regardless of its reliability and completeness, and thereby end up with data elements that will be used only rarely and, worse, be of questionable value when they are used.

Part of the problem is that analysts will have little experience with such data elements and may make incorrect assumptions about their reliability or about how to interpret values correctly. Another part of the problem is that some data, although currently collected routinely because an entry must be made in a box on a form, are not used for anything by anyone. Such data will likely have a very low level of accuracy. A commonly cited example relates to information on hospital diagnoses in the Medicare program; diagnoses were often doubtful before the advent of the DRG-based PPS (see Gardner, 1990). When diagnostic data began to figure in decisions about reimbursement, studies of quality of care, choices in clinical care, or analyses about productivity, the situation changed. After 1983 hospitals came to be paid on the basis of DRGs (which obviously are diagnosis based), and diagnostic information improved markedly, although some problems persist. Similar problems of suspicious (missing, wrong, or even fraudulent) information on insurance claims forms for outpatient care exist to this day; the underlying problem is that payment mechanisms do not depend so heavily on outpatient diagnostic data—that is, the information is not used in the same way as inpatient data—so little incentive exists to record diagnoses accurately.[17] The least that can happen in these instances is that those data elements consume computer memory; the worst is that the data will be used in ways that contaminate an entire study or cause unwarranted harm to individuals, groups, or practitioners.

Second, data must be accurate and analyzable. Sometimes these points are couched in terms of reliability and validity of data.[18] More generally, the accuracy and completeness of data elements that will be used extensively must be guaranteed if they are to be useful. Among the problems one must guard against are the following: missing data; out-of-range values for quantitative data (e.g., age of patient; charges; even laboratory values in the most advanced databases of the future); unrealistic changes in parameters over time (e.g., the doubling of a patient's weight between office visits); clearly erroneous information (e.g., wrong sex); and miscoded information on diagnostic tests, actual diagnoses, surgical procedures, medications, and the like. Analysts must also be cautious about their interpretation of patient care events—for example, not misconstruing the reasons for or timing of a particular diagnostic procedure when interpreting events in the course of treatment of a life-threatening emergency.

Third, the committee also believes that structural aspects of health data-

----

[17] One example of the problem of diagnostic coding for insurance claim purposes was provided during a study site visit. A member of an internal medicine group noted that he used essentially six outpatient (office visit) diagnoses because "they work" and because he would otherwise be questioned or second-guessed too much by insurers if he recorded more, or more detailed, diagnostic codes. Because reimbursement is keyed to length and complexity of a visit, rather than to diagnosis, he had a clear conscience about this practice.

[18] Reliability in this context relates to the need for data to be reasonably accurate and complete—that is, essentially free of missing values, systematic bias in what data are captured or recorded and how those data are coded, and random errors. Validity concerns relate to the issue of whether analyses done on a given database are appropriate for the questions being asked and whether those analyses will provide defensible answers that are internally consistent and externally generalizable. According to Palmer and Adams (1993), measures of quality can be reliable if the rate of random error is low, although they may still contain systematic error (meaning that some attribute is being captured but that it may not be the one intended); for quality measures to be valid, both random and systematic error must be low. These considerations of random and systematic error mean that the level of reliability of a measure (or the underlying data) place a ceiling on the level of validity that can be attained; unreliable measures or information can never be valid.

bases should be emphasized as conducive to high-quality data and information. Databases should be built around a core of uniformly reported (or translatable) data that is relevant and can be shown to be accurate and valid for the HDO's intended analyses (in keeping with the comments just above). In addition, HDO should have an easily implemented capacity to supplement core data elements. The committee and other experts agree on the significant tension that exists between the desire for comprehensive databases and the consequently broad uses to which HDO data might be put and the wisdom of a certain parsimony in the actual gathering of person-identifiable information.

Although the committee realizes that the federal government may have to take the lead in standards development and improved coding systems, the committee urges HDOs to foster, encourage, and work toward national standards for coding and definitions for (at least) core data elements.[19] Government leadership is indispensable in matters of coding and data uniformity, but widespread input from the private sector is desirable. The reason is that the costs of momentous or frequent changes (in terms of money, loss of comparability of data, potential incompatibility of clinical and payment coding, and incentives for fragmentation and upcoding of services) can be significant; consultation between the public and private sectors can help avert excessive or unnecessary costs of these types.

Fourth, the committee takes the position that the basic structure and content of these databases ought to be carefully designed from the beginning, but they must have sufficient capacity for expansion and change as health care reform, effectiveness and outcomes research, and other dynamic aspects of the health care sector evolve in coming years. This requirement implies that due attention will be paid to the quality of new categories of data that may become available for HDOs in the future.

RECOMMENDATION 2.1 ACCURACY AND COMPLETENESS

To address these issues, **the committee recommends that health database organizations take responsibility for assuring data quality on an ongoing basis and, in particular, take affirmative steps to ensure: (1) the completeness and accuracy of the data in the databases for which they are responsible and (2) the validity of data for analytic purposes for which they are used.**

Part 2 of this recommendation applies to analyses that HDOs con-

---

[19] AHCPR has explored the feasibility of linking administrative databases for effectiveness research and urged the development of uniform messages and vocabulary standards (USDHHS, 1991). See also Aronow and Coltin (1993).

**duct. They cannot, of course, police the validity of data when used by
others for purposes over which the HDOs have no a priori control.**

Until HDOs can demonstrate the quality of their data, the committee
cautions that their proponents must guard against promising too much in the
early years, particularly in the area of improving quality of care and conducting research on the appropriateness and effectiveness of health services.
The committee returns to this point in Chapter 4 in a discussion of data
protection and data integrity.

As many investigators have pointed out, the absence of sufficient clinical information in most databases today (and likely for tomorrow) is a
critical limitation (Roos et al., 1989; Hannan et al., 1992; Chassin, 1993b;
Krakauer and Jacoby, 1993). Efforts to acquire such information through
manual abstraction of relevant information in hospital records, which is the
basis of various patient classification programs (e.g., MedisGroups or HCFA's
proposed Uniform Clinical Data Set), are costly and time-consuming. Some
means of obtaining such information more directly from patient records will
be needed.

Clinical data should be obtained, whenever practical, to validate analyses. The committee does not regard the clinical data found in medical
records, whether computerized or not, as always sufficiently comprehensive, accurate, or legible to characterize them as a "gold standard," but they
are a valuable, and sometimes indispensable, touchstone against which to
judge the less rich administrative data on which many types of health policy
and health services research are and must be based.

The validity of elements in a database must be matched with the kinds
of inferences that can be drawn. The committee believes that the best
method of enhancing the *comprehensiveness* of HDO databases and the
accuracy and completeness of data elements is to move toward CPRs in
which the desired variables themselves, rather than high-level abstraction
and proxy coding systems, could be accessed. This committee does not
wish to convey the impression that the transition to CPR systems is anything but an extraordinarily difficult task. Although the progress made in
establishing a CPR Institute is laudable, much remains to be done for that
organization to realize even the main objectives set forth for it in the IOM
report on CPRs and CPR systems. In addition, planning efforts by the
Computer Science and Telecommunications Board (a unit of the Commission on Physical Sciences, Mathematics, and Applications of the National
Research Council) on the national information infrastructure and its role in
health care (and health care reform) make clear that both the health care and
the computer and information sciences communities have a considerable
way to go even in agreeing on details about the directions that policies and

technical advances should take in addressing major issues in this critical area.

In its April (1993) report to the Secretary of DHHS, the Work Group on Computerization of Patient Records supported the development of national standards for documenting and sharing patient information. It also called on the American National Standards Institute Healthcare Information Standards Planning Panel to coordinate the development, adoption, and use of national information standards for patient data definitions, codes and terminology, intersystem communication, and uniform patient, provider, and payer identifiers.

RECOMMENDATION 2.2 COMPUTER-BASED PATIENT RECORD

Accordingly, the committee recommends that health database organizations support and contribute to regional and national efforts to create computer-based patient records.

The committee acknowledges the importance of computer-based patient records with uniform standards for connectivity, terminology, and data sharing if the creation and maintenance of pooled health databases is to be efficient and their information accurate and complete. The committee urges HDOs to anticipate the development of CPRs and to contribute to the development and adoption of these standards. HDOs should take a proactive stance, by joining efforts by the CPR Institute and other organizations working to facilitate implementation of CPRs, helping in standards-setting efforts, and otherwise becoming full participants in the multidisciplinary effort that is now under way.

SUMMARY

Much of the thrust of this report concerns how to maximize the benefits that this committee believes can be realized from the construction and operation of *inclusive* and *comprehensive* health databases. In examining these questions, the committee has focused on what it calls *health database organizations*. HDOs are emerging entities of many different characteristics in states and other geographic regions of the country; the committee made two key assumptions about them: (1) HDOs have access to and possibly control considerable amounts of person-identifiable health data outside the care settings in which those data were originally generated and (2) the chief mission of HDOs is public release of data and results of studies about health care providers or other health-related topics.

The broad-based value of HDOs and their databases might be said to be the provision of reliable and valid information in a reasonably timely manner to address all the major questions in health care delivery—access, costs, quality, financing and organization, health resources and personnel, and research—facing the nation today and in the coming years. The chapter also details the narrower benefits that might accrue to a variety of potential users, including patients and their families, health care providers, purchasers and payers, employers, and many other possible clients in the public and private sectors.

In assembling the data that will go into products for all such users and uses, the committee had sobering concerns about the quality of those data. Thus, it recommends that HDOs take responsibility for assuring data quality on an ongoing basis, and in particular take affirmative steps to ensure: (1) the completeness and accuracy of the data in the databases for which they are responsible and (2) the validity of data for analytic purposes for which they are used [by HOOs] (Recommendation 2.1). The committee also recommends that HDOs support and contribute to the regional and national efforts to create CPRs and CPR systems (Recommendation 2.2).

Initially, HDOs will attempt to provide data for particular users and uses to answer particular kinds of questions. Nevertheless, advances in the creation and operation of computer-based databases, whether centralized or far-flung, can be expected in the coming years. The committee believes that thoughtful appreciation of their potential and anticipation of their potential limitations will hasten that progress. The development of HDOs— their structure, governance, and policies on disclosure as well as on protection of data—must be designed for the achievement of these long-term goals.

The next chapter takes up the major responsibilities of HDOs in carrying out a critical mission: furnishing information to the public on costs, quality, and other features of health care providers in a given region or community. The committee adopted two strong assumptions as it began to consider this topic. The first is that considerable benefits will accrue to interested consumers and to the public at large from having access to accurate and timely information on these aspects of the health care delivery system with which they deal; this has been the thrust of the present chapter. The other assumption is that HDOs supported by public funds ought to have a stated mission of making such information available, and this will be a core element of several committee recommendations. The committee also assumes, however, that harms can arise from some uses of the information in such databases. For this reason, in the next chapter the committee considers administrative and other protections that it believes HDOs should put in place.

3

Public Disclosure of Data on Health Care Providers and Practitioners

Previous chapters have discussed a wide array of users, uses, and expected benefits of information held by health database organizations (HDOs). Such organizations are presumed to have two major capabilities. One is the ability to amass credible descriptive information and evaluative data on costs, quality, and cost-effectiveness for hospitals, physicians, and other health care facilities, agencies, and providers. The other is the capacity to analyze data to generate knowledge and then to make that knowledge available for purposes of controlling the costs and improving the quality of health care—that is, of obtaining value for health care dollars spent. Another benefit derived from HDOs is the generation of new knowledge by others.

In principle, the goals implied by these capabilities are universally accepted and applauded. In practice, HDOs will face a considerable number of philosophical issues and practical challenges in attempting to realize such goals. The IOM committee characterizes the activities that HDOs might pursue to accomplish these goals as *public disclosure.*

By *public disclosure*, this committee means the timely communication, or publication and dissemination, of certain kinds of information to the public at large. Such communication may be through traditional print and broadcast media, or it may be through more specialized outlets such as newsletters or computer bulletin boards. The information to be communicated is of two varieties: (1) descriptive facts and (2) results of evaluative studies on topics such as charges or costs and patient outcomes or other

91

quality-of-care measures. The fundamental aims of such public disclosure, in the context of this study, are to improve the public's understanding about health care issues generally and to help consumers select providers of health care.[1]

These elements imply that HDOs should be required to gather, analyze, generate, and publicly release such data and information:

- in forms and with explanations that can be understood by the public;
- in such a manner that the public can distinguish actual events (i.e., primary data) from derived, computed, or interpretive information;
- in ways that reveal the magnitude of any differences among providers as well as the likelihood that differences could be the result of chance alone;
- in sufficient detail that all providers can be easily described and compared, not just those at the extremes;
- with descriptions and illustrations of the steps necessary to predict outcomes in the present or future from information relating only to past experience; and
- with statements and illustrations about the need to particularize information for an individual in the final stages of decision making.

Acceptance of HDO activities and products relating to public disclosure will depend in part on the balance struck for fairness to patients, the public in general, payers, and health care providers. Fairness to patients involves protecting their privacy and the confidentiality of information about them, as examined in Chapter 4. Fairness to the public involves distributing accurate, reliable information that is needed to make informed decisions about providers and health care interventions; the broader aims are to promote universal access to affordable and competent health care, enhance consumer choice, improve value for health care dollars expended, and increase the accountability to the public of health care institutions. Fairness to payers may be a subset of this category. They should receive the information that is available to the public at large, but perhaps in more detail or in a more timely manner. Finally, fairness to providers entails ensuring that

---

[1] SEC. 5003 of the HSA (1993) calls for a National Quality Management Council to develop a set of national measures of quality performance to assess the provision of health care services and access to such services.

SEC. 5005 (1) requires health alliances annually to publish and make available to the public a performance report outlining in a standard format the performance of each health plan offered in the alliance and the results of consumer surveys conducted in the alliance.

data and analyses are reliable, valid, and impartial; it also means that providers are given some opportunity to confirm data and methods before information is released to the public, and offered some means of publishing their perspectives when the information is released.

This chapter deals chiefly with issues relating to trade-offs between fairness to providers and fairness to the public at large (including patients) insofar as public disclosure of information is concerned. The considerations just noted appear simple and noncontroversial on the surface; in the context of real patients, providers, and data, they become technical, complex, and occasionally in conflict. The appendix to this chapter offers a brief illustration of the difficulties that HDOs might face in discharging their duties of fairness to all groups.

PREVIOUS STUDIES

This report is not the first treatment of issues related to providing health-related information to the public. Marquis et al. (1985) reviewed what was known about informing consumers about health care costs—considered then and now a less difficult challenge than informing them about quality of care—as a means of encouraging them to make more cost-conscious choices. In an extensive literature review, the authors documented the wide gaps in cost (or price) information available to consumers, especially for hospital care.[2] They reported evidence that some programs to help certain consumer groups, such as assisting the elderly in purchasing supplemental Medicare coverage, have had salutary effects on the choices people make. Despite new efforts at that time by employers, insurers, business coalitions, and states to collect and disseminate such information, the authors concluded that, "it remains uncertain whether disclosure of information about health care costs will do much to modify consumers' choices of health plans,

---

[2] In all likelihood, people will have more, and be more attentive to, information about their own health insurance plans than about cost or quality information on health care providers. Marquis (1981) studied consumers' knowledge about their health insurance coverage as part of the RAND Corporation Health Insurance Experiment. She determined that, although most families understand some aspects of their insurance policies, many lack detailed knowledge of benefits, especially about coverage of outpatient medical services. Greater exposure to information about an insurance plan, measured by the length of time the family was insured and whether the family had a choice of plans, increased the family's knowledge, which suggests that more experience with information or formal efforts to educate will improve the general level of knowledge. Left unanswered, however, is the question of the extent to which people will act on that knowledge, especially to change insurance plans. These findings raise cautions, therefore, about what actions people might take in response to receipt of quality and cost information.

hospitals, or other health care providers" (p. xii). The authors emphasized that understanding how consumers use information in making health care choices is critical to the design of effective data collection and disclosure interventions but that such basic knowledge was lacking. It is not clear that the knowledge gap has been closed.

More recently, the congressional Office of Technology Assessment (OTA, 1988) produced a signal report on disseminating quality-of-care information to consumers. It examined the rationales that lie behind the call for more public information; evaluated the reliability, validity, and feasibility of several types of quality indicators;[3] and advanced some policy options that Congress could use to overcome problems with the indicators. Also presented was a strategy for disseminating information on the quality of physicians and hospitals using the following components: stimulate consumer awareness of quality of care; provide easily understood information on the quality of providers' care; present information via many media repeatedly and over long periods of time; present messages to attract attention; present information in more than one format; use reputable organizations to interpret quality-of-care information; consider providing price information along with information on the quality of care; make information accessible; and provide consumers the skills to use and physicians the skills to provide information on quality of care (OTA, 1988, pp. 40-47).

The OTA study did not wholly endorse any one quality measure or approach, and specifically noted that "existing data sets do not allow routine evaluation of physicians' performance outside hospitals" (p. 30). The report also concluded that "informing consumers and relying on their subsequent actions should not be viewed as the only method to encourage hospitals and physicians to maintain and improve the quality of their care. Even well-informed lay people . . . must continue to rely on experts to ensure the quality of providers. Some experts come from within the medical community and engage in self regulation, while others operate as external reviewers through private and governmental regulatory bodies" (p. 30). It may be said that many, if not most, of the issues raised by the OTA report are germane to today's quite different health care environment, including the development of regional HDOs.

---

[3] Quality indicators in the OTA (1988) report included: hospital mortality rates; adverse events; disciplinary actions, sanctions, and malpractice compensation; evaluation of physicians' performance (care for hypertension); volume of services in hospitals or performed by physicians; scope of hospital services (external standards and guidelines); physician specialization; and patients' assessments of their care.

IMPORTANT PRINCIPLES OF PUBLIC DISCLOSURE

A significant committee stance should be made plain at the outset: the public interest is materially served when society is given as much information on costs, quality, and value for health care dollar expended as can be given accurately and provided with educational materials that aid interpretation of that information. Indeed, public disclosure and public education go hand in hand. Much of the later part of this chapter, therefore, advances a series of recommendations intended to foster active, but responsible, public disclosure of information by HDOs.

One critical element in this position must be underscored, however, because it is a major caveat: public disclosure is acceptable *only* when it: (1) involves information and analytic results that come from studies that have been well conducted, (2) is based on data that can be shown to be reliable and valid for the purposes intended, and (3) is accompanied by appropriate educational material. As discussed in Chapter 2, data cannot be assumed to be reliable and valid; hence, study results and interpretations, and resulting inferences, cannot be assumed always to be sound and credible. Thus, a position supporting public disclosure of cost, quality, or other information about health care providers must be tempered by an appreciation of the limitations and problems of such activities. In Chapter 2 the committee advanced a recommendation about HDOs ensuring the quality of their data so as to minimize the difficulties that might arise from incomplete or inaccurate data.

Apart from these caveats, the committee's posture in this area leads to three critical propositions. First, it will be crucial for HDOs or those who use their data to avoid the harms that might come from inadequate, incorrect, or inappropriately "conclusive" analyses and communications. That is, HDOs have a minimum obligation of ensuring that the analyses they publish are statistically rigorous and clearly described.

Second, HDOs will need to establish clear policies and guidelines on their standards for data, analyses, and disclosure, and this is an especially significant responsibility when the uses in question are related to quality assurance and quality improvement (QA/QI). The committee believes that HDOs can produce significant and reliable information and that the presumption should be in favor of data release. Such guidelines can help make this case to those who would otherwise oppose public disclosure efforts with the argument that reasonable and credible studies cannot be conducted.

Third, in line with these principles, the committee advises that HDOs establish a responsible administrative unit or board to promulgate, oversee, and enforce information policies. The specifics of this recommendation are discussed in Chapter 4, chiefly in relationship to privacy protections. The committee wishes here simply to underscore its view that HDOs cannot responsibly or practically carry out the activities discussed in the remainder of this chapter without formulating and overseeing such policies at the highest levels.

IMPORTANT ELEMENTS OF PUBLIC DISCLOSURE

Several elements are important to the successful public disclosure of health-related information. Among them are the topics and types of information involved, who is identified in such releases, differing levels of vulnerability to harm, and how information might be disclosed. How these factors might be handled by HDOs is briefly discussed below.

Topics for HDO Analysis and Disclosure

In theory, virtually any topic may be subject to the HDO analyses and public disclosure activities under consideration in this chapter. In practice, the topics that figure most prominently in public disclosure of provider-identified health care data thus far have been extremely limited. Perhaps the best-known instance of release of provider-specific information is the Health Care Financing Administration's (HCFA) annual publication (since 1986) of hospital-specific death rates; these have been based on Medicare Part A files for the entire nation (see, e.g., HCFA, 1987; OTA, 1988, Chapter 4; HCFA, 1991; and the discussion in Chapter 2 of this report).[4]

This activity has had three spin-offs (not necessarily pertaining just to hospital death rates). The first is repackaging and publishing the HCFA data in local newspapers, consumer guides, and other media. The second is similar analyses, perhaps more detailed, more timely, or more locally pertinent, carried out by state-based data commissions. Examples of statewide work include the published data on cardiac surgery outcomes in New York (cited in Chapter 2), the work of the Pennsylvania Health Care Cost Containment Council on hospital efficiency (PHCCCC, 1989) and on coronary artery bypass graft (PHCCCC, 1992), and the publication of a wide array of information on hospitals, long-term care facilities, home health agencies,

---

[4] As this report was being prepared, the HCFA administrator announced a moratorium of indeterminate length on publication of hospital-specific mortality data (Darby, 1993). The main issues appear to be the adequacy of risk adjustors in the statistical model and the concern that mortality-related data do not provide meaningful information about the true levels of quality of care in the nation's hospitals (or at least in certain types, such as inner-city institutions). Some attention may thus be turned to other indicators, such as length of stay or hospital-acquired complications. Even more ambitious goals may involve reporting on volume of services and patient satisfaction. The ultimate desirability of making reliable and valid information available to consumers is not in question.

and licensed clinics by the California Health Policy and Data Advisory Commission (California Office of Statewide Health Planning and Development, 1991). The files of the Massachusetts Health Data Consortium have been a rich source of information for various health services research projects (Densen et al., 1980; Gallagher et al., 1984; Barnes et al., 1985; Wenneker and Epstein, 1989; Wenneker et al., 1990; Ayanian and Epstein, 1991; Weissman et al., 1992). The third spin-off is exemplified by the special issues of *U.S. News & World Report* (1991, 1992, 1993) that have reported on top hospitals around the country by condition or speciality. The underpinnings of these rankings, however, are not HCFA mortality data but, rather, personal ratings by physicians and nurses.

Longo et al. (1990) provide an inventory of data demands directed at hospitals, some of which originate with entities like the regional HDOs envisioned in this study (e.g., tumor and trauma registries and state data commissions). Those requesting data would like, for example, to compare hospitals or hospital subgroups during a specific calendar period, to control or regulate new technologies or facilities, and to help providers identify and use scarce resources such as human organs.

Local activities, such as those for metropolitan areas or counties, are exemplified by the release of the *Cleveland-Area Hospital Quality Outcome Measurements and Patient Satisfaction Report* (CHQC, 1993), as described in Chapter 2. (Nearly a decade ago, the Orange County, California, Health Planning Council developed a set of quality indicators for local hospitals, which was considered at the time to be a pioneering effort; see Lohr, 1985-86.) In 1992 (Volume 8, Number 3), *Washington Checkbook* presented information on pharmacy prices for prescription drugs and for national and store-brand health and beauty care products; it also reported on hospital inpatient care quality (judged in terms of death rates) and pleasantness (evaluated in terms of staff friendliness, respect, and concern) (Hospital Inpatient Care, 1992). In October 1993 *The Washingtonian* offered a review of top hospitals and physicians serving the Washington D.C. metropolitan area (Stevens, 1993). Another local publication, *Health Pages* (1993, 1994), covers selected cities or areas of the country. It tries to help readers choose doctors, pick hospitals, and decide on other services such as home nursing care. Its Spring 1993 issue provides a consumer's guide to several metropolitan areas of Wisconsin; included are practitioners; hospital services, procedure rates, and prices; and an array of other kinds of health care.[5] A similar issue released in Winter 1994 focused on metropolitan St.

---

[5] Quality of care becomes problematic for these types of publications. *Health Pages* (1993), for instance, states explicitly: "There is little objective information available enabling us to judge the quality of care provided [about physicians]" (p. 3).

Louis. Sources of the information in these publications include surveys, price checks, and HCFA mortality-rate studies; only the last approximates the uses that might be made of the data held by regional HDOs today, but clearly more comprehensive HDOs in the future may have price information, survey data, and the like.

The brief examples above illustrate areas in which analyses that identify providers have been publicly released. Other calls for public disclosure, however, may actually be intended for more private use by consulting firms; health care plans such as health maintenance organizations (HMOs), independent practice associations (IPAs), and preferred provider organizations (PPOs); and other health care delivery institutions such as academic medical centers or specialized treatment centers. Requests may include analyses of the fees charged by physicians for office visits, consultations, surgical procedures, and the like, and the requests may be for very specific ICD-9-CM (International Classification of Diseases, ninth revision, clinical modification) and CPT-4 (Current Procedural Terminology, fourth revision) codes. Yet other inquiries come from clients concerned with the market share of given institutions or health plans in a region as part of a more detailed market assessment. Questions may also be focused on patterns of resource utilization by certain kinds of patients, for instance, those with advanced or rare neoplastic disease. In general, because these applications are unlikely to lead to studies with published results, they are not discussed here in any detail.

Some internal studies are intended for public release, however, for use by regulators, consumers, employers, and other purchasers. These include the so-called quality report cards being developed by the National Committee on Quality Assurance, by Kaiser Permanente, the state of Missouri, and others. The Northern California Region of Kaiser Permanente, for instance, has released a "benchmarked" report on more than 100 quality indicators such as member satisfaction, childhood health, maternal care, cardiovascular diseases, cancer, common surgical procedures, mental health, and substance abuse (Kaiser Permanente, 1993a, 1993b).

Who Is Identified

The main objects of such requests and the ensuing analyses tend to be large health plans to hospitals, physician groups, individual physicians, and nursing homes. Most of the debate in the past few years has centered on hospitals, especially in the context of the validity and meaningfulness of hospital-specific death rates (Baker, 1992). Generally, arguments in favor of the *principle* of release of such information on hospitals have carried the day; controversy persists about the reliability, validity, and utility of such information when the underlying data or the sophistication of the analyses can be called into question.

More recently, the debate has turned to release of information on the hospital-based activities of particular physicians—for example, death rates associated with specific surgical procedures. Here the principle of public disclosure also seems to have gained acceptance, again with caveats about the soundness of the analyses and results. Nevertheless, because of the much greater difficulty of ensuring the reliability and validity of such analyses, especially on the level of individual physicians, many observers remain concerned about the possible downside of releasing information on specific clinicians. This criticism is especially pertinent to the extent that this information is a relatively crude indicator of the quality of care in hospitals or of that rendered by individual physicians, especially surgeons.

In the future, attention can be expected to shift to outpatient care and involve the ambulatory, office-based services of health plans and physician groups in primary or specialty care and of individual physicians. In these cases the stance in favor of public disclosure may become more difficult to adopt fully, for three reasons: the problems alluded to above for hospital-based physicians become exponential for office-based physicians; the clear, easy-to-count outcomes, such as deaths, tend to be inappropriate for office-based care because they are so rare; and quality-of-life measures, such as those relating to functional outcomes and physical, social, and emotional well-being, are more significant but also more difficult to assess, aggregate, and report.

Other types of providers and clinicians also must be considered in this framework. These include pharmacies and individual pharmacists; home health agencies and the registered nurses and therapists they employ; and durable medical device companies, such as those that supply oxygen to oxygen-dependent patients and the respiratory therapists they employ. Stretching the public-disclosure debate to these and other parts of the health care delivery environment may seem farfetched; to the extent that their data will appear eventually in databases maintained by HDOs, however, the prospect that someone will want to obtain, analyze, and publicize such data is real. This may illustrate the point raised in Chapter 2 that simple creation of databases may lead to applications quite unanticipated by the original creators.

Finally, some experts foresee the day when HDOs might do analyses by employer or by commercial industry or sector with the aim of clarifying the causes and epidemiology of health-related problems. Cases in point might be the incidence of carpal tunnel syndrome in banks, accidents in the meatpacking or lumber industry, or various types of disorders in the chemical industry. Here the issue is one of informing the public or specific employers in an economic sector about possible threats to the health and well-being of residents of an area or employees in a particular commercial enterprise.

Vulnerability to Harm

The examples above can be characterized by level of aggregation: large aggregations of health care personnel in, for instance, hospitals or HMOs, as contrasted with individual clinicians. The committee believes that, in general, public disclosure can be defended more easily when data involve aggregations or institutions than when they involve individuals. Vulnerability to harm is the complicating factor in this controversy, and some committee members affirm that it should be carefully and thoughtfully taken into account before data on individuals are published.

To an individual, the direct harms are those of loss of reputation, patients, income, employment, and possibly even career.[6] Hospitals and other large facilities, health plans, and even large groups are less vulnerable to such losses than are individuals. Higher-than-expected death rates for acute myocardial infarction or higher-than-expected caesarean section rates are not likely to drive a hospital out of business unless the public becomes convinced that these rates are representative of care generally and are not being addressed. By contrast, reports of higher-than-expected death rates for pneumonia or higher-than-expected complication rates for cataract replacement surgery could disqualify an individual from participating in managed care contracts and eventually spell ruin for the particular physician.

How one regards harms and gains may depend in part on whether one views public disclosure of evaluative information about costs or quality as a zero-sum game. In a highly competitive market, which may have the characteristics of a zero-sum game, clear winners and losers may emerge in the provider and practitioner communities. Furthermore, in theory this is what one would both expect and desire. Nevertheless, when markets are not highly competitive—for instance, when all hospital occupancy rates are high or when the number of physicians in a locality is small—the information may less directly affect consumer choice, although it may well influence provider behavior by changing consumer perceptions. In this situation, clear winners and losers are neither expected nor likely, but establishing benchmarks that all can strive to attain should, in principle, contribute to better performance across all institutions and practitioners.

---

[6] The prospect that particular institutions, health plans, or individual practitioners might rate less well than others, but not necessarily poorly, and thereby lose patients to others is possible (and perhaps probable), but in the committee's view it did not warrant special attention. Similarly, the possibility of gain, when publicly disclosed data or other ratings are superior and thereby enhance reputation or bring additional patients, seems likely but not of sufficient weight to merit further discussion.

Methodological and Technical Issues

Several factors influence the degree of confidence one can have in the precision of publicly disclosed analyses, and this dictates how securely one can interpret and rely on published levels of statistical significance and confidence intervals and generalize from published information. Two factors involve the quality of the underlying data and the analytic effort, as introduced in Chapter 2. Others, discussed below, involve the level of aggregation in published analyses, the appropriateness of generalizing from published results to aspects of care not directly studied, and the difficulty of creating global indexes of quality of care.

In the committee's view, proponents of public disclosure have an obligation to insist that the information to be published meet all customary requirements of reliability, validity, and understandability for the intended use. Such requirements vary, to some degree, according to the numbers of cases or individuals included in the report—that is, according to the *level of aggregation*, from a single case or physician to dozens or hundreds of cases from multiple hospitals. When HDOs cannot satisfy these technical requirements, they should not publish data in either scientific journals or the public media. The committee was not comfortable with the idea that publication might go forward with explanatory footnotes or caveats, on the grounds that most consumers or users of such information are unlikely to accord the cautions as much importance as they give to the data themselves and may thus be unwittingly led to make erroneous or perhaps even harmful decisions.

This position may not be sustainable in all cases, however. The New York Supreme Court rejected the argument "that the State must protect its citizens from their intellectual shortcomings by keeping from them information beyond their ability to comprehend" (*Newsday, Inc. and David Zinman v. New York State Department of Health, et al.*) and ruled that physician-specific mortality rate information be made public pursuant to a Freedom of Information Law request. In this particular case it could be argued that the data and analyses met all reasonable expectations of scientific rigor. In the future, however, one cannot assume this will be the case. One solution in problematic circumstances may be for HDOs to disclose information only at a much higher level of aggregation than that at which the original analyses may have been done.[7]

---

[7] To overcome some of these objections to public disclosure of information with weak reliability and validity, especially stemming from small sample sizes, various statistical disclosure limitation procedures might be considered (NRC, 1993). For example, if data or results are in tabular form *and* if the data are themselves questionable, then information on individual

Generalizability is a related methodologic matter with ramifications for the harms and gains noted above. It refers here to the proposition that information on one dimension of health care delivery and performance will in some fashion predict or otherwise relate to other dimensions of performance. For hospitals, for instance, the thought might be that information on adult intensive care can be generalized to adult cardiac care, pediatric intensive care, neonatal intensive care, or even to orthopedics, obstetrics, or ophthalmology. A similar proposition might hold that information on the management of patients with acute upper respiratory infections in the office setting can in some manner predict care of patients with long-standing conditions such as chronic obstructive lung disease, congestive heart failure, or even diabetes mellitus.

Those involved in public disclosure of evaluative information must take care to reflect expert opinion on this matter—inferences about one aspect of care cannot always successfully be drawn from information, whether positive or negative, about another aspect of care. The point is complex because some extrapolation or generalization may be supportable. For example, good or bad ratings for a hospital on death rates for congestive heart failure or acute myocardial infarction might well be generalizable to that hospital's performance on pneumonia or chronic obstructive pulmonary disease (Keeler et al., 1992b), but they might well be completely irrelevant to ratings for asthma in children, hip replacement, or management of high-risk pregnancies. The committee thus believes that HDOs will have a duty to make clear the limits of one's ability to draw conclusions about quality of care beyond the precise conditions and circumstances reported for analyses.

A related problem involves the understandable desire to reduce several separate measures of quality of care into a *single, global index* intended to represent the performance of an entire hospital, plan, or individual provider. The presumption is that an index measure will be easier for HDOs to report and for the public to understand. Developing index measures is extremely difficult for conceptual reasons, which mainly relate to the difficulty of aggregating measures that come from a variety of sources or represent disparate variables (essentially an "apples and oranges" or even "apples and giraffes" problem); quantitative and statistical problems are also significant. In practice, developing index measures for quality-of-care analyses rarely if

---

practitioners, or indeed even specific plans, hospitals, and so forth, might be suppressed according to a "concentration rule" (an N,K rule); in this, if "n" number of providers (e.g., a small number, such as two) dominate a given cell (e.g., account for "k" percentage of a given cell, where "k" is a large figure such as 80 percent), then information on those particular providers would not be made public. This is a form of protection against the "statistical identification problem" as well.

ever has been successful,[8] although at least one committee member believes that the general level of *intra*hospital correlation is probably underestimated.

How Information Is Publicly Disclosed

Assuming that some of the above issues have been adequately addressed, one arrives at the question of the content and appearance of publicly disclosed information. The structure, level of detail, and other properties of such information will differ by the disclosure media used, by the nature of the information, by the type of provider or practitioner under consideration, and by the level of confidence that can be placed in the numbers, statistics, and inferences to be presented. Some of the more problematic factors in presenting data are noted here. The committee does not take a formal stand on how these matters might be resolved, however, because it believes that those decisions need to be governed by local considerations.

One difficulty in presenting data involves *how and in what order HDOs elect to identify or list institutions, clinicians, or other providers.* The most obvious choice is to do so alphabetically. This option has the advantage of making it easy to find a given provider and would probably be the likely approach when publicly disclosed information is purely descriptive. It has the related disadvantage, however, of complicating the task of comparison when the issues of interest involve evaluative information.

Other approaches are nonalphabetic. HDOs might, for instance, order providers of interest on a noncontroversial or descriptive variable; for a given region, these might be the number of beds for institutions, the number of free-standing clinics for HMOs, or the number of primary care physicians for PPOs. This method, however, does not have the advantages of alphabetic ordering and still has the disadvantages noted above. A variant is to sort providers on the basis of an essentially descriptive variable, such

---

[8] As evidence of the difficulty of developing index measures in quality analyses, Cleveland Health Quality Choice (CHQC, 1993) has attempted to avoid the methodological pitfalls of trying to combine independent measures of quality. In its recent report, the Cleveland group provides data separately for various quality measures, which include intensive care mortality and length of stay (LOS), medical mortality (for acute myocardial infarction, congestive heart failure, stroke, pneumonia, and chronic obstructive pulmonary disease) and LOS, and surgical mortality and LOS. The group did report global patient satisfaction measures, in addition to separate indicators of satisfaction with such elements of care as admissions, ancillary services, billing, food, and nursing care, but in this case the entire approach to assessing patient satisfaction (including the estimation of a global measure) is based on known instruments with proven reliability and validity.

as charges for a particular service, that has the potential of some evaluative content.

Yet another option is to list providers in order from high to low (or vice versa) on a particularly sensitive evaluative variable, such as death or complication rates. This option may be the least desirable or the most open to misinterpretation, as exemplified by *PrimeTime Live's* referral to such an arrangement as a "surgical scorecard" (*PrimeTime Live*, ABC, June 4, 1992).

Some choices in the category of other-than-alphabetic ordering present special problems or considerations. For one, the distinction implied above between descriptive and evaluative information may be incorrect or not always applicable. What for some consumers may be purely informational, noncontroversial, or irrelevant—for instance, numbers of specialists or fees charged for a procedure—may for others be a significant or decisive matter in choosing or leaving providers. Opting to list providers or practitioners by these variables may thus reflect the biases or predispositions of those publicizing the data and may not serve all consumers equally well.

Rankings—for instance, from highest to lowest on some variable—may imply greater differences than are truly warranted, and indeed may be positively misleading. This is especially the case when adjacent ranks differ numerically but the differences have no clinical meaning or statistical significance (stated degree of certainty). The committee believes that those disclosing such information must indicate where no statistical differences exist between ranks.

Mixed approaches—for instance, grouping into thirds, quartiles, quintiles, or essentially equivalent ranks and then ordering alphabetically within the groups—are of course possible. Scores, indexes, or other combinational calculations may be appealing for publication purposes, but they often have technical or methodologic weaknesses that will be difficult to convey to the public.

Other aspects of public disclosure involve *whether information is representational or symbolic*. Data can be presented quantitatively as numbers, rates, dollars, and so forth. Alternatively, data can be rendered qualitatively—for example, as one to five stars or dollar signs; open, half-open, or closed circles; or other symbolic figures. Combinations of such approaches are possible. Exactly which approaches convey what kinds of information best, with the least implicit bias, is open to question and deserves empirical study.

Another aspect of disclosure involves *how analyses are released*. Up to the present time, most observers would expect HDOs to release analyses in printed form; in the future, however, electronic outlets, such as CD-ROM diskettes or computer bulletin boards, may come into play. A computer-based approach may speed information to some audiences, which would be a positive outcome. Depending on the extent to which the underlying data accompany analytic results in computer-based media, however, some opportunity may arise for unauthorized analysis of data that could distort the original information. From the viewpoint of HDOs, this would be an undesirable outcome.

A final set of factors concerns the *extent of explanatory information and technical footnotes*. When public disclosure relies on judgmental or symbolic approaches, more explanatory and definitional material is probably needed than when information is given in straightforward, nonqualitative ways. Some of this information might best be left to a technical report for researchers and other very knowledgeable readers. In any case, the committee agrees that HDOs involved in public disclosure must make available, in clear language, the key elements of their methods, including discussion of possible threats to the internal validity and generalizability of the work that analysts believe they have dealt with adequately.

COMMITTEE FINDINGS AND CONCLUSIONS

To this point the committee has considered issues of public disclosure of information, particularly descriptive or evaluative data on costs or quality, by or under the auspices of HDOs. Its views do not extend to certain other kinds of data banks or repositories, such as computer-based patient record systems of individual hospitals and health plans or internal data files of commercial insurance carriers. Furthermore, the positions advanced here logically depend on the databases in HDOs being regional in nature (i.e., serving entire states or large metropolitan areas) and both *inclusive* and *comprehensive* within that region as those terms were used in Chapter 2.

The committee further believes that public disclosure of such information, particularly evaluative or comparative data, must give due regard to the possible harms that may unfairly be suffered by institutions and individuals. In the committee's view, disclosure of information about larger aggregations of health caregivers, such as hospitals, will generally be less prone to causing undeserved losses of reputation, income, or career than disclosure of information on individual practitioners. The committee thus takes the position that public disclosure is a valuable goal to pursue, to the extent that it is carried out with due attention to accuracy and clarity and does not undermine the QA/QI programs that health care institutions and organizations conduct internally.[9]

---

[9] According to a reviewer of this report, the laws establishing the PHCCCC provide that a violation of the law would occur if cost data were provided without associated quality data, or vice versa. The committee did not consider this specific requirement in its deliberations about disclosure policies for HDOs, but arguably the Pennsylvania provision could be seen as an effort to strengthen the "fairness" principle.

RECOMMENDATIONS

The stance favoring public disclosure presented so far includes two requirements. One is that the HDOs *themselves* ought to carry out some minimum number of consumer-oriented studies and analyses and publish them routinely. That view proceeds directly from the definition of HDO developed for this study—that HDOs are entities that have as one of their missions making health-related information publicly available. In elaborating this position, the committee offers a series of recommendations under the general rubric of advocacy of analyses and public disclosure of results. The second requirement is that HDOs make appropriate data available for *others* to use in such studies and analyses, with the expectation that the results of the work will be publicly disclosed; that is the thrust of a recommendation on advocacy of data release. Finally, to promote these aims, the committee has urged that HDOs keep prices for providing data and related materials as low as possible, as noted in the section on related issues

Advocacy of Analyses and Public Disclosure of Results

RECOMMENDATION 3.1 CONDUCTING PROVIDER-SPECIFIC EVALUATIONS

The committee recommends that health database organizations produce and make publicly available appropriate and timely summaries, analyses, and multivariate analyses of all or pertinent parts of their databases. More specifically, the committee recommends that health database organizations regularly produce and publish results of provider-specific evaluations of costs, quality, and effectiveness of care.

The subjects of such analyses should include hospitals, HMOs and other capitated systems, fee-for-service group practices, physicians, dentists, podiatrists, nurse-practitioners or other independent practitioners, long-term care facilities, and other health providers on whom the HDOs maintain reliable and valid information. In all cases the identification of providers and practitioners in publicly released reports should be only at a level of disaggregation that will support statistically valid analyses and inferences. In this context, *publish* or *disclose* is intended to mean to the public, not simply to member or sponsoring organizations. This may be easier to state as a principle than to effect in practice. For HDOs with clear public-agency mandates, such as those created by state legislation or governmental fiat or charter and supported with public funds, the requirement to provide information to the public would seem clear, but the use of public funds to support private HDOs could be made contingent on the dissemination of such analyses. Some HDOs may be based in the private sector, operate chiefly for the benefit of for-profit entities, and have no connection with or mandate from states or the federal government. In these cases, the imperative to make information and analytic results available to the public on a broad scale is much less clear. This committee hopes that such groups would act in the public interest and not just in support of parochial or member interests.

This committee assumes that policy and economic forces already exist to encourage HDOs to conduct such studies and to release information to the public. As implied above, however, this presupposition may be in error, particularly if HDOs are supported largely by private interests or professional groups that may have reasons not to want such information publicly disclosed or that may believe that proprietary advantage may be lost by disclosure. Professional groups may have different, but equally self-interested, reasons for wanting information on their members to remain private.

In the committee's view, therefore, the charters of such HDOs ought to include firm commitments to conduct consumer-oriented studies. Furthermore, no public monies or data from publicly supported health programs (for example, Medicare and Medicaid at the federal level, or Medicaid or various health reform efforts at the state level) ought to be available to HDOs that do not subscribe to such principles (except when such data are otherwise publicly available). Where state legislation is used to establish HDOs or similar entities (e.g., data commissions), the enabling statutes themselves should contain such requirements.

RECOMMENDATION 3.2 DESCRIBING ANALYTIC METHODS

The committee recommends that a health database organization report the following for any analysis it releases publicly:

* **general methods for ensuring completeness and accuracy of their data;**
* **a description of the contents and the completeness of all data files and of the variables in each file used in the analyses;**
* **information documenting any study of the accuracy of variables used in the analyses.**

The committee expects HDOs to accompany public disclosure of provider-specific information with the following kinds of information: (1) clear descriptions of the database, including documentation of its completeness and accuracy; (2) material sufficient to characterize the original sources of the data; (3) complete descriptions of all equations or other rules used in risk adjustments, including validations and limitations of the methods; (4) explanations of all terms used in the presentations; and (5) description of appropriate uses by the public, payers, and government of the data and analyses, including notice of uses for which the data and analyses are *not* valid. When certain disclosures are relatively routine (e.g., appearing quarterly or annually), such information might be made available in some detail only once and modified or updated as appropriate in later publications.

With respect to the quality and accuracy of data, HDOs that do not cover the majority of patients, providers, and health care system encounters—such as those operated mainly for the interests of self-selected employers—will have less to say about cost, quality, and other evaluative matters for the full range of providers in the community. Public disclosure of the results of evaluative investigations in these circumstances may be less important; indeed, it may even be undesirable if the information is open to oversimplification, misinterpretation, or misuse. As noted previously, therefore, it will be crucial to provide explanatory material and clear caveats about how the data might be appropriately applied or understood. Publicizing descriptive facts on providers who do render health care services to the populations covered by these smaller HDOs will, however, likely be a useful step.

Minimizing Potential Harms

Up to this point, the committee has taken an extremely strong pro-disclosure stance toward comparative, evaluative data, but it sees some potential for harm in instantaneous public release of comparative or evaluative studies on costs, quality, or other measures of health care delivery. This might be the case, for example, if those doing such work fail to provide information to hospitals, physician groups, or other study targets in advance of release, even to permit them to check the data or develop responses. Disclosure proponents assume that such studies will be done responsibly, and the public has every right to expect that to be the case. To the extent that is true, the generators of the work will be believed and the public interest will have been served.

What is not clear is how well such initiatives will be carried out and what brake or check will exist to ensure high-quality studies. One option is to require HDOs to exercise formal oversight over their work and, insofar as possible, over work done with data they provide. For instance, HDOs might be expected to impose an expert review mechanism on their own analyses before public release, or to require that such peer review be done for analyses performed by others on HDO data, or both.

Alternatively, reliance might be placed on an essentially market-driven set of checks and balances. This approach holds that poor, biased, or otherwise questionable work will eventually be discovered and those carrying it out discredited, because the "marketplace of ideas" has its own discipline to prevent reckless analysis. Studies cost money and are likely to be done only by organizations large enough to have a reputation to protect; poorly done analyses will be criticized and discounted in the press; analysts will fear diminishment of their professional reputations; and fear of lawsuits for defamation can be a powerful dissuader.

The committee did not, in the end, wish to rely solely on marketplace correctives; it believed that a more protective stance was needed.

RECOMMENDATION 3.3 MINIMIZING POTENTIAL HARM

The committee recommends that, to enhance the fairness and minimize the risk of unintended harm from the publication of evaluative studies that identify individual providers, each HDO should adhere to two principles as a standard procedure prior to publication: (1) to make available to and upon request supply to institutions, practitioners, or providers identified in an analysis all data required to perform an independent analysis, and to do so with reasonable time for such analysis prior to public release of the HDO results; and (2) to accompany publication of its own analyses with notice of the existence and availability of responsible challenges to, alternate analyses of, or explanations of the findings.

This set of recommendations reflects what might be regarded as a fairness doctrine. It holds that an important safeguard for providers, especially individual practitioners, dictates that they be allowed to check their own data and comment thereon.

Meeting a fairness principle could take the form simply of giving the subjects of analyses prerelease copies of the publication or at least of the information about them. Such subjects would not be given a veto over whether their data are used, nor would they necessarily be afforded an opportunity to have their data amended in public studies, but their comments would be maintained by the HDO so that interested parties could review them. The committee assumed that HDOs might well choose to append such comments to their own reports and publications. HCFA adopted this approach for its mortality-rate releases, for instance, as did Cleveland Health Quality Choice for its first data release.

The committee actually has gone further, however, to advise that HDOs give providers and practitioners (or their representatives) the relevant data and sufficient time to analyze them, should such requests be made. Because such situations will differ among HDOs in the future, the committee did not develop specific guidance on these points. For example, it cautions that HDOs will have to devise ways, in conveying such data to one requestor, to conceal the identities of other providers or practitioners in the data files to be transferred, but the committee believes that HDOs can accomplish this.

In addition, the committee did not reach any consensus on what constitutes sufficient time, believing that this would vary by the nature, size, and scope of the analysis in question, but common sense about the difficulties of data analysis and fairness to all parties might dictate the length of waiting time; a week's, or a year's, delay would doubtless fail both tests, two months might not. The committee also thought that the time permitted for reanalysis might be longer in the earlier years of HDO operations, when all parties are developing procedures and skills in this area, and for approximately the first year of any new or especially complicated analyses.

This discussion began with the premise that potential harms to institutions and individual practitioners need to be prevented or minimized, and the steps recommended above have that intent. The committee believes, however, that a benefit for HDOs of requiring them to make such data available for review and possible reanalysis is that feedback from providers may reveal problems with data quality and study methods that HDOs would want to remedy.

Advocacy of Data Release

Promoting Wide Applications of Health-related Data

To this point, the chapter has focused on what HDOs might do internally to analyze and publish information on providers and practitioners in their regions. Consistent with the discussion in Chapter 2, however, HDOs might well be expected to do more in the public interest to promote responsible use of health-related data. Specifically, they can serve as a key repository of data to which many other groups should have access.

RECOMMENDATION 3.4 ADVOCACY OF DATA RELEASE: PROMOTING WIDE APPLICATIONS OF HEALTH-RELATED DATA

To foster the presumed benefits of widespread applications of HDO data, the committee recommends that health database organizations should release non-person-identifiable data upon request to other entities once they are in analyzable form. This policy should include release to any organization that meets the following criteria:

- **It has a public mission statement indicating that promoting public health or the release of information to the public is a major goal.**
- **It enforces explicit policies regarding protection of the confidentiality and integrity of data.**
- **It agrees not to publish, redisclose, or transfer the raw data to any other individual or organization.**
- **It agrees to disclose analyses in a public forum or publication.**

The committee also recommends, as a related matter, that health database organizations make public their own policies governing the release of data.

In referring to "non-person-identifiable data," this recommendation is intended to protect the confidentiality of person-identifiable information in HDO databases. The latter pertains to specific patients or other individuals and might include persons residing in the community who appear in population-based data files but have not received health care services. The distinction is made because individual practitioners or clinicians, who might well appear in the databases as patients or residents of the area, *could* be identified or identifiable by their professional roles (in line with earlier recommendations in this chapter). Chapter 4 of this report explores issues of privacy and of confidentiality of person-identifiable data in more detail.

The committee debated at length the desirability and propriety of advocating that HDOs make data available to all requestors, rather than constraining the transfer of data as in the above recommendation. It was uncomfortable with flat prohibitions on all transfers of data, but it was equally uncomfortable with the possibility of open-ended or blanket transfers of data to a wide variety of groups who would not be expected to place public dissemination of information high on a list of organizational objectives. To thread a path through this dilemma, therefore, the committee advocated that HDOs make data available to those entities that can demonstrate their clear goal of public disclosure of descriptive or evaluative information and their ability to realize this goal. HDOs should not place prior restraints on which entities might receive such data simply on the grounds that others may conduct analyses or release findings that dispute those of the HDOs themselves.[10]

To characterize such entities, therefore, the committee devised the criteria in the above recommendation for two purposes. The first is to underscore its view that databases held by HDOs (or at least those mandated by law or supported by public funds) should be available for science and the public good. The second is to constrain the use of such data purely for

---

[10] One of the reviewers of this report noted that the ability of individuals and institutions to obtain information from public HDOs under state or federal Freedom of Information Act (FOIA) legislation is going to become more problematic and troublesome as HDO releases become more widespread, especially if courts uphold the view that (1) anything known to the requestor is available through FOIA procedures, (2) any analyses can be requested as long as they do not require excessive time to perform, and (3) data can be obtained at any stage (before analysis, before cleaning or editing, even before the end of data collection). The reviewer suggested that consideration of federal preemptive FOIA legislation that is cognizant of new challenges posed by public data disclosures by the HDOs might be wise.

private gain, particularly in anticompetitive actions. Examples of this second concern might be employers, insurers, PPOs, hospitals, or other health care delivery organizations in a given region using data for price collusion. Thus, it is expected that those requesting data tapes from an HDO will perform and publish analyses that can be said to serve science and/or the public interest.

The committee recognized that a tension may develop between the understandable desire on the part of HDOs to hold data until they have completed studies they wish to conduct and the need to be responsive to requests from eligible organizations for reliable, valid, and up-to-date data. Responding to such requests might even delay or prevent studies and publications by the HDOs themselves. The committee believes, therefore, that HDOs might consider developing independent units; one group could be responsible for data management and release of data to authorized recipients, and the other could take the lead for the HDOs' own internal analyses and public disclosure activities.

Requiring Recipients to Protect Data Privacy and Confidentiality

The committee debated at some length the advisability and feasibility of recommending that HDOs require recipients of their data to protect the confidentiality of the information. Ultimately, the committee elected simply to observe that such behavior on the part of HDOs might be desirable; it is certainly desirable on the part of data recipients. It concluded, however, that the practical aspects of insisting that HDOs police the actions of their data recipients were too difficult to make this step an integral part of HDO operations.

Certain kinds of database organizations, already in existence for some years, have long experience in designing descriptive, public-use data tapes that are consistent with all the principles of privacy and confidentiality advanced in Chapter 4. Thus, to the extent that any affirmative action is required of HDOs, it should at a minimum include that they create data files according to well-known precepts and methods for public-use tapes and transfer data only through those means. Further steps are examined in Chapter 4. In sum, HDOs can probably not be expected to police the proper and responsible use of their data beyond their own walls. They can, however, cut off from further access to their data any users who have abused these principles, and the committee advises that HDOs be authorized or empowered to do so.

Using Valid Analytic Techniques

This chapter has dealt chiefly with descriptive or evaluative studies and related activities that HDOs might pursue and then release publicly; it has also considered the responsibilities that HDOs might have to make data available to others for private QA/QI programs and for other analytic purposes. Consistent with the discussion of data quality in Chapter 2, however, the committee wishes to emphasize that valid studies will require valid analytic techniques, often multivariable methods.

Such techniques are powerful, complex, and arguable in details among experts, but they are easily understood in principle. Properly used, they provide the best methods for comparing institutional, provider, plan, or clinician performance. This is so because only such approaches can isolate performance from the potentially confounding effects of differences in the prevalence of disease, severity of illness, presence of large numbers of elderly or poor patients, and so forth. Variables that reflect these factors are often termed severity-, risk-, or case-mix-adjustors.

Serious criticisms can be leveled at studies with inadequate or inappropriate adjustors and analyses;[11] such studies, and the organizations that conduct them, can readily be discredited. The consequences could be devastating to the entire public-disclosure effort. To help protect against such criticisms, the committee advises that HDOs use only proper statistical techniques—particularly multivariable analyses—for comparisons released to the public.

In addition, the committee holds that HDOs ought to use only severity- and risk-adjustment techniques and programs that are available for review and critique by qualified experts. It also believes that HDOs would do well to require, as a condition of data release, that entities or investigators conducting secondary analysis of these data adopt the same precept.

---

[11] Moses (1990, p. 187) argues that such adjustments can be quite difficult, as follows: "To be fully effective, it [such severity- or risk-adjustment] requires three things: (a) recognition of what variables are influential on outcomes; (b) measured values of these variables for each subject; and (c) understanding of how those adjustments are to be made correctly. . . . The promise of adjustment is hard indeed to realize, even in principle, and the practical problems of unrecognized and unmeasured influential variables, incomplete data, and necessarily ad hoc adjustment strategies compound the difficulties." With respect to these practicalities, for example, Greenfield et al. (1988), Iezzoni (1989), Iezzoni et al. (1992), and Greenfield (1993) all provide useful reviews of issues relating to comorbidity, case mix, and risk adjustment. Greenfield (1993) emphasizes the distinction between presence of a comorbid condition and the severity of that condition in the context of analyses that might be done on data from the end-stage renal disease (ESRD) program or from individual ESRD treatment units.

Related Issues

Privacy Protections for Person-identifiable Data

Chapter 4 deals with the issues of privacy and confidentiality of person-identifiable data in depth. In advocating release of data to providers, researchers, or others, however, the committee recognizes the possibility that information identifying patients or other persons may be inadvertently revealed to those with neither a right nor a need to know. This brief commentary on how privacy might be protected is intended to signal the committee's strong view that it *must* be protected.

Generally, committee members believe that encrypting, encoding, and aggregating patient data can go a long way toward protecting the identity of patients and other persons in HDO databases. Although no one can ever guarantee zero probability that an individual can be identified through concerted effort and ingenious devices, these methods make it possible to issue assurances about privacy at a reasonable level of confidence. Such assurances are stronger regarding tabular or aggregated information than data in discrete records, but they might still be reasonably strong at the level of tapes and other disaggregated databases.

Some committee members were not convinced that such steps will be sufficient to ensure anonymity and protect the identity of patients. They argued that a less ambitious goal—that of protecting the identity of patients to the extent feasible—is more realistic. It has the further advantage of conveying to the public that absolute protection of the identity of individuals when their information is in a computerized data bank is very difficult, if not impossible.

Consistent with the principles developed in Chapter 4 on access to person-identifiable information for researchers, the committee argues that appropriately qualified, institution-based researchers with approvals from their institutions' Institutional Review Boards can receive data with intact identifiers. The committee suspects that most investigators will not wish to acquire data tapes on analyses that HDOs have already performed. Rather, they will wish to obtain data that permit original analyses on a broad array of topics relating to the effectiveness and appropriateness of health care interventions. The committee does make provision in Chapter 4 for researchers interested in HDO data for these purposes to receive person-identifiable information.

Constrained Staff Capabilities

This chapter assumes that HDOs will have an affirmative responsibility to carry out analyses and public dissemination activities. Clearly, however, what studies they choose to do and how actively they pursue communication of results will be constrained by available resources and dictated by their own perceptions of critical issues. HDOs, for reasons of political disinclination, lack of staff, or other factors, may not wish or not be able to conduct certain analyses that outside requestors, such as consumer groups or newspapers, regard as extremely significant or timely. Such outside requestors might even be able to pay for such work, or at least to underwrite the costs of acquiring the data; HDOs may still find it impossible or unattractive to attempt to respond to such requests. The committee developed no consensus on how these problems might be addressed, beyond the points made earlier that HDO charters ought to mandate consumer-oriented studies.[12]

Obligations to Correct Analyses or Retract Information

A complex issue that proponents of HDOs need to consider is what incentives are required to ensure the accuracy of their analyses and subsequent publications. The market for the work may act as one corrective, as discussed earlier. In theory, if it becomes known that an HDO has published information demonstrated to be false, wrongly interpreted, or inappropriate, then political, economic, and social support for the HDO will falter. In practice, the committee was not convinced a market-oriented solution like this would have much effect on an HDO's later performance— there is essentially no evidence on the point—and it was even less persuaded that harms to individuals could be prevented or redressed in this manner.

An alternative, more activist approach may be to require that HDOs publish retractions in the same way and through the same media that published the original erroneous material. Some remedies for injury to individuals or providers might be available through civil litigation when false

---

[12] To overcome some of the difficulties HDOs might face in responding to outside requests for studies (e.g., staffing constraints or inability to price analytic services appropriately to recoup costs), one committee member proposed that HDOs might contract with at least three "analysis consultants," who will have the same clearance to see patient identifiers as HDO staff. These analysis consultants would compete to do analyses for any outside requestor and to release to the requestor analysis results that do not permit or include patient identification. The rationale for this suggestion is that "outsiders," such as newspapers, employers, consumer organizations, or other nonacademic organizations, will find it difficult to meet the Institutional Review Board requirements for direct access to patient-identified data (a condition elaborated in Chapter 4 on privacy and confidentiality); such entities may also find it difficult to identify experts (within academic institutions) who can or would be willing to do such studies. The full committee was divided on whether this approach was either desirable or feasible but regarded it as worth consideration.

information has done material harm to their reputations, incomes, or careers, although bringing libel actions that demonstrate malicious intent or foreknowledge of the falsity of the information may be extremely difficult. A further drawback to this strategy is the same feeling that inhibits individuals whose privacy has been breached from bringing lawsuits—the disinclination to make public *again* what was painful, defamatory, or otherwise harmful when it first was publicized.

A related question is what to do when data are corrected long after they have been processed, used in analyses, or transferred to other users. For example, should HDOs notify users or recipients of their data when something has been augmented, corrected, or changed? Ought they go further and insist that the users alert the public or others to whom they have disclosed study results or transferred data of such matters? The committee did not develop considered opinions on these questions, but it did believe that individual HDOs should be prepared to devise policies to address these issues in anticipation of the day when the questions will arise in their own operations.

STRENGTHENING QUALITY ASSURANCE AND QUALITY IMPROVEMENT PROGRAMS

Data Feedback

The primary focus of this chapter has been on actions HDOs might take to make reliable, valid, and useful information on health care providers and practitioners easily available to the public. The committee concluded that HDOs could help improve the quality of health care through more direct assistance to health care institutions, facilities, and clinical groups. One technique to accomplish this is termed *feedback*, namely, efforts to make available to providers and practitioners—in as nonthreatening, nonconfrontational, and constructive a way as possible—the data used or the results of evaluative studies about themselves and their peers.

Despite high hopes and some years of experience with public disclosure of provider-specific information, QA/QI experts are not yet clear whether and how an uninhibited approach to public disclosure will foster better QA/QI initiatives in the health care community. To the best of the committee's knowledge, no systematic or rigorous analysis of the short- or long-term effects of public disclosure has been conducted. Anecdotal evidence suggests that some provider groups may seize the opportunity to take a hard look at their own operations and act aggressively on what they find, whereas others may adopt an essentially defensive posture. Nevertheless, virtually no conclusive information indicates whether public disclosure activities materially improve quality of care or QA/QI programs or, for that matter, make any lasting impact on the public's mind.[13] On balance, the committee believes the risk of damage to QA/QI efforts—for instance, if public disclosure forces institutions to divert QA/QI funds to efforts to defend themselves against negative publicity—is likely to be less than the gain from timely public disclosure of such information, but this proposition remains a question for empirical study.

To support advances in QA/QI, the committee advises that HDOs make available to provider organizations the information they need to conduct their own internal QA/QI programs more assertively. This might mean, for example, that HDOs would supply hospitals with their own data and equivalent, but probably nonidentified, data on their peers (e.g., all other hospitals in the region, or all other hospitals of certain types). The notion is generalizable to virtually all kinds of entities that deliver health care in a region, from small fee-for-service practices of physicians, to large multispecialty health plans, to pharmacies and nursing homes. Here the intent is more to transfer raw data than to transmit results of evaluative studies, although in principle HDOs could develop a set of reports that would personalize such results for each of the specific institutions or clinicians included in the study.

Some HDOs may elect to take a lower-profile, less pro-disclosure position. For example, they may opt to postpone public release of their own evaluative studies or insist on delay by groups to whom they provide data until the information has been made available to providers for their use in QA/QI programs. This option would probably entail more delay before public disclosure than is assumed for the earlier recommendation about supplying such data for providers to reanalyze for possible challenge to or comment on HDO studies. Consistent with its stance above, however, the committee would urge HDOs to assess carefully the pros and cons of operating in this manner, with particular attention to whether they are thereby supplying a useful *public* service or acting more in the interests of the health care community.

---

[13] The focus here is on provider-specific information made available in lay media to the public at large. Some experience suggests that providers identified through database analyses as delivering poor care can be targeted for follow-up of various sorts (e.g., patient chart review or more intensive analysis of information in the databases) by QA/QI programs (see, e.g., Des Harnais, 1990; Dubois, 1990; IOM, 1990). This is certainly the philosophy underlying shifts in the Medicare Peer Review Organization (PRO) program scope of work in the mid-1990s (Wilensky and Jencks, 1992), although the feasibility of new plans for changing provider behaviors through applications of data, feedback, and continuous quality improvement methods has been called into question (Nash, 1992).

Quality Assurance and Quality Improvement

The committee assumed that the QA/QI activity prompted by HDO data would occur chiefly as a part of or an adjunct to the formal QA/QI process that various providers and plans might themselves conduct.[14] Information on identified providers and individual clinicians concerning questionable, and perhaps quite poor, performance would be made available to organizations' QA/QI programs so that they could act constructively on that information; information on superior accomplishments as well as on average performance should also be forthcoming. Such feedback implies that health care institutions and individual practitioners will review, analyze, and make judgments about this information and use it to improve the quality of care.

Of course, QA/QI programs can be (and are often accused of being) ineffective. For instance, they may not act meaningfully or in a timely way on information about poor providers and clinicians; and efforts that should be taken to improve performance or remove substandard providers from the scene may be delayed. Here, it is argued, is where near-real-time public disclosure of information can play a significant sentinel role, illuminating problems and perhaps encouraging, if not forcing, provider groups and health institutions to take actions they would otherwise have softened, postponed, or not initiated.

Nevertheless, the committee believes that the health care community today is moving more forcefully toward meaningful QA/QI efforts. Contemporary QA/QI philosophy would call HDOs to provide information that will accomplish several tasks equally well: identifying poor providers, identifying superior providers, *and* improving average levels of practice. The committee would encourage HDOs to give these quality-of-care goals equal weight.

Privileging

On a narrower point, quality-related information can be used to grant practitioners various kinds of privileges, for instance, to admit patients to

---

[14] This committee was not constituted to explore issues of quality of care *per se*; it has opted to use a hybrid phrase, quality assurance and quality improvement (QA/QI), to refer to the wide set of approaches to assessing, maintaining, and strengthening the equality of health care in this country. For a comparison of the two generic approaches, see IOM (1990). For a recent description of industrial quality improvement systems, see Blumenthal (1993). Other seminal publications of the past quarter-century include: Donabedian, 1966, 1980, 1982, 1985; Brook, 1973; Brook and Appel, 1973; Williamson, 1978; Palmer, 1983; *Inquiry*, 1988; Batalden and Buchanan, 1989; Berwick, 1989; Goldfield and Nash, 1989; Berwick et al., 1990; Couch, 1991.

hospital and perform certain kinds of invasive, diagnostic, or therapeutic procedures. This process can also be used to withdraw privileges in certain circumstances, such as for specific surgical procedures. It is applied most often to physicians but can be directed at other clinicians as well. Related applications in this area involve various forms of selective contracting, in which physicians or other providers are selected for or excluded from participation in certain types of health plans.[15]

HDOs may be asked to provide information on specific practitioners on a private basis to health plan and group administrators, precisely for formal privileging or contracting purposes. Some potential for harm to physicians does exist in this application of HDO data; the particulars depend on who actually receives such information and the presence or absence of due process, in addition to the quality of the information *per se*. The committee believes that when privileging procedures are used creatively, they are compatible with QA/QI efforts. It cautions, nonetheless, that HDOs need to be alert to the possible drawbacks of making information privately available in these circumstances and to take appropriate steps to minimize them.

Peer Review Information

Some kinds of quality-related information, developed through formal QA/QI and peer review efforts, are not covered by this discussion.[16] The content of private peer review efforts, for instance, those of hospital QA committees or other investigative or disciplinary actions, are protected from

---

[15] Issues relating to selective contracting for HMOs, IPAs, PPOs, and other types of health plans that may emerge in the coming years of health care reform go well beyond those mentioned in Chapter 2. Selective-contracting decision making on the part of health plan managers is likely to differ in philosophical, operational, legal, and other ways from steps that patients and consumers take to choose (or drop) plans, providers, or physicians. In this context, one might speculate that patients and consumers would use information obtained through public disclosure to make judgments or choices about health plans, providers, or physicians, whereas plan executives might rely more on information developed internally. Nevertheless, HDOs (and policymakers) should not underestimate the sensitivity that health plan executives may have to public opinion and image, however, and this factor may have a synergistic or leveraging effect on the effectiveness of HDO disclosure activities.

[16] The rules governing due process and other aspects of quality assurance and peer review are too complex to explore here, but see the IOM report on confidentiality of peer review information in the Professional Standards Review Organization (IOM, 1981) and other work by Gosfield (1975). The IOM report on a quality assurance strategy for Medicare describes the PRO program in detail and reinforces the extent to which information on substandard performance of physicians and hospitals will be kept confidential through many steps before a more public "sanction" step is begun (IOM, 1990).

disclosure.[17] In 1981 an IOM committee issued a study (*Access to Medical Review Data*) on disclosure policy for Professional Standards Review Organizations (PSROs, which were the precursor organizations to Medicare Peer Review Organizations, or PROs); it addressed several questions about the types of information that PSROs collected and generated and the potential benefits and harms of disclosing individual institutional and practitioner profiles and other data. That committee concluded that the protection of patient privacy must be a primary component of any disclosure policy and, indeed, is not really at issue. By contrast, major problems do arise in the context of data about facilities, institutions, systems, and practitioners that can be identified individually. The study concluded that disclosure of utilization data about identified *institutions* could be justified on the grounds of public benefits such as enhanced consumer choice and public accountability of health care institutions. Conversely, that study did not conclude that utilization data on identified practitioners ought to be released because of concerns about "unwarranted harm to professional reputations caused by misleading or incomplete data, and the likelihood of a chilling effect on peer review stemming from physician fears of data misuse" (p. 8). Finally, that committee decided that when the data in question relate to quality of care, "the potential harms of requiring public disclosure [by PSROs] in identified form would outweigh the potential benefits" (p. 8).

A decade later, essentially the same approach is in place for PROs. PROs clearly provide considerable information to individual physicians under review and to the hospitals where they practice. PRO regulations, however, hold most quality-related information to be confidential and not subject to public disclosure,[18] and PROs are exempted from the require-

---

[17] Privacy protections for individual practitioners are also part of the procedures followed by the National Practitioner Data Bank, which was created by the Health Care Quality Improvement Act of 1986 (P.L. 99-660). Providers such as hospitals and state physician disciplinary boards are mandated to report to the data bank information on physicians and dentists involved in cases of malpractice (judgments or settlements) or other disciplinary actions that last more than 30 days. Organizations with a peer review process (e.g., hospitals and medical and dental plans) must make inquiries about such information concerning physicians or dentists who apply for employment, admitting privileges, or additional privileges. Except for the physicians who can query the data bank to check on the accuracy of its information about them, no others, including the public, are permitted access. Questions have been raised about: (1) the handling of sensitive material by the data bank (related to handling of mail and mailing to incorrect addresses; see GAO, 1993b), and (2) requests to physicians by PPOs and insurers to query the database and turn over information about themselves (Doyle, 1992).

[18] Confidential information includes, among other things, data that explicitly or implicitly identify an individual patient, practitioner, or PRO reviewer; reports from the PRO on sanctions and other recommendations; and other PRO deliberations. "Implicitly identifies" means that "the data are sufficiently unique or the numbers so small" that identification of the patient, practitioner, or reviewer would be easy (IOM, 1990, p. 202; also see Blum et al., 1977).

ments of the Freedom of Information Act. PROs are required to disclose some confidential information to appropriate authorities in cases of risk to public health or fraud and abuse.

Public Disclosure and Feedback

Some readers may believe that a tension exists between public disclosure and feedback, but the committee believes that both will be important tools available to HDOs to improve quality and foster informed choices in health care. Thus, it voices support for both functions, believing that one activity does not—or at least need not—discredit the other and that effective combination strategies can be designed. It sees public disclosure as a powerful motivator for physicians to participate more fully in their organizations' QA/QI activities.

The challenge to HDOs may be to decide on policies that will foster the greatest improvements in quality of care, patient outcomes, and use of health care resources. Some advances will be achieved more by public disclosure, particularly actions that aim to get useful descriptive data to the public in a timely way, but others may be aided chiefly by private feedback in the QA/QI context. This clearly is not an either/or situation. Combinations of approaches will probably be the most desirable strategy, and the exact combinations are likely to differ by type of provider, geographic area, nature of the data under consideration, and similar factors.

SUMMARY

This chapter has addressed the challenges posed for HDOs in two critical sets of activities: *public disclosure* of quality and cost data and information and *private feedback* of similar information to health care providers in efforts to help them monitor and improve their own performance. The HDO will have to have an impeccable reputation for fairness, evenhandedness, objectivity and intellectual rigor. This will be hard to earn and hard to maintain but essential if HDOs are to play the key roles envisioned for them.

The committee believes that public disclosure of information, particularly evaluative or comparative data, must give due regard to the possible harms that may unfairly be suffered by institutions and individuals. The committee thus takes the position that public disclosure is a valuable goal to pursue, to the extent that it is carried out with due attention to accuracy and clarity and contributes to the QA/QI programs that health care institutions and organizations conduct internally.

The committee identified several important aspects of public disclosure. These included: topics for HDO analysis and release, who is identified in material so released, questions of the vulnerability to harm of providers and clinicians so identified, various methodologic questions about analysis, alternative approaches to public disclosure, and specific considerations about using quality-of-care data in QA/QI programs and the protections accorded peer review information.

In explicating its findings and conclusions, the committee advanced several recommendations advocating analyses and public disclosure of results. It specifically recommended that HDOs produce and make publicly available appropriate and timely summaries, analyses, and multivariate analyses of all or pertinent parts of their databases. The committee recommends that HDOs regularly produce and publish results of provider-specific evaluations of costs, quality, and effectiveness of care (Recommendation 3.1). Furthermore, the committee recommends that a health database organization report the following for any analysis it releases publicly: its general methods for ensuring completeness and accuracy of their data; a description of the contents and the completeness of all data files and of the variables in each file used in the analyses; and information documenting any study of the accuracy of variables used in the analyses (Recommendation 3.2).

In protecting against harms to individuals or institutions by the publication of evaluative studies, the committee also recommended that HDOs adhere to several principles apart from those just noted. It recommends that to enhance the fairness and minimize the risk of unintended harm from the publication of evaluative studies that identify individual providers, each HDO should adhere to two principles as a standard procedure prior to publication: (1) make available to and upon request by institutions, practitioners, or providers identified in an analysis all data required to perform an independent analysis, and do so with reasonable time for such analysis prior to public release of the HDO results; and (2) accompany publication of its own analyses with notice of the existence and availability of responsible challenges to, alternate analyses of, or explanations of the findings. To foster QA/QI efforts, the committee argues that HDOs ought to make available to provider organizations the information they need to conduct their own internal programs.

Consistent with its public interest stance, the committee also states some recommendations intended to promote wide applications of health-related data. HDOs should release non-person-identifiable data upon request to a variety of other entities that meet certain criteria; these criteria involve public missions to promote public health and publicly released information and explicit policies about data protection. The committee also recommends that HDOs make public their policies governing data release (Recommendation 3.4).

This chapter has only tangentially touched on privacy and confidentiality matters as they relate to person-identified and person-identifiable data. The next chapter presents those issues in some detail.

APPENDIX 3A
FAIRNESS AND PUBLIC DISCLOSURE OF DATA

Chapter 3 advances the proposition that an appropriate balance must be found concerning fairness to the public and to providers in the public disclosure of health-related information by health database organizations. The committee notes that this balance may be more difficult to attain than is commonly appreciated, in part because of inappropriate reliance on technical and statistical decisions and methods. This appendix attempts to illustrate the pitfalls that may confront even relatively straightforward public disclosure activities, using information that is in the public domain from the statewide study in New York State on hospital-specific deaths following coronary artery bypass graft (CABG) in 1991.

Actual Numbers, Computed Values, and Risk Adjustment

When HDOs attempt to disseminate information about providers in ways useful to the public, they are likely to rank providers according to data that either report actual events or reflect computed values. The former might include the number of patients who undergo CABG in each hospital in New York State and the number of patients who die in hospital following CABG (Figures 3A-1 and 3A-2); these numbers describe actual events and, barring inaccurate reporting, are certain. The computed or derived information might include the percentage of patients undergoing CABG who died in hospital (Figure 3A-3).

Such information is likely to be of some use to the public, but the limitations should be clearly stated. For example, suppose that 2 percent of patients in Hospital A and 8 percent of patients in Hospital B died in a given year and that this information is made available to the public at large. An individual contemplating an elective operation might conclude that she should go to Hospital A. Suppose further, however, that Hospital A had only very low-risk patients undergoing elective procedures, whereas Hospital B had a large number of high-risk patients or patients undergoing emergency operations and a mortality of only 0.5 percent among its low-risk elective patients. Suppose yet further that this information was *not* publicly disclosed. With this additional information, reasonable persons might well conclude that the expertise of Hospital B for the type of operation the individual needs might be greater than in Hospital A, despite Hospital A's lower overall hospital mortality.

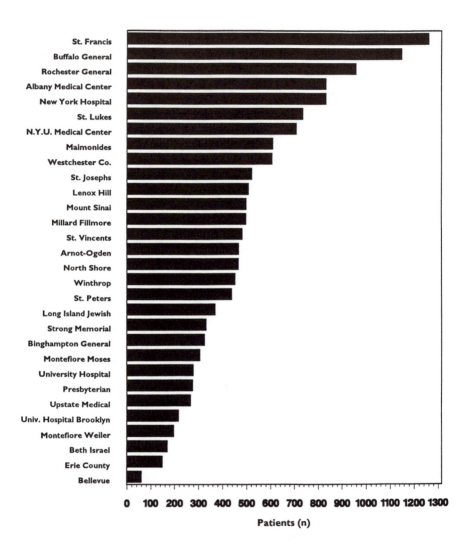

FIGURE 3A-1 The number of patients undergoing coronary artery bypass graft in each hospital in New York State, 1991.

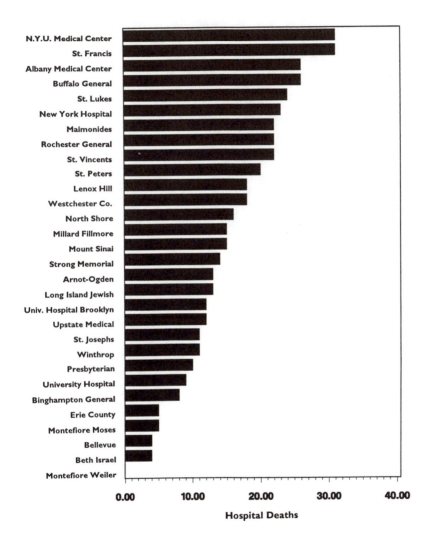

FIGURE 3A-2 Actual (observed) number of patients who died in the hospital after coronary artery bypass graft in each hospital in New York State, 1991.

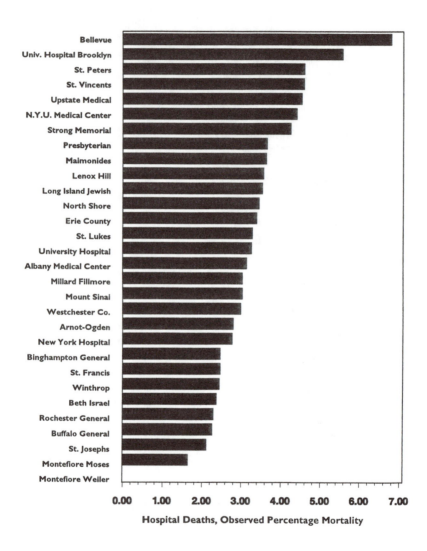

FIGURE 3A-3 Actual (observed) proportion of patients who died in the hospital after coronary artery bypass graft in each hospital in New York State, 1991.

Releasing data only on actual mortality rates clearly is unfair to the public; it is equally unfair to the providers in question. For example, more and more patients would seek care from Hospital A, and these actions collectively might render Hospital B's cardiac surgical program sufficiently underutilized that it would be closed. This would serve the interests neither of future low-risk patients, for whom expected mortality would be lower in Hospital B than in Hospital A, nor of future high-risk emergency patients, with whom Hospital A has no experience.

This kind of unfairness had led to the process generally referred to as risk adjustment. This may be defined as a process that allows the effect of a variable of interest on patient outcomes, such as a hospital or a surgeon, to be isolated from the effect of all other variables believed to influence that outcome. This commonly is accomplished by multivariate analysis to determine simultaneously the variables that, with a stated degree of uncertainty, determine the outcome in question in the population under study.[1] In the example just above, the question would be the effect of hospital on the outcomes of patients undergoing elective or emergency CABG. The analysis would be used to risk-adjust actual hospital mortalities for Hospitals A and B so that they reflect only—or at least largely—the effect of the expertise of the hospitals on patient outcomes. By extension the same process can be applied to determine physician-specific outcomes; in this example, mortality rates by surgeon.

It can be argued that properly risk-adjusted hospital mortality rates, and their conversion by one or another means to inferences about quality of care, is a fair method of comparing providers. Some would counter, however, that random assignment of treatment (e.g., CABG or no CABG in the example at hand) is the only reliable method of risk adjustment. Whether or not this argument is persuasive in theory, random assignment is not practical in many situations, including the one under consideration here. The conclusion to this point might be, however, that HDOs should publicly release not just actual numbers of events but also the results of appropriately risk-adjusted analyses.

Certainty, Probability, and Correct Inferences

Even with all these refinements all derived information and comparisons inherently have only a degree of certainty, not absolute certainty. The

---

[1] Risk adjustment can also be approached by polling expert opinion about indications for an intervention—as for example, in the indications of appropriateness for CABG that have been developed by the RAND Corporation (Chassin et al., 1986b; Leape et al., 1991)—and then stratifying groups of (actual) patients in the analysis according to those indications.

reason is that such analyses yield information and inferences relating to a hypothetical group or population on the basis of investigation of a presumably randomly selected sample of that population. Simple "secure" facts, such as those cited in the figures above for Hospitals A and B, do give some of the information required for fair comparisons, reliable predictions, and secure inferences. Nonetheless, comparisons, predictions, and inferences require something more, and that something more always has a degree of uncertainty. Thus, the comparisons, predictions, and inferences must take into account both the amount or magnitude of any differences displayed by derived information (as well as that shown in actual information) and the related degree of certainty (or uncertainty). This IOM committee has asserted that HDOs have a responsibility to ensure that public disclosures of their data and analyses done with their data clearly portray these considerations. Again, it may suffice to include detailed warnings concerning how not to use the data.

One pitfall that HDOs should avoid is releasing only that information they regard as critically—or statistically significantly—important. They may do this when the multiplicity of providers and computations produces such a large amount of information that not all of it can be published, but doing so may be unfair both to providers and the public. For example, studies might show, with a high degree of certainty, that in a group of 30 hospitals, hospitals X, Y, and Z are the only ones determined to have less good results than the remaining 27 institutions. This degree of certainty, or criterion for differentiating between one subset of the whole group and another, is conventionally defined as a "P-value less than 0.05."

Assume, in this example, that no other members of this group of 30 hospitals are shown with a high degree of certainty to be different from one another. A public release containing only this information is an attractive option on practical grounds, but it may not be fair. Some readers will intuitively realize that one or more other institutions may also have somewhat inferior outcomes, and thus are different from the others in the group, but this conclusion will not have as high a degree of certainty as for hospitals X, Y, and Z.

In short, the use of P-values and establishment of criteria using degrees of certainty are based on arbitrary decisions. The point is illustrated in Table 3A-1, which shows the usual tabular form of public disclosure of hospital deaths after CABG for the purpose of identifying hospitals with poor outcomes. The single asterisk in the figure identifies the only three institutions (here, St. Peter's, St. Vincent's, and University Hospital of Brooklyn) that the analyses showed to be different from all others in risk-adjusted mortality rates with a high degree of certainty ($P < 0.05$).

Although technically this portrayal may be correct, is it fair? That is, should the public be left with the general impression—which may not be accurate—that the other institutions were not different one from the other? As can be seen in Figure 3A-4, three other hospitals (Bellevue, Erie County, and Upstate Medical) had less good outcomes as well, but with slightly less certainty than the three already noted. The arbitrary designation of a *P*-value (here of less than 0.05, but it could be any a priori *P*-value) has led to the erroneous general impression that only the first-named three hospitals are somehow "different" and are to be regarded as outliers.

The criticism can be generalized: Why should "the ruler"—in this case an arbitrary *P*-value—not be placed so that St. Luke's, Arnot-Ogden, and Long Island Jewish are included as outliers? Where, indeed, ought the ruler, if applied to Figure 3A-4, be brought to rest?

The Educational Content of Public Information Dissemination

Public release of information about the variability in the ranks of various hospitals that is produced by different methods of analysis helps the public to understand the degree of uncertainty in overall inferences about "the best place to go for surgery." Much of this can be expressed in some combined index (in Figure 3A-4, this is the risk-adjusted percentage mortality). Depicting other information, and displaying information in bar diagrams (see, for instance, Figures 3A-5, 3A-6, and 3A-7) encourages, if not forces, the public to see how complex a matter it is to distinguish between the best and the worst (or better and poorer) hospitals. It also portrays the small differences that sometimes separate these facilities. Thus, this committee believes that HDOs must realize that the fairest approach to the public release of evaluative information involves disclosing rankings—of all actual data as well as derived data—along with appropriate explanations.

The knowledge base on effective ways to communicate and disseminate quality-related information to consumers is comparatively scanty, yet much health policy today presumes that health care policymakers and providers understand how to carry out such efforts. To overcome gaps in this area, more than one research agenda in the quality-of-care arena has specifically called for work on information dissemination techniques (IOM, 1990; VanAmringe and Shannon, 1992). The committee endorses these calls for additional research on these topics.

TABLE 3A-1 Hospital Deaths Following Coronary Artery Bypass Graft (CABG) in New York State, 1991

Hospital	Patients (n)	Hospital Deaths		Expected % Mortality	Risk-Adjusted Mortality	
		Number	Actual (Observed) % Mortality		%	95% Confidence Limits (CL)
Albany Medical Center	831	26	3.13	2.85	3.38	2.20-4.95
Arnot-Ogden	466	13	2.79	2.14	4.01	2.13-6.85
Bellevue	59	4	6.78	2.81	7.42	2.00-19.00
Beth Israel	169	4	2.37	3.05	2.39	0.64-6.11
Binghamton General	325	8	2.46	3.35	2.26	0.98-4.46
Buffalo General	1,151	26	2.26	2.52	2.76	1.80-4.04
Erie County	148	5	3.38	1.93	5.39	1.74-12.59
Lenox Hill	507	18	3.55	3.17	3.45	2.04-5.45
Long Island Jewish	369	13	3.52	2.70	4.02	2.14-6.88
Maimonides	608	22	3.62	3.63	3.07	1.92-4.64
Millard Fillmore	496	15	3.02	2.44	3.82	2.14-6.30
Montefiore Moses	305	5	1.64	2.82	1.79	0.58-4.18
Montefiore Weiler	196	0	0.00	2.29	0.00[a]	0.00-2.51
Mount Sinai	497	15	3.02	2.84	3.28	1.83-5.40
New York Hospital	831	23	2.77	3.77	2.26	1.43-3.39
North Shore	465	16	3.44	3.25	3.25	1.86-5.28
NYU Medical Center	707	31	4.38	5.38	2.51	1.70-3.56
Presbyterian	275	10	3.64	2.95	3.80	1.82-6.99
Rochester General	959	22	2.29	3.40	2.08	1.30-3.15

St. Francis	1,261	31	2.46	3.10	2.44	1.66-3.47
St. Joseph's	521	11	2.11	2.56	2.53	1.26-4.54
St. Luke's	734	24	3.27	2.44	4.12	2.64-6.13
St. Peter's	437	20	4.58	2.12	6.64[b]	4.06-10.26
St. Vincent's	481	22	4.57	2.13	6.61[b]	4.14-10.01
Strong Memorial	331	14	4.23	3.64	3.57	1.95-5.99
Univ. Hosp. Brooklyn	216	12	5.56	2.37	7.21[b]	3.72-12.59
Univ. Hosp. Stony Brook	277	9	3.25	5.27	1.90	0.87-3.60
Upstate Med. Ctr. Syracuse	266	12	4.51	2.71	5.12	2.64-8.95
Westchester County	605	18	2.98	2.66	3.44	2.04-5.44
Winthrop	451	11	2.44	4.24	1.77	0.88-3.17
Total	14,944	460			3.08 (95% CL = 2.81%-3.37%)	

NOTE: This is the usual New York State tabular form of public disclosure of hospital deaths after CABG, with each hospital being identified. Although the ranking here is alphabetical, the media often reranks the institutions according to the risk-adjusted mortality. The *number of* patients and the *number* of hospital deaths are the only happenings depicted that occurred and about which there is no uncertainty. The *actual* percent mortality is a derived datum, obtained from the previous two numbers by computation. The *expected* percent mortalities and the *risk-adjusted* percent mortalities depend upon computations using a multivariable logistic risk-factor equation and have a degree of uncertainty. The uncertainty in the risk-adjusted percent mortality is expressed here in the 95% confidence limits. Note that the *public's attention* is called primarily to three institutions whose risk-adjusted percent hospital mortalities are nearly certainly higher than those of the state as a whole. (This is essentially the same as those hospitals with nearly certainly larger actual mortality than expected mortality.) The decision as to which hospital is to receive the designations in footnotes *a* and *b* is entirely arbitrary (although based on conventional criteria), as will be seen later.

[a]The only hospital whose lower than statewide risk-adjusted percent mortality is unlikely to be due to chance alone (*P* < 0.05).
[b]*P* < 0.05.

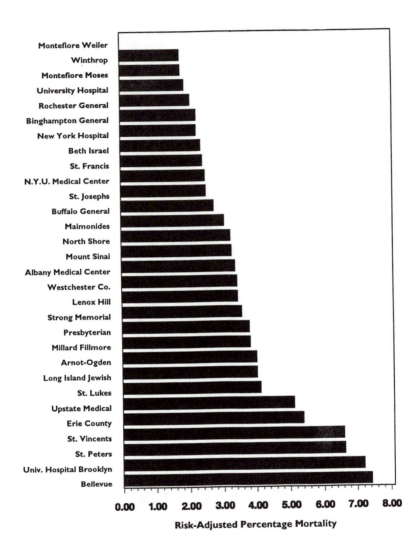

FIGURE 3A-4 The risk-adjusted percent mortality from coronary artery bypass graft in New York State, 1991, shown numerically in Table 3A-1. The higher the risk-adjusted percent mortality, the less the perceived expertise of the institution.

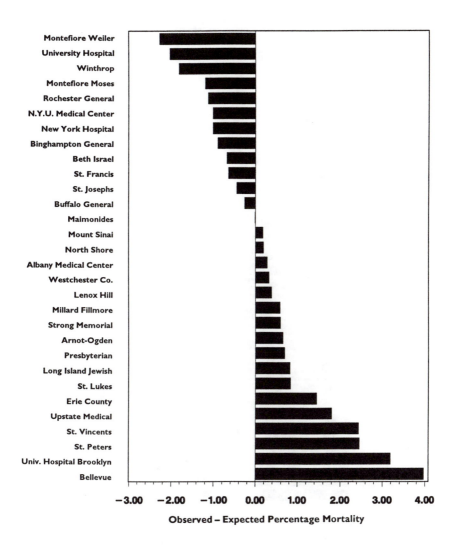

FIGURE 3A-5 The computed difference between the observed (actual) and the expected percent mortality from coronary artery bypass graft in New York State, 1991. The hospitals with lower (negative) differences can be held to have greater expertise than the state as a whole; those with higher (positive) differences can be held to have less expertise.

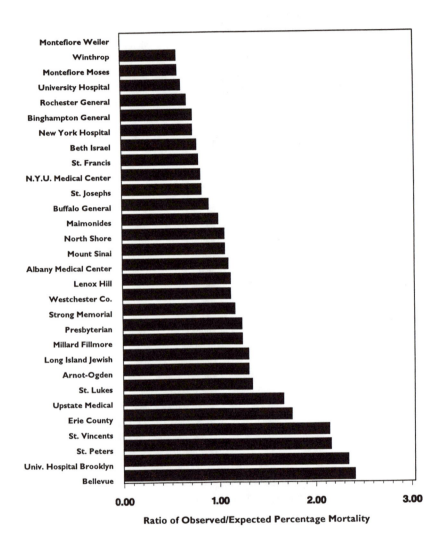

FIGURE 3A-6 The computed ratio between observed (actual) and expected (computed) percent mortality. The smaller the ratios, the greater the expertise of the institution.

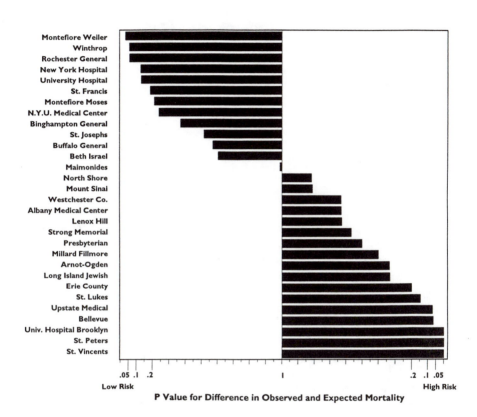

FIGURE 3A-7 The *P*-value for the difference in observed and expected mortality from coronary artery bypass graft in each institution in New York State, 1991. This says nothing about the amount of the difference shown in Figure 3A-5 and Figure 3A-6, but speaks only to the degree of certainty (believability) that the difference is not due to chance alone.

4

Confidentiality and Privacy
of Personal Data

Earlier chapters introduced the Institute of Medicine (IOM) committee's conceptualization of health database organizations (HDOs), outlined their presumed benefits, listed potential users and uses, and examined issues related to the disclosure of descriptive and evaluative data on health care providers (institutions, agencies, practitioners, and similar entities). This chapter examines issues related to information about individuals or patients—specifically, what this committee refers to as person-identified or person-identifiable data. It defines privacy, confidentiality, and security in the context of health-related information and outlines the concerns that health experts, legal authorities, information technology specialists, and society at large have about erosions in the protections accorded such information. It pays particular attention to the status that might be accorded such data when held by HDOs.

Existing ethical, legal, and other approaches to protecting confidentiality and privacy of personal health data offer some safeguards, but major gaps and limitations remain. The recommendations at the end of this chapter are intended to strengthen current protections for confidentiality and privacy of health-related data, particularly for information acquired by HDOs.

HISTORICAL PERSPECTIVES AND GENERAL OBSERVATIONS ON DISCLOSURE OF INFORMATION

The Privacy Protection Study Commission (PPSC) was created by the Privacy Act of 1974 to investigate the personal data recordkeeping practices of governmental, regional, and private organizations. In its landmark 1977 report, *Personal Privacy in an Information Society* (PPSC, 1977a), the commissioners noted that:

> Every member of a modern society acts out the major events and transitions of his life with organizations as attentive partners. Each of his countless transactions with them leaves its mark in the records they maintain about him.

The report went on to point out that:

> . . . as records continue to supplant face-to-face encounters in our society, there has been no compensating tendency to give the individual the kind of control over the collection, use, and disclosure of information about him that his face-to-face encounters normally entail.

The warnings implicit in the commissioners' statement are even more pertinent today. The emergence of HDOs in the 1990s comes at a time when the American public is expressing growing concern about threats to personal privacy. A 1993 Louis Harris poll found that 79 percent of the American public is "very" (49 percent) or "somewhat" (30 percent) worried about the threat to personal privacy (Harris/Equifax, 1993).[1] This response has remained stable since 1990 when it rose sharply from a figure of 64 percent cited for 1978. There was agreement by 80 percent of respondents that "consumers have lost all control over how personal information about them is circulated and used by companies." The 1992 survey also asked about the effect of computers on privacy. Sixty-eight percent agreed strongly or very strongly that "computers are an actual threat to personal privacy," and almost 90 percent agreed that computers have made it much easier to obtain confidential personal information improperly (Equifax, 1992).

Many privacy experts have described the ready availability of personal information (e.g., see Piller, 1993). Rothfeder (1992) asserts that about five billion records in the United States describe each resident's whereabouts and other personal information. He also claims that such information is moved from one computer to another about five times a day (pp. 22-23):

> Information about every move we make—buying a car or a home, applying for a loan, taking out insurance, purchasing potato chips, requesting a government grant, getting turned down for credit, going to work, seeing a

---

[1] In October 1993, Equifax, a credit reporting company, released the results of a Louis Harris poll, the most recent in a series of surveys commissioned by Equifax and conducted periodically since 1978. For the first time, the 1993 survey assessed the beliefs and attitudes about privacy and disclosure of health information of a sample of the public and of "health leaders." A number of the survey questions bear directly on the issues addressed in this chapter.

doctor—is fed into . . . databases owned by the credit bureaus, the government, banks, insurance companies, direct-marketing companies, and other interested corporations. And from these databases it's broadcast to thousands . . . of regional databanks as well as to numerous information resellers across the country.

Rothfeder believes that such pervasive data acquisition and exchange can lead to a feeling of powerlessness in the face of privacy intrusion. His language is evocative (p. 30):

Increasingly, people are at the whim of not only pressure groups, but also large organizations—direct marketers, the credit bureaus, the government, and the entire information economy—that view individuals as nothing but lifeless data floating like microscopic entities in vast electronic chambers, data that exists [sic] to be captured, examined, collated, and sold, regardless of the individual's desire to choose what should be concealed and what should be made public.

It may be that the increasing aggregation of personal data documenting the details of our physical attributes and defects, behaviors, desires, attitudes, failings, and achievements creates a virtual representation of us. Some have called this a "computerized alter ego" or a "digital version of each of us to go with our public personae" (Rothfeder, 1992, p. 16, citing Miller). To the extent this is so, the privacy of this "virtual person" requires protection.

Recently the U.S. Congress has given serious attention to reform of the Fair Credit Reporting Act (Public Law [P.L.] 102-550; see below). It has also looked at technology-driven privacy issues: most pertinent are legislative proposals to restrict caller I.D. programs (S. 652; H.R. 1305; also see, House Report No. 102-324, 102nd Congress 2d Session), junk telephone calls and junk faxes (P.L. 102-243, "Telephone Consumer Protection Act of 1991"). Some congressional efforts, such as bills related to DNA testing and genetic profiling (S. 1355, "DNA Identification Act of 1991"; H.R. 2045, "Human Genome Privacy Act"), were intended to protect individuals against threats posed by medical technologies or initiatives. In October 1991, the Committee on Government Operations of the U.S. House of Representatives, Subcommittee on Government Information, Justice, and Agriculture, held hearings on genetic privacy issues, and in April 1992 it issued a report calling for reforms related to the privacy of genetic information.

Both the U.S. Congress and the Administration have undertaken activities related to the protection of medical information. In October 1993 the Senate Committee on the Judiciary held hearings on High Tech Privacy Issues in Health Law, and in November, the Subcommittee on Government Information, Justice, and Agriculture of the Committee on Government Operations held a hearing on a report prepared by the Office of Technology

Assessment (OTA, 1993) at the request of that subcommittee and the Senate Subcommittee on Federal Services, Post Office, and Civil Service. The former committee has also been drafting legislation to protect the privacy of health information.[2]

A Task Force on Privacy was established in 1990 by the Assistant Secretary for Planning and Evaluation to report on the privacy of private sector health records. Another DHHS group established at the same time, the Workgroup on Electronic Data Interchange (WEDI, 1991) also addressed the protection of information when medical insurance claims are handled electronically. The recommendations of that workshop are discussed later in this chapter.

Two of President Clinton's Health Care Reform Task Forces met during the spring of 1993. They considered the implications of and generated plans for the protection of health-related data that would be acquired and held under the administration's proposal for health reform. The legislative proposals in the Health Security Act contain specific privacy protection provisions.[3]

---

[2] The OTA report was released just as the IOM report was being completed.

[3] The Administration's Health Security Act (HSA, 1993) calls for the development of Health Information System Standards within two years of its enactment to promulgate standards and security safeguards for the privacy of individually identifiable health information that is in the health information system (see Footnote 1, Chapter 2). The proposed legislation states the following principles: (1) All disclosures of individually identifiable health information by an individual or entity shall be unauthorized unless (a) the disclosure is by the enrollee identified in the information or whose identity can be associated with the information; (b) the disclosure is authorized by such enrollee in writing in a manner prescribed by the Board; (c) the disclosure is to Federal, State, or local law enforcement agencies for the purpose of enforcing this Act or an Act amended by this Act; or (d) the disclosure otherwise is consistent with this Act and specific criteria governing disclosure established by the Board. Further, disclosure of individually identifiable health information shall be restricted to the minimum amount of information necessary to accomplish the purpose for which the information is being disclosed. It would require that any individual or entity who maintains, uses, or disseminates individually identifiable health information implement administrative, technical, and physical safeguards.

It stipulates that an enrollee (or an enrollee representative) has the right to know (a) "whether any individual or entity uses or maintains individually identifiable health information concerning the enrollee; and (b) for what purposes the information may be used or maintained" (Sec. 5120). It also specifies a right to access to see, copy, and have entered a notation of any amendment or correction of his or her information. It specifies a right to receive a written statement concerning (1) the purposes for which individually identifiable health information may be used or disclosed by, or disclosed to, any individual or entity; and (2) the right of access described above. The legislation also calls for the use of a unique identifier to be used in transmitting information. It further specifies that individually identifiable health care information may not be used in making employment decisions.

Sec. 5121 calls for the National Health Board to sponsor (1) research relating to the privacy and security of individually identifiable health information; (2) the development of consent

State legislatures have also been active. In the past three years, for example, many states have adopted legislation that prohibits employers from discriminating against applicants and employees on the basis of off-the-job, lawful activity or some specific subset of lawful activity, such as cigarette smoking.

SOURCES OF CONCERNS ABOUT PRIVACY
AND THE CONFIDENTIALITY OF HEALTH RECORDS

Two somewhat distinct trends have led to increased access to the primary health record and subsequent concerns about privacy. One has to do with primary health records regardless of how they are created and maintained; the other involves health records stored electronically.

Health Care Records

The quantity and type of health care information now collected has also increased dramatically in recent years. The participation in health care delivery of many different individuals and groups of providers exerts strong pressures to document in ever greater detail. The expanding numbers of available technologies for diagnosis and therapy mean that details that a provider could at one time recall must now be recorded and thus become available for inspection by others. Further, information on lifestyle (e.g., use of tobacco or alcohol), family history, and health status have become of greater interest and relevance as we learn more about the relationship of these factors to overall health and well-being. In addition, genetic data are becoming more readily available, not only for prenatal testing but also for assessing an individual's degree of risk for an inherited condition.[4]

The more detailed the information about an individual or class of individuals, the more appropriate, one hopes, is the treatment they will be given. Further, documentation of care and risk factors are essential to promoting

---

forms governing disclosure of such information; and (3) the development of technology to implement standards regarding such information. It should also establish education and awareness programs, foster adequate security practices, train personnel of public and private entities in appropriate practices.

Sec. 5122. calls for a proposal not later than three years after enactment of the HSA to provide a comprehensive scheme of Federal privacy protection for individually identifiable health information that would include a Code of Fair Information Practices and provide for enforcement of the rights and duties created by the legislation. (Health Security Act. Title V. Part 2. Privacy of information.)

[4] An IOM report on assessing genetic risk explores these issues in considerable detail and develops a strong pro-privacy stance (IOM, 1993b).

continuity of care over time and among providers. It is also a first defense against charges of malpractice.

The primary health record is no longer simply a tool for health care providers to record their impressions, observations, and instructions. Rather, it serves many purposes beyond direct health care. Third-party payers access patient record information to make payment determinations, and managed care organizations access patient records for precertification and case management.

Other parties external to the healing relationship seek person-identified information and assert socially beneficial reasons for access. What was once the "business" only of patients and possibly their physicians has now become the business of such groups as: (1) officers of government entitlement programs checking on eligibility, and on patient and provider fraud and abuse; (2) agencies granting security clearance; (3) attorneys bringing criminal or civil charges; and (4) social service workers protecting possibly abused children, to name only a few. Others access secondary health records or obtain portions of the medical record when making decisions about hiring, granting a license, or issuing life, health, or disability insurance.

Electronic Records

Other trends give rise to particular concerns about the confidentiality of health information that is stored electronically. First is the ability to access, transmit, and copy large volumes of data easily. Photocopying paper records is, of course, possible, but it is hardly feasible for large numbers of geographically dispersed medical records. Electronic storage and transmittal of data, by contrast, enable interested parties to aggregate information for individuals over time and across institutions and providers of care.

Second, databases were at one time discrete—often held in physically secure rooms on tape drives—with identifiers that were unique to a given institution or insurer. Now, however, data from diverse sources can be combined and linked. Once data are stored electronically, networks of databases can be explored almost imperceptibly from remote locations. Unless security systems are designed to record access, the curious, entrepreneurial, or venal can enter databases without leaving evidence of having done so.

Third, computer-based health data have become a very valuable commodity. Some companies obtain information from physicians' computers and pharmacy records for sale to pharmaceutical companies in return for incentives such as low-cost computer hardware and software. These companies gather such identifying variables as age, sex, and Social Security numbers even if patient names are either not taken or are later stripped off (Miller, 1992).

Other companies resell information from prescription or claims databases to companies that sort it by physician for marketing purposes. For example, Health Information Technologies, Inc., helps automate private physicians' insurance claims. When it transmits claims and payments between the insurance company and the physician, it retains electronic copies of these records, and it can later sell them (presumably without physician or patient names) for pharmaceutical and other related kinds of marketing (Miller, 1992).

In August 1993, Merck & Company purchased Medco Containment Services, a mail-order prescription firm. The purchase price, $6 billion, was based in part on the value of the information in its databases to influence physician prescribing practices (Tanouye, 1993). HDOs will control a gold mine of information, and they may find it difficult indeed to resist economic benefits from allowing access to their data files by third parties.

Finally, because developers of HDOs have compared claims transmittal to electronic funds transfer (EFT), it is helpful to examine how the Privacy Protection Study Commission regarded confidentiality in EFT. The commissioners were alert to problems that might result if records created by EFT could not be controlled by institutions. Noting that automated clearinghouses centralize information that would otherwise be segregated among diverse depository institutions, their report (PPSC, 1977a) expressed worry about threats posed by the accumulation and centralization of the financial information that flows through such clearinghouses. The commissioners also recognized that the resulting pools of information would become attractive sources of person-identifiable information for use "in ways inimical to personal privacy" (p. 121). They urged that adequate protections be established for person-identifiable information flowing through an EFT data communications network and that such account information be retained for as limited a period of time as was essential to fulfill operating requirements of the service provider. Thus, in contemplating EFT, the commissioners did not foresee, and certainly did not encourage, the creation of an information repository now contemplated under the concept of an HDO.

DEFINITIONS

Below, the committee offers definitions of critical terms—privacy (especially informational privacy), confidentiality, security, and health-related information.

Privacy

The most general and common view of privacy conveys notions of withdrawal, seclusion, secrecy, or of being kept away from public view, but with no pejorative overtones. By contrast, an *invasion of privacy* occurs when there is intentional deprivation of the desired privacy to which one is entitled. In public policy generally and health policy in particular, privacy takes on special meanings, some derived from moral theories, others from legal doctrine, and one from the widespread use of health information.

Privacy is sometimes characterized as the "right to be left alone" (Cooley, 1880; Warren and Brandeis, 1890; Elison and Nettiksimmons, 1987; Turkington, 1987; Herdrich, 1989). Many experts, however, have objected that such a definition is too broad to be helpful in the health context. There are innumerable ways of not being left alone that arguably have nothing to do with privacy (Thomson, 1975; Reiman, 1976; Parent, 1983), such as when an individual is subjected to aggressive panhandling on a city street. Consequently, theorists have sought to refine their conceptions of privacy. Their aim has been to isolate what is unique about privacy, to identify what constitutes its loss, and to distinguish among a variety of conceptually related but separable senses of privacy (Gerety, 1977; McCloskey, 1980; Schoeman, 1984).

The development and application of the concept of privacy in American law encompasses three clusters of ideas.[5] First, privacy embodies autonomy interests; it protects decisions about the exercise of fundamental constitutional liberties with respect to private behavior, such as decisions relating to marriage, procreation, contraception, family relationships, and child-rearing. This is frequently characterized as decisional privacy (Tribe, 1978). Second, privacy protects against surveillance or intrusion when an individual has a "reasonable expectation of privacy." Examples include protections against unlawful searches of one's home or person and unauthorized wiretapping. Third, privacy encompasses informational interests; this notion is most frequently expressed as the interest of an individual in controlling the dissemination and use of information that relates to himself or herself (Shils, 1966; Westin, 1967), or to have information about oneself be inaccessible to others. This last form—informational privacy—is the main subject of this chapter.

Informational Privacy

Informational privacy—*"a state or condition of controlled access to personal information"* (Schoeman, 1984; Allen, 1987; Powers, 1993)—is infringed, by definition, whenever another party has access to one's personal information by reading, listening, or using any of the other senses. Such loss of privacy may be entirely acceptable and intended by the indi-

---

[5] In the United States, privacy is restricted to real persons. In Europe, legal persons are generally included.

vidual, or it may be inadvertent, unacceptable, and even unknown to the individual.

This definition of privacy thus reflects two underlying notions. First, privacy in general and informational privacy in particular are always matters of degree. Rarely is anyone in a condition of complete physical or informational inaccessibility to others, nor would they wish to remain so. Second, although information privacy may be valuable and deserving of protection, many thoughtful privacy advocates argue that it does not, in itself, have moral significance or inherent value (Allen, 1987; Faden, 1993).

Nonetheless, informational privacy has value for all in our society, and it accordingly has special claims on our attention. In his pivotal book, *Privacy and Freedom*, Westin (1967) described it as "the claim of individuals, groups, or institutions to determine for themselves when, how, and to what extent information about them is communicated to others" (p. 7). This definition served as the foundation for the Privacy Act of 1974 (P.L. 93-579; 5 U.S.C. § 552a). This act, arguably the most significant step to protect privacy in recent decades, was enacted to control use of personally identifiable information maintained in federal government databases.

Recordkeeping Privacy

In recent decades, discussions about privacy have almost exclusively addressed the use of information about people to make decisions about some right, privilege, benefit, or entitlement—so-called "recordkeeping privacy." This focus was of particular interest to those framing the Privacy Act of 1974.

More recently the desire for informational privacy has become an important expectation, not because of a benefit or entitlement sought, but for its own sake. Information may be created as a byproduct of some event—for example, an individual's geographic location becomes available when he or she uses a bank card for a financial transaction; similarly, one's preferences are known when one buys goods by mail order or uses a check-verification card at the local supermarket. In yet other cases, information derives from aggregating data from many sources, including public records; such aggregation can also include data that have been derived from computer processing (e.g., buying profiles or dossiers).

Data subjects want informational privacy to be respected in such contexts as well. Many people in the United States would like to believe that data collected about them legitimately, in connection with some transaction or incidentally through participation in the general activities of society, will not be exploited for secondary purposes such as advertising, soliciting, telemarketing, promotional activities, or other actions that are distinct from and unrelated to the activities for which the data were originally collected (see Harris/Equifax, 1993). As should be clear from the discussion in this chapter, however, these hopes are often not realized in general or in relation to health information.

Privacy Rights

To assert a right is to make a special kind of claim. Rights designate some interests of the individual that are sufficiently important to hold others under a duty to promote and protect, sometimes even at the expense of maximizing or even achieving the social good (Raz, 1986). Two interests are widely cited as providing the moral justification for privacy rights: the individual's interest in autonomy and the instrumental value that privacy may have in promoting other valuable human goods.

With respect to *autonomy*, privacy fosters and enhances a sense of self (Reiman, 1976). Respecting privacy enhances an individual's autonomy (Westin, 1967; Benn, 1971; Bloustein, 1984). It allows the individual to develop the capacity to be self-governing or "sovereign," a notion analogous to the sense in which autonomous states are sovereign (Beauchamp and Childress, 1989). The loss or degradation of privacy can enable others to exercise an inordinate measure of power over the individual's economic, social, and psychological well-being (Gavison, 1980; Parent, 1983).

With respect to the value of privacy to promote other ends, its *instrumental value*, privacy permits the development of character traits and virtues essential to desirable human relationships. These include trust, intimacy, and love. Without some measure of privacy, these relationships are diminished or may not be possible (Fried, 1968; Rachels, 1975).

The existence of informational privacy rights means that someone is under a duty either not to disclose information or to prevent unauthorized access to information by others. Dworkin (1977) has argued that for a right to be meaningful implies that any policy or law overriding such duties must withstand rigorous scrutiny and that considerations of social utility alone are inadequate grounds to override it. That is, to take rights seriously is to recognize some limits on the prerogative of government or others to mandate the common good at the expense of the individual. This is not to say, however, that rights function as an absolute barrier to the pursuit of collective goals; indeed, the tension between individual and social goals is reflected in the issues raised in Chapter 3, as well as in this chapter.

Balancing Benefits of HDOs Against Loss of Informational Privacy

There cannot be much doubt that HDOs will serve legitimate societal interests as described in Chapter 2. Nevertheless, because HDOs will represent one of the most comprehensive and sensitive automated personal record databases ever established, they inevitably implicate interests protected by informational privacy principles. Accordingly, HDO advocates will be well served from an ethical as well as legal viewpoint if they consider what social goods justify possible loss of privacy and such loss can be minimized or prevented.

Whether HDOs can achieve their potential for good in the face of their possible impact on privacy will likely turn on the interplay of three considerations. First, to what extent do the HDOs provide important (and perhaps irreplaceable) health care benefits to their regions and perhaps to the nation? Second, do the societal benefits resulting from the implementation of HDOs outweigh the privacy risks? Third, to what extent have adequate privacy safeguards been incorporated into the HDOs?

Federal and State Privacy Protection

No explicit right to privacy is guaranteed by the Constitution of the United States; in fact, the word "privacy" does not appear. The presumed right as the basis of a civil action is based on legal opinion written by Justice Louis D. Brandeis in 1890, and its constitutional status derives from various amendments to the Bill of Rights.

The issues surrounding the constitutional status of privacy protection are too numerous and controversial to explore in detail here. Most constitutional scholars agree that federal constitutional protections are unlikely to provide the first line of defense for privacy of health information. The Constitution generally has not provided strong protection for the confidentiality of individual health care information; the constitutional protection for informational privacy is thus very limited and derived from case law interpreting the Constitution.

The courts have made clear that, at least theoretically, information privacy principles based on the Constitution limit a government agency's collection and use of personal information to situations in which the use bears a rational relationship to a legitimate governmental purpose. The government's interest in the information program must outweigh the threat to personal privacy posed by the program.[6]

In *Whalen* v. *Roe* (429 U.S. 589 [1977]), for example, the Supreme Court balanced the privacy threat posed by a New York State law against the statute's benefits. The New York State statute required pharmacists and physicians to report sensitive health record information to state officials, in

---

[6] See, *Plante* v. *Gonzalez*, 575 F. 2d 1119, 1123 (5th Cir. 1978). However, in *J.P.* v. *DeSanti*, 653 F. 2d 1080, 1090 (6th Cir. 1981), the Sixth Circuit held that the Constitution's right-to-privacy standard does not extend to the disclosure of personal information.

this case prescriptions for controlled drugs. It required physicians to report the names of patients receiving certain types of prescription drugs to a state agency. The court concluded that the statute was constitutional on two grounds: the societal interests served by the statute (combating the illegal use of otherwise legal drugs) and extensive privacy and confidentiality protections in the law (redisclosure of the drug information, for example, was prohibited). The court suggested that if the statute had lacked these confidentiality protections it would have been found to violate constitutional privacy principles (Chlapowski, 1991). Thus, privacy rights are to be considered derived and not explicit rights.

In *United States v. Westinghouse Electric Corp.* (638 F. 2d 570, 578 [3rd Cir. 1980]), the Third Circuit identified seven factors that should be weighed in determining whether to permit a government agency to collect personal information and thus undertake a program that infringes privacy. These were the type of record requested; the subject matter of the information; the potential for harm in a subsequent nonconsensual disclosure; the damage to the relationship in which the record was generated; the adequacy of safeguards to prevent unauthorized disclosure; the degree of need for access; and whether there is an express, statutory mandate, articulated public policy, or other recognizable public interest tilting toward access.

Various state constitutional provisions offer more protection. For one to have a claim for a violation of a constitutional privacy right, however, the individual generally must show that state action caused the violation. California's constitution (Cal. Const., Art. 1, § 1) is an exception to this general rule because it makes privacy rights explicit. California courts have held that the state's constitutional privacy provision can be asserted against private parties who infringe on citizens' privacy; see, for instance *Heda v. Superior Court*, 225 Cal. App. 3rd 525 (Cal., Dist. Ct., App. 1990) and *Soroka v. Dayton Hudson Corp.*, 1 Cal. Rptr. 2nd 77 (1991). Other common law and statutory remedies, as well as institutional policies and practices, will be of greater immediate importance. This and the relevance of existing laws to HDOs is discussed in the next section.

Confidentiality

Confidentiality relates to disclosure or nondisclosure of information. Historically a duty to honor confidentiality has arisen with respect to information disclosed in the context of a confidential relationship, such as that between an individual and his or her physician, attorney, or priest. In such relationships, the confidante is under an obligation not to redisclose the information learned in the course of the relationship. Now the law applies such duties to some holders of information who do not have a confidential relationship to a patient. In the health sector, this includes such holders as utilization management firms in many states and local, state, or federal health agencies that receive reports of communicable diseases.

When one is concerned about data disclosure, whether or not any relationship exists between a data subject and a data holder, an essential construct is that of *data confidentiality*. Data confidentiality is the status accorded data indicating that they are protected and must be treated as such. In the federal Freedom of Information Act (FOIA, 5 U.S.C., Section 552), certain categories of data are specified as confidential and thus not disclosable; for instance, Exemption 6 states that FOIA is not applicable to "personnel and medical files and similar files, the disclosure of which would constitute clearly unwarranted invasion of personal privacy." Data confidentiality is discussed in more detail in a later section.

Confidentiality Obligations in Health Care

Professional obligations to privacy and confidentiality. The importance of confidentiality to the medical profession is reflected in the physician's "Oath of Hippocrates." Adopted in roughly the fourth century B.C.E., it remains a recognized element of medical ethics:

> Whatsoever things I see or hear concerning the life of men, in my attendance on the sick or even apart therefrom, which ought not to be noised abroad, I will keep silence thereon, counting such things to be as sacred secrets (Bulger, 1987).

In similar fashion, the American Medical Association *Principles of Medical Ethics* (AMA, 1992, Section 5.05) states that "The information disclosed to a physician during the course of the relationship between the physician and patient is confidential to the greatest possible degree . . . The physician should not reveal confidential communications or information without the express consent of the patient, unless required to do so by law."

Within the healing relationship, four justifications may be offered for medical confidentiality (adapted from Faden, 1993). First is a respect for privacy and patient autonomy. In the earliest practice of medicine, physicians treated patients in their homes, and medical privacy was an extension of the privacy of the home. The Hippocratic Oath, for instance, does not justify confidentiality on any ground other than respect for privacy. If information concerning a patient's mind and body are viewed as extensions of the patient, than the concept of autonomy requires that the patient be able to control disclosure and use of that information. The value placed on personal autonomy gives rise to the notion of informed consent. As Justice Benjamin N. Cardozo wrote in his opinion in *Schloendorff* v. *Society of New York Hospital,* 211 N.Y. 125, "Every human being of adult years and sound mind has a right to determine what shall be done with his body."

A second justification related to respect for privacy is the implicit and sometimes explicit expectation or promise of confidentiality. Third is the special moral character of the doctor-patient relationship, which is characterized by trust and intimacy. Confidentiality can be instrumental in fostering patients' trust in their physicians; when this trust encourages patients to speak freely and disclose information they would otherwise keep secret, it facilitates diagnosis and treatment. Fourth, respecting confidentiality protects patients from harm that might befall them if the information were to become widely available and indiscriminately used.

Legal obligations of confidentiality. Various federal and state laws impose a duty to preserve the confidentiality of personal health information. These laws can be divided into two categories: those imposing confidentiality obligations on recordkeepers and those protecting health information that is deemed highly sensitive. Examples of the former include general confidentiality statutes about health care information such as the Uniform Health Care Information Act (National Conference, 1988) and the California Confidentiality of Medical Information Act (Cal. Civil Code §§ 56-56.37 [1992]), as well as various state laws and Medicare and Medicaid regulations. Laws and regulations imposing confidentiality requirements for sensitive personal health information include those related to alcohol and drug abuse records and laws governing nondisclosure of records of patients with acquired immunodeficiency syndrome (AIDS), the results of antibody tests for human immunodeficiency virus (HIV), psychiatric and developmental disability records, and information concerning results of genetics screening and testing.

Courts have also recognized a legal obligation to maintain the confidentiality of personal health care information. In response to harm resulting from unauthorized release of personal health information, courts have granted legal relief under a number of theories: breach of trust, breach of confidence, breach of implied contract, invasion of privacy, defamation, and negligence (Waller, 1992).

Disclosure of Health Information

As one looks beyond the protected sphere of the patient-provider relationship, it is not always clear who is rightly in the community of "knowers," nor is there universal agreement on principles that ought to control disclosure. With the growth of managed care, utilization review, third-party payment systems, and claims administration for self-insured health plans, information sharing for purposes of adjudicating claims and managing high-risk or high-cost cases has become part and parcel of the provision of health care. Westin has described these supporting and administrative activities as

"Zone 2" in comparison to "Zone 1," which refers to information flow to support direct medical care (Westin, 1976; Harris/Equifax, 1993). These wide-ranging claims of need for sensitive health information, which are emblematic of modern health care, raise difficult problems for the preservation of privacy and maintenance of confidentiality.

Patients generally understand that, with consent, information in their medical records will be shared widely within a hospital and for insurance and reimbursement purposes. They also expect that data collected about them will be used only for the purpose of the initial collection and that such data will be shared with others only for that same purpose. Outside the health care institution, patients expect that confidential data will not be shared with people or organizations not authorized to have such information and that legitimate users of the data will not exploit such access for purposes other than those for which the information was originally obtained (e.g., see Harris/Equifax, 1993).

Consent. Such exceptions to the rule of confidentiality as described above are rationalized as being conducted by consent of the patient or a patient representative. A patient may be asked to accede to disclosure by signing a blanket consent form when applying for insurance or employment. In such cases, however, consent cannot be truly voluntary or informed. Such authorizations are often not *voluntary* because the patient feels compelled to sign the authorization or forego the benefit sought, and they are not *informed* because the patient cannot know in advance what information will be in the record, who will subsequently have access to it, or how it will be used.

Although consent may be the best-recognized way to permit disclosures of private information, consent is so often not informed or is given under economic compulsion that it does not provide sufficient protection to patients. As will be seen in the recommendations section of this chapter, this committee generally does not regard "consent" procedures as sufficient to protect sensitive information from inappropriate disclosure by HDOs, although they are a necessary adjunct to other autonomy protections.

Mandatory reporting and compulsory process. Other situations exist in which sensitive health information about individuals *must* be disclosed to third parties. Such sharing of health information for socially sanctioned purposes may be truly voluntary; it may also be required through mandatory reporting or coerced by court order.

Mandatory reporting requirements are justified by society's need for information; these include filing reports of births and deaths, communicable diseases, cancer, environmental and occupational diseases, drug addiction, gunshot wounds, child abuse, and other violence-related injuries. Some statutes requiring that records be retained for 10 to 25 years in some cases make past diagnoses retrievable long after they no longer accurately describe the patient. Another type of reporting requirement involves the expectation that third parties require warning about threats to their life.[7]

Physicians and others may also find themselves compelled to divulge patient information when they would otherwise choose not to do so. Such requirements—sometimes termed "compulsory process"—may take the form of subpoenas or discovery requests and may be enforced by court order. In some instances personal health care information may be protected from disclosure in court and administrative proceedings by virtue of the physician-patient privilege, which may be mandated by statute or derive from the common law. Information that is so privileged cannot be introduced into evidence and is generally not subject to discovery.

Weaknesses of Legal Protection for Confidentiality

Legal and ethical confidentiality obligations are the same whether health records are kept on paper or on computer-based media (Waller, 1992). Current laws, however, have significant weaknesses. First, and very important, the degree to which confidentiality is required under current law varies according to the holder of the information and the type of information held.

Second, legal obligations of confidentiality often vary widely within a single state and from state to state, making it difficult to ascertain the legal obligations that a given HDO will have, particularly if it operates in a multistate area. These state-by-state and intrastate variations and inconsistencies in privacy and confidentiality laws are well established among those knowledgeable about health care records law (e.g., see Powers, 1991; Waller, 1991; WEDI, 1992; Gostin et al., 1993; OTA, 1993; for examples ranging across many types of professionals, institutions, and ancillary personnel). This is important because some HDOs will routinely transmit data across state lines. Interstate transmission already occurs with data such as claims or typed dictation. When confidential data are transmitted across state lines, it is not always clear which state's confidentiality laws apply and which state's courts have jurisdiction over disputes concerning improper disclosure of information.

Third, current laws offer individuals little real protection against redisclosure

---

[7] In a California case, *Tarasoff* v. *Regents of the University of California,* 17 Ca. 3d 425,551 P.2d (1976), a psychiatrist who was told of a patient's homicidal fantasies regarding the patient's girlfriend did not warn her because he believed that confidentiality constraints prevented him from doing so. Soon after, the patient killed the woman. The court found that the physician had a duty to warn third parties in such circumstances.

of their confidential health information to unauthorized recipients for a number of reasons. Once patients have consented to an initial disclosure of information (for example, to obtain insurance reimbursement), they have lost control of further disclosure. Information disclosed for one purpose may be used for unrelated purposes without the subject's knowledge or consent (sometimes termed secondary use). For instance, information about a diagnosis taken from an individual's medical record may be forwarded to the Medical Information Bureau in Boston, Massachusetts (MIB, 1989; and see Kratka, 1990) and later used by another insurance company in an underwriting decision concerning life insurance. Redisclosure practices represent a yawning gap in confidentiality protection.

As a practical matter, policing redisclosure of one's personal health information is difficult and may be impossible. At a minimum, such policing requires substantial resources and commitment. With the use of computer and telecommunications networks, an individual may never discover that a particular disclosure has occurred, even though he or she suffers significant harm—such as inability to obtain employment, credit, housing, or insurance—as a result of such disclosure. Pursuing legal remedies may result in additional disclosure of the individual's private health information.[8]

Fourth, in some instances federal law preempts state confidentiality requirements or protections without imposing new ones. For example, the Employment Retirement Insurance Security Act (ERISA) preempts some state insurance laws with respect to employers' self-insured health plans, yet ERISA is silent on confidentiality obligations. Because 74 percent or more of employers with 1,000 or more employees manage self-insured health plans (Foster Higgins, 1991, in IOM, 1993e), such preemption is particularly troublesome.

Last, enforcing rights through litigation is costly, and money damages may not provide adequate redress for the harm done by the improper disclosure.

Security

In the context of health record information, confidentiality implies controlled access and protection against unauthorized access to, modification of, or destruction of health data. Confidentiality has meaning only when the

---

[8] A suit brought by an AIDS patient under the name John Doe against Shady Grove Adventist Hospital resulted in the hospital's trying to force the patient to reveal his true name to the press and public (*John Doe v. Shady Grove Adventist Hospital, et al.*, 89 Md. App. 351, 598 A.2d 507 [1991a]).

data holder has the will, technical capacity, and moral or legal authority to protect data—that is, to keep such information (or the system in which it resides) secure (NRC/CBASSE, 1993). Data security exists when data are protected from accidental or intentional disclosure to unauthorized persons and from unauthorized or accidental alteration (IOM, 1991a).

In computer-based or computer-controlled systems, security is implemented when a defined system functions in a defined operational environment, serves a defined set of users, contains prescribed data and operational programs, has defined network connections and interactions with other systems, and incorporates safeguards to protect the system against a defined threat to the system, its resources, and its data. More generally, protective safeguards include:

- hardware (e.g., memory protect);
- software (e.g., audit trails, log-on procedures);
- personnel control (e.g., badges or other mechanisms to control entry or limit movement);
- physical object control (e.g., logging and cataloging of magnetic tapes and floppy disks, destruction of paper containing person-identifiable printouts);
- disaster preparedness (e.g., sprinklers, tape vaults in case of fire, flood, or bomb);
- procedures (e.g., granting access to systems, assigning passwords);
- administration (e.g., auditing events, disaster preparedness, security officer); and
- management oversight (e.g., periodic review of safeguards, unexpected inspections, policy guidance).

The collective intent of these safeguards is to give high assurance that the system, its resources, and information are protected against harm and that the information and resources are properly accessed and used by authorized users.

Health-Related Information

In a study that focuses on the protection of health-related data about individuals, defining which items are health related is more difficult than one might initially think. The most obvious categories are medical history, current diagnoses, diagnostic test results, and therapies. Other pieces of information are more distantly related to health—because of what one might infer about a person's health. Examples include type of specialist visited, functional status, lifestyle, and past diagnoses. Nevertheless, not everything in a medical record is relevant to health status or is health related.

Insurance coverage and marital status are cases in point. Some elements could nevertheless be considered sensitive because of the social stigma that could result if they are revealed. Examples include sexual preference, address, or the receipt of social services.

The same disclosure might be harmful to one individual but not another, or harmful to an individual in one circumstance but not in another. Personal data, particularly health-related personal data, are not inherently sensitive, but they become so because of the harmful way(s) in which they might be used. Thus, any data element in medical records, and many data items from other records, *could* be considered either health-related or sensitive, or both. Where the boundaries for the protection of personal health information lie is not at all obvious. In considering the actions of HDOs, this committee takes a relatively broad view of health-related data; it proceeds from an assumption that *all* information concerning an individual and any transactions relating directly or indirectly to health care that HDOs access or maintain as databases must be regarded as potentially requiring privacy protections.[9]

EXPANDED DEFINITIONS

The foregoing discussions of confidentiality are based on historical, ethical, and legal usage and have served to guide legislators and practitioners. Legally and medically, confidentiality has been treated as arising from a relationship such as that between physician and patient or attorney and client. Such usage may not be as useful to administrators, vice presidents for data processing, or system designers who must design HDO systems and are working not with relationships but with access to secondary records.

The committee suggests, therefore, that an expanded interpretation using a taxonomy that is not derived from interpersonal or interprofessional relationships might be more helpful to those responsible for protection of information in these HDOs. In this taxonomy one begins with *data confidentiality*, defined as the status accorded *data that have been declared to be sensitive and must be protected and handled as such.* The rationale for the statement about sensitivity is based on potential harm to people, potential invasion of privacy, and potential loss of entitlements or privileges.

Two consequences flow from defining data as sensitive and requiring protection. First, the data must be made secure; second, access must be controlled. As described earlier, data security includes system and network

---

[9] Waller (1991) provides a detailed discussion of legal considerations affecting computer-based patient records, including privacy rights.

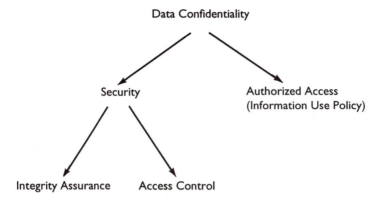

FIGURE 4-1 A new taxonomy of data confidentiality, security, and informational privacy.

protection and assures the integrity of data—such that they are not altered or destroyed accidentally or intentionally. Some system security safeguards (e.g., control of personnel) also assure data integrity.

The second consequence of declaring data sensitive—the need for access control—is related to the concept of informational privacy described above. Access control can be operationalized by HDO planners and legislators in a form that this committee would term "information-use policy." Information-use policy in the automated system context gives rise to decisions about who can do what, with which data, and for what purpose. It leads to policymaking about who may be allowed to use health-related information and how they may use it. It also requires decisions about how health information can be used as a matter of social policy and might also include consideration of whether some data should be collected at all.

The three issues—data confidentiality, security, and information use— are obviously related (Figure 4-1) They overlap to some extent and collectively represent the area of direct concern in this report. One reason to keep the three issues separate is that different remedies are relevant to each.

Data confidentiality is a matter of law and regulation. Legislation would be required to establish that health-related information is confidential, to spell out the rationale for the position, and to clarify the ramifications and consequences of attaching protection to health data.

Security is a matter of technology, management controls, procedures, and administrative oversight. In the public sector, the action agents are regulators; in the HDO, a policy and oversight board could establish security policies. Implementation and management would be provided by technical and system design personnel.

Informational privacy (information use) is the most difficult to sort out.

The nation needs to agree on the proper use of health-related information. It is not yet clear how this will or can be done, nor is it obvious who the action agents will be. At the level of the HDO, information use would be decided by the governing board. At a regional or national level, federal agencies, legislators, professional bodies, consumer advocates, and industrial lobby groups are all likely to be involved.

In the remainder of this chapter, the terms *confidentiality* (rather than the more cumbersome *data confidentiality*), *privacy* (rather than *informational privacy*), and *security* continue to be used, but the committee intends that they be understood in the context just described. The committee believes this conceptualization will make it easier to translate recommendations into policies and procedures that can be implemented and enforced.

HARM FROM DISCLOSURE AND REDISCLOSURE
OF HEALTH RECORD INFORMATION

Very little systematic or empirical evidence supports the widespread perception of the threat or the reality of harm from disclosure and redisclosure of health-related information. This is because the origins of the information may not be known by the person harmed, because of the natural preference not to further publicize confidential information about oneself, and because inquiry in this area has been to date more anecdotal than systematic.

This section presents examples of the potential confidentiality and privacy problems that might be encountered with health data, either in patient record form or in databases accessed or held by HDOs. Although these concerns cannot easily be quantified, reports to the committee during this study, cases mentioned in media such as the *Privacy Times* and the Internet-based *Privacy Forum Digest*, incidents known to or recounted to committee members, and similar inputs make clear that the threats and potential harm are real and not numerically trivial.

Health leader respondents to the 1993 Harris/Equifax survey showed that 71 percent were somewhat or very concerned about threats to the confidentiality of medical records, and 24 percent were "aware of violations of the confidentiality of individuals' medical records from inside an organization that embarrassed or harmed the individual." Respondents identified test results and diagnostic reports as the most frequently disclosed information.

Of the responding public, some 27 percent believed that their own medical records had been improperly disclosed. That group identified health insurers most often as having been responsible (15 percent). Fewer respondents identified hospitals or clinics (11 percent), public health agencies (10 percent), and employers (9 percent).

This section describes three categories of disclosure of patient information common today and the problems and harm that may result: (1) common disclosures that are breaches of confidentiality; (2) covert, illegal, or unethical acquisition and use of information; and (3) harm from disclosure of inaccurate data. It also raises questions about unforeseen uses of databases accessed by HDOs.

"Common" Disclosures

Three types of common disclosures pose threats: inadvertent, routine, and rerelease to third parties.

Inadvertent Release

A form of disclosure that the committee has termed "unthinking" often occurs within medical institutions. Examples include discussions with or about patients within earshot of other patients in waiting areas and discussions of cases in elevators, halls, cafeterias, and social settings. Disclosure related to the human penchant for gossip and carelessness in leaving medical records "lying around" or leaving information displayed on computer terminals is common. Westin (1972) concluded that such disclosures (sometimes to patients' relatives or friends) were less likely to be related to automated databases than to common indiscretion by hospital workers and health care providers. As the nation moves into yet more sophisticated telecommunication systems, such disclosure can include leaving detailed patient information on answering machines, sending information on fax transmissions that accumulate in common areas, or holding conversations about patients or dictating patient histories or notes about patient visits over cellular telephones.

If the diagnosis stigmatizes or indicates a disabling or fatal condition, harm can be especially serious. The harm can be great both to the famous and "VIP" patient and to noncelebrities, especially for coworkers or patients in a small community. One well-known case involved a staff physician whose HIV status became known in his hospital when his diagnosis was discussed by hospital personnel (*Estate of Behringer* v. *Medical Center at Princeton*, 249 N.J. Super. 597, 592 A.2d 1251 [1991]).

The committee believes many safeguards exist that can and should be put in place in any health care institution or HDO to anticipate and prevent disclosures of this sort. Preventing disclosure requires greater sensitivity to confidentiality issues and better training of health care workers. The Mayo Foundation, for example, has successfully developed and maintained a culture of adamant protection of the confidentiality of its patients' health information (Mayo Foundation, 1991).

"Routine" Releases or Uses in Accordance with Prevailing Practices

Health information is frequently shared *without* knowledge of the individual based on "uninformed" or "blanket" consent. In addition to the consent to disclose information routinely obtained from a patient before care is administered or when enrolling in a health insurance plan, another example of data disclosure is the wholesale photocopying of medical records that are forwarded to insurers, when much of the information does not pertain to the given insurance claim. The committee believes that the ability to prevent inappropriate release and use (misuse) must be strengthened. Such protections for data in HDOs are at the heart of this report and its recommendations.

Rerelease to Third Parties Without the Subject's Knowledge or Consent (Secondary Use)

The "secondary use" principle is an important component of fair information practices. It reflects the notion that when personal information is collected for a particular purpose the information should be used for only that purpose or a compatible one.[10]

An especially troublesome problem is the difficulty of confining the migration of information to third, fourth, or fifth parties without the individual's knowledge or consent. Examples include the sharing of health record information within organizations in one industry (e.g., between the health insurance and life insurance division of a company or between the personnel benefits division and the personnel or supervisory unit of an employer). Other examples include sharing between organizations in one industry (e.g., between the Medical Information Bureau and a second insurer). Yet a third sort of sharing can occur between organizations in two different industries (e.g., between insurer and credit bureau or between a current employer and a potential employer). A final example involves sharing genetic information with relatives who are at risk of an inherited disorder.

A major concern among commentators writing about the collection and storage of genetic information is that there will be increased pressure on the holders of such information to reveal to other patients and their physicians

---

[10] The report of the Secretary's Advisory Committee on Automated Personal Data Systems, *Records, Computers and the Rights of Citizens* (USDHEW, 1973) was a ground-breaking report of the Secretary of Health, Education, and Welfare that articulated five fair information practice principles, including the secondary use principle. The Federal Privacy Act at 5 U.S.C. § 552a(b) reflects the secondary use principle by permitting nonconsensual secondary uses of personal data only for purposes that are consistent with the purpose for which the data were first collected.

information gained about family members. These individuals might want to assess their own genetic risks of inheritable disease or use the information when making reproductive decisions. Some indeed have argued that there is an exception to physician duties of confidentiality analogous to that of duties to warn (or protect) people at risk from those with psychiatric disorders or HIV infection.

Given the growth in fringe benefits offered by employers and their subsequent stake in managing the costs of such benefits, there are few limitations on information that can be gathered for use in administering health, disability, and pension plans. Committee members were told repeatedly that self-insured employers are given access, when they insist, to patient-identified health claims information. Indeed, some third-party administrators (TPAs) provide human resources personnel with dial-in capability to perform their own analyses of data concerning a firm's employees and dependents (personal communication, third-party software and services vendor, 1993). Whether employers have the right to data incident to the health care for which they have paid is highly debatable, but this rationale is commonly accepted by TPAs under the pressure of competition, and there is great risk that data will not be partitioned from use in personnel actions. The 1993 Harris/Equifax survey confirmed the public's concern about this problem. Forty percent were somewhat or very concerned that their job might be affected if their medical claims information was seen by their employer. Another example of information that is in some ways mandated and also creates a database of problematic information is that which is compiled by medical review officers in connection with employee drug-testing programs.

Although corporate and professional ethics tend to discourage abuse, few barriers exist to an employer's use of its employees' medical and insurance claims records. The threat of liability under the Americans with Disabilities Act has served as a brake on some employers' access to and use of their employees' health records. In addition, some state laws limit access. Employers, however, may be required by federal or state regulations to access records in order to identify employees who pose threats to security. Information available under such permission may pertain to spouses and dependents as well as employees.

The committee believes secondary use of medical information by employers is common and may be increasing as employers seek to find ways to manage high-cost cases, to adjust their benefit packages to control their health care exposure,[11] and perhaps even to identify or terminate high-cost

---

[11] A recent case upheld the right of any employer to change (and thereby reduce) its health insurance benefits to reduce exposure. In *McGann v. H&H Music Co*, 742 F. Supp. 392, *aff'd* 946 F.2d 401, after a current employee was diagnosed with AIDS, his employer changed the health benefit plan to become self-insured and subsequently established a $5,000 limitation on AIDS-related medical expenses.

employees or those with high-cost dependents. Real or potential harm ranges from the inconsequential to the calamitous. It is likely that the ability to limit secondary use can be strengthened, and ways to accomplish this are at the heart of the committee's concerns.

Covert Acquisition and Use of Data for Illegal or Unethical Purposes

Another problem involving acquisition and use of medical information occurs covertly through illegal or unethical means. Examples include information brokers who tap into computerized systems by using false names or by bribing database employees to supply information about celebrities or the names of individuals with certain characteristics. In health care institutions, there is also a risk that employees will browse through medical records out of curiosity (as tax and credit bureau employees have done).

The character of the threat to confidentiality posed by the aggregation of databases is altered. Celebrities have long been vulnerable to loss of privacy through both paper and computerized searches as documented by Rothfeder (1992). The new vulnerability posed by computerized searches is to those who until now have been (relatively) anonymous. That is, information brokers seek to identify information not about an identified individual but about the identities of individuals with given characteristics (e.g., those with a diagnosis of AIDS or women who have had an abortion).

Isikoff (1991) describes the growth of the information-broker industry, which boasts instant access to a range of confidential computer data—credit reports, business histories, driver's license records, Social Security records, and criminal history backgrounds. Some of these records are public, but some are in government and private computer databases; in the latter, illegal access may involve insiders (e.g., employees of the Social Security Administration, police and other law enforcement employees). Of particular concern is the problem of unauthorized disclosure by often low-paid individuals who have legitimate access to information but who use it to facilitate illegitimate searches or to profit from the sale of records—a practice some have termed "insider information trading" and known to data system security specialists as the "insider threat."

Hendricks (1992) described a recently published hacker's manual for penetrating TRW's credit bureau database; it was complete with dial-up numbers, codes, and methods for persuading credit bureau subscribers to divulge their passwords over the phone. He described how the traditionally youthful hackers have been supplanted by profit-oriented criminal enterprises and the emergence of individuals who, in this case, proclaim the right of the individual to conquer and destroy the "system" and its laws and to damage individuals for excitement and profit. Those who are determined to break into a system can be thwarted only with thoughtful and comprehensive system safeguards.

Although harm from this source is likely to occur rarely in comparison with others, the harm can be great because so many individuals are affected. Further, the data holder can be severely damaged in the public's eye. One goal for an HDO must be to assure the public of reasonable, if not absolute, safety.

Release of Inaccurate Data

A different harm can result from release of information when data are incomplete, inaccurate, or out of date. Examples are medical records or insurance claims on which diagnoses are listed or coded incorrectly (e.g., mastectomy for myringotomy). Other problems involve diagnoses that were considered at one time and ruled out but are still listed as a final diagnosis, incorrect inferences drawn from diagnostic tests, and clinical distortions that result from coding limitations. Data inaccuracies also arise from actions that are intended to be beneficial—for example, to protect the patient from a stigmatizing diagnosis, to permit insurance reimbursement for a test or procedure that might otherwise not be covered (as in the case of preventive and screening tests), or to allow a frail patient to be treated on an inpatient rather than outpatient basis.

The committee does not know how often these irregularities occur. Studies of the accuracy of medical records consistently show unintentional and sometimes intentional errors (Burnum, 1989), and medical records personnel and researchers report that errors and omissions are extremely common in all health records. Harm from such problems may range from trivial to severe. Any reliance on databases for such social benefits as credit ratings or life insurance means that data that are incomplete, inaccurate, or false (for example, when records of several different people are combined) are not merely useless, they are pernicious. Such errors and omissions were not a major focus of the study committee. It should be noted, however, that the converse of this problem is that the more accurate and comprehensive the databases, the more pressure there will be for access, which in turn raises the chances of harm in the other categories already discussed.

Harm resulting from inaccurate or out-of-date data can be mitigated or prevented in a number of ways, including adequate and regular attention to the reliability and validity of database contents as described in Chapter 3. Allowing individuals to obtain, challenge, and correct their own records can also help to improve their accuracy.

PRIVACY INTERESTS AND HDOs

HDOs may pose a threat to privacy interests in four ways. The first arises through harm from secondary use. This includes the potential for stigmatizing and embarrassing patients; adversely affecting their opportunities for employment, insurance, licenses, and other benefits; undermining trust and candor in the health care provider-patient relationship; and defeating patients' legitimate expectations of confidentiality. Second is the unpredictable effect that will be produced by the mere existence of HDOs as described. Third, HDOs may exacerbate societal concerns about the emergence of national, centralized personal record databases, which may be perceived as a national identification system or dossier. Issues concerning the Social Security number and its analogs are especially pertinent here. Finally, HDOs will need to be mindful of the possible effect that research uses may have on privacy.

Foreseen and Unforeseen Circumstances

In addition to the current risk of breaches of confidentiality and the risk of harm from inaccurate data inherent in the paper record, the existence of any accumulation of valuable data will spawn new users, new demands for access, and new justifications for expanded access.

HDOs may unintentionally create a heightened risk of disclosure resulting with the new forms of data becoming available through the HDOs, new inquiries and types of inquirers, new uses, and new legal and governance structures. The mere presence of the HDO may, over time, encourage new practices or changes that may be harmful to at least some segments of the population.

HDOs must also realize that the more information it holds or can access, and the more valuable that information, the greater the temptation will be for others to acquire and covertly use the information. An HDO database becomes, in some sense, like a swimming pool or an abandoned refrigerator to a child—an overwhelming opportunity or, in legal terms, an attractive nuisance.

Computerization poses problems for the protection of privacy and confidentiality, but it also offers new opportunities for protection. For example, access to records and to defined parts of records can be granted, controlled, or adapted on a need-to-know (or function-related) basis; this means that users can be authorized to obtain and use only information for which their access is justifiable. It will also be possible to implement authentication procedures (discussed below) and to implement and publicize the use of methods to permit the HDO to know if anyone has browsed in the databases, who has done so, and which data were accessed. Automation could also greatly mitigate the disclosure that now occurs when, for instance, an entire medical record is copied to substantiate a claim for a single episode of care, and software could prevent the printing or transfer of database information to other computers.

A National Identification System or Dossier

Privacy advocates can be expected to express sharp concerns about the potential for HDOs to be linked with one another or with other types of personal databases such as the financial, credit, and lifestyle databases maintained by consumer reporting agencies and information services. One particular threat is the possible contribution of linked databases to development of a *de facto* national identification (and data) system. Such a system would comprise a comprehensive, automated dossier on virtually every citizen.

Conventional wisdom holds that after a personal information database is established, some consequences are inevitable (Gellman, 1984): expansions in permissible uses of the database; demands to link the database with complementary databases to improve the database product; and relaxations of confidentiality restrictions. With respect to HDOs, privacy advocacy groups and the media are likely to be concerned that over time various regional HDOs will establish telecommunications links and that these entities will become a national network linkable to other financial and government records such as those serving the Social Security Administration or the Internal Revenue Service.

As potential *users* of HDO data files, many persons in these groups might regard this scenario as desirable and beneficial; as potential record *subjects*, however, most would probably be uncomfortable with this threat to their privacy. Once such a system were in place, some fear that both those with and without bona fide access would be able to call up a remarkably comprehensive and intrusive dossier comprising detailed biographic information, family history information, employment information, financial and insurance information, and, unless prevented, of course, medical record information about every citizen participating in the system.

In the view of many, this development would bring the nation perilously close to a national identification database. Indeed, at that point the "national" network would lack only a means of positive identification and a requirement that all citizens participate to constitute such a national identification system.[12] HDOs will need to take steps to be certain that they do not contribute to these developments.

---

[12] For a history of the national identification debate in this country, see Department of Justice, 1976; Burnham, 1983; U.S. Senate, Subcommittee on Courts, Committee on the Judiciary, 1983; and Shattuck, 1984; Eaton, 1986.

Although many people carry credit or health insurance cards and have no objection to doing so, others would view any requirement that a special identification card must be carried by participating consumers with special alarm because such an instrument is thought to connote totalitarian values. In the former Soviet Union, for instance, all Soviet citizens were required to carry an internal passport and to produce this passport upon request. In this way, the passport served not only to regulate internal travel but as a means of identification and social control (Pipko and Pucciarelli, 1985). The Harris/Equifax survey found that the great majority of the public (84 percent) is willing to accept a personal identity card but had mixed feelings about being assigned a number—perhaps reflecting concern about whether such a number could be used to link their health information to other databases.

Admittedly, a few Western democracies employ national population registries and automated and centralized personal record data banks, but virtually all these systems are principally statistical and research systems, rather than systems that are used for administrative or investigative purposes. Moreover, even these primarily statistical and research systems "inspire fears about the expanded power of central government, vis-à-vis the legislature, the local administration, the private sector and most especially the citizen" (Bennett, 1992, p. 49). In Sweden, for example, the press harshly criticized the linkage of cancer registry databases and abortion record databases for medical research purposes (Stern, 1986).

Moreover, European democracies that use unique personal identification numbers assigned at birth for each citizen have a history of the use of personal, numerical codes. Even in Sweden and Germany, two European democracies that make extensive use of personal identification numbers to track individuals and link databases, personal identification numbers are not used as a standard universal numeric identifier for participation in all aspects of the society. In addition, reports are increasing of popular resistance in these countries to the use of universal numeric identifiers (Stern, 1986). As Bennett (1992) comments in *Regulating Privacy*:

> The issue in these countries [Sweden and Germany] has been the incremental and surreptitious use of these numbers for ends unrelated to those for which they were created. Where proposals have been introduced for a new universal identifier accompanied by a personal identification card, such as in Germany and Australia, they have been met with strong resistance because of the belief that non-uniformity and non-standardization with all the attendant problems for administration, are vital to the maintenance of personal privacy. (p. 51)

Over the years the Congress, the press, and privacy advocates have fiercely resisted any proposal for the development of databases that appeared to facilitate establishment of a national identification or database system.

Some observers urge that entities like HDOs eschew the use of any type of positive identification, such as a biometric identifier, and avoid the use of the Social Security number. The aim is to minimize the likelihood that HDOs will contribute intentionally or unintentionally to a national identification system or to the development of a standard universal identifier (USDHEW, 1973). If the HDO initiative is viewed by opinion leaders as a precursor to the establishment of any type of automated, national identification or dossier system, the initiative will likely fail.

HDO proponents should take every practicable step to assure advocacy groups, the media, legislators, and the American people that the emergence of HDOs will not contribute to the development of a centralized, automated national dossier system or a national identification system through linkage with non-health-related databases or the gradual relaxation of confidentiality policies.

Personal Identifiers and the Social Security Number

The personal identifier (ID) used by an HDO to label each of the individuals in the database is a crucial issue. It is related not only to past practices but will also be strongly influenced, if not mandated, by the health care reform actions now under way in the nation.

Of necessity, identifiers are used in present health care systems. For practical purposes the identifier in many systems is either the person's Social Security number (SSN) or, as in Medicare, the Social Security number of an individual with a letter appended. Issues relating to the Social Security number are examined below (see also USDHEW, 1973).

An Ideal Personal Identifier

The ideal personal identifier must, whatever its design, minimize or eliminate the risk of misidentification. An ideal identifier would meet certain requirements, including the six discussed below.

First, it must be able to make the transition easily from the present recordkeeping environment to one that will prevail in HDOs (and under national health care reform). Further, organizations will need to know where to apply for new numbers, to verify numbers that patients give verbally, to track down uncertainties in identification, to find current mailing addresses, and to be able to backtrack errors and correct them. This requirement also has technical dimensions. For example, if a new identifier contains more digits or characters (or both) than the 10 used for the Medicare identifier, there will be software repercussions in many systems, and redesign of data-capture forms may be necessary.

Second, the identifier must have error-control features to make entry of a wrong number unlikely. Control implies that errors of many kinds are detectable and possibly correctable on the basis of the digits and characters in the ID alone. Ideally it will protect against transpositions of characters and against single, double, or multiple errors. At a minimum the error-control features must be able to indicate whether the ID is valid and to do so with high confidence (USDHEW, 1973).

Error control is certain to be a system-wide requirement in any automated system. It will involve not only the structure of the ID itself, but also the processing software (or the residual manual processes) in every system that will have to use and verify the ID.[13]

Third, the ID will have separate identification and authentication ele-

---

[13] The term *check digits* is often used as short hand for error correcting and detecting codes used extensively in modern computers and communications systems. It is sometimes suggested, almost casually as though it were a magic solution, that the addition of a check digit to the Social Security number would allow the verification of its accuracy. The addition of extra characters could in principle accomplish a number of tasks, including:

1. Identifying that something is wrong, but not indicating the error,
2. Detecting and locating a single error,
3. Detecting and locating multiple errors,
4. Detecting, locating, and correcting single errors, and
5. Detecting, locating, and correcting multiple errors.

The number of additional characters needed depends on the degree of error detection and correction that designers think is necessary for the circumstances. For example, a single check digit can identify an error but does not locate which digit is wrong or how. Moreover, it would not catch the common manual error of transposed characters. A simple single-digit check can sometimes say a bad message is good. For such reasons, a single check digit is not a very strong error control mechanism.

The issue of designing error codes becomes complex rapidly. It is essential, however, to realize that any error correction feature added to an established number such as the SSN will have hardware and software consequences—or both. The data fields in storage will have to be longer; the software will have to be modified to handle the longer data fields; additional software—or hardware or both—will have to be added to do whatever calculations the particular error-detection/correction scheme requires.

Error control is a system-level problem, not just an issue of the identifier per se. If one can arrange procedures so that the identifier is always known to be correct at the time it is entered into the automated system, then the problem within the system itself becomes simpler. The method of providing the identifier will result in higher or lower assurance of its accuracy: an individual's memory is probably the least assurance of correctness; an embossed card is better; and an electronic reader for the card is better still.

The present health care information infrastructure runs largely without external visible error controls. Although mainframes and communications equipment almost certainly have error controls to catch equipment malfunctions and communication faults, there is no error control on some, possibly much, of the data in the data base. It relies, instead, on people outside the system to detect errors—providers and patients—and risks major mistakes in processing.

ments. The distinction between identification and authentication is made where strong security is required. "Identification" implies that (in this case) an individual indicates who he is, but authentication is a separate process with different parameters (known only to the individual) that allow the system to verify with high confidence that the identification offered is valid. Banks, for example, sometimes require an individual to provide his mother's maiden name; a personal identification number (PIN) is another authenticator. In many, perhaps most, medical systems this distinction is not made, and a simple identifier (e.g., insurance plan identification number) is presumed to be correct. In the future, however, some consideration should be given to separating these functions.

Fourth, the ID must work in any circumstance in which health care services are rendered, whether or not the situation was anticipated in the design of the system. At a minimum, the ID must never be an impediment to the prompt, efficient delivery of health care. For example, it must work when the patient requiring health care is not able to cooperate (e.g., is unconscious or does not speak the same language as the health care personnel) and regardless of the patient's mental and physical abilities.

Fifth, the ID must function anywhere in the country and in any provider's facilities and settings. By extension, it must also be able to link events that have occurred at multiple providers.

Sixth, the ID must help to minimize the opportunities for crime and abuse and perhaps help to identify their perpetrators.

Issues Relating to the SSN

When the initial Social Security law was passed in 1935, the SSN was called the SSAN, the number of one's "account" with the Social Security Administration (SSA). The SSA has always held that the SSN is not to be used as a personal identifier.[14]

In 1943 President Franklin Roosevelt signed an executive order requiring federal agencies to use the SSN whenever a new record system was to be established. The Department of Defense adopted it as a military identification number during World War II, and in 1961 the Internal Revenue Service (IRS) adopted it as the taxpayer identification number. When Medicare legislation was passed in the 1960s, the government adopted the SSN plus

---

[14]The most comprehensive treatment of the SSN as a recordkeeping personal identifier in the government is in the PPSC report (1977a) and the report of the Secretary's Advisory Committee (USDHEW, 1973). An examination of the latter also examines the role of the SSN in some commercial and private-sector circumstances. Hibbert (1992) gives a brief overview of the SSN in recordkeeping with advice for the individual in controlling its use.

an appended letter as the Medicare health insurance number. Many experts regard this as a serious undermining of privacy protection because the many recordkeeping activities associated with health care delivery act to disseminate a piece of information that differs from the SSN by only an appended letter.

In the Privacy Act of 1974—largely in response to the position of a Department of Health, Education, and Welfare (USDHEW, 1973) committee that had studied the issue—Congress prohibited states from using the SSN for enumeration systems other than by authority of Congress; however, states already using it were allowed to continue. The Tax Reform Act of 1976 undermined this position, however, by authorizing the states to use the SNN for a variety of systems: state or local tax authorities, welfare systems, driver's license systems, departments of motor vehicles, and systems for finding parents who are delinquent in court-imposed child-support payments (OTA, 1986).

In short, the government has caused the proliferation in the use of the SSN, sometimes by positive actions but sometimes by indifference or congressional failure to act. Some government decisions, notably to use the SSN as the taxpayer identification number and as the basis of the Medicare number, forced its wide diffusion throughout the private sector through financial transactions and benefits payments. In this way—partly deliberately and partly inadvertently—a very sensitive item of personal information has become widely disseminated.

SSN Uses for Other Than Medical Payments

Organizations that use the SSN as a personal ID and that most citizens will deal with frequently include federal government agencies (e.g., the Social Security Administration for benefits, the Internal Revenue Service for taxes and withholding, the Health Care Financing Administration and its contractors for Medicare payments, and the Securities and Exchange Commission); educational institutions, which frequently use it as a student identifier for campus-wide purposes; state governments (e.g., for state taxes, property and other local taxes, driver and vehicle registrations, real property records, financial transactions, and Medicaid payments); and private organizations (e.g., providers for health care services, industry-support databases such as the Medical Information Bureau, mortgage and loan agencies, credit reporting organizations, real property records, and banks).

Organizations, especially those in the private sector, choose to use the SSN for a number of pragmatic reasons and for expediency. Organizations already hold the number legally in connection with tax, financial, and wage matters. Moreover, there are no prohibitions against its use as a personal identifier in the private sector. Individuals usually have an SSN, or they can get one easily. In addition, people have become accustomed to willingly providing an SSN when asked; hence, its acquisition is a matter of merely asking, not legal compulsion.[15] Finally, administration of an enumeration system can be burdensome, and the choice of SSN shifts that consequence onto the government.

Although federal, state, or local governments usually require the SSN under law, private-sector requests serve the purposes and motivations of the organization. The essential point is that the SSN is in extraordinarily wide use as a personal identifier. As a result, any given person is indexed in a huge number of databases by his or her SSN, and an unknown number of linkages and data exchange among such databases are routine business.

If health care reform were to mandate a patient ID that is either the SSN or a closely related number, it will in effect have forced the last step of making the SSN into a truly universal personal ID. This is the issue that launched the DHEW committee in 1970 (PPSC, 1977a).

Shortfalls of the SSN as an Identifier

The choice of a personal ID that is satisfactory for the operational needs of health care delivery, but at the same time assures the confidentiality of medical data and the privacy of individuals is neither easy nor casual. Superficially, the choice would be the SSN, Medicare number, or something similar simply because people are accustomed to using them, systems are used to handling them. The government would bear the burden of administering the enumeration system but would avoid the cost of creating a new one. For information management, however, the shortfalls of the SSN are well known. The following list is representative of the problems.

1. Any 9-digit number rendered with hyphens in the appropriate places—that is, XXX-XX-XXXX—has a high likelihood of being a legitimate SSN that belongs to someone or at least appears to. This provides little security, and data commingling can occur that would result in erroneous records, mistaken conclusions and actions, and incorrect payments.

2. The allowable entries in each of the three groups in a SSN are well known. Thus, it is easy to counterfeit an SSN and have a high probability that it will not be challenged.

3. It has no error-correcting features. It is fallible to transpositions and single- or multiple-digit mistakes.

4. The SSN is not coupled to an authenticator. Some organizations,

---

[15] For example, some large-volume retail stores in the Washington, D.C., area routinely ask for a customer's Social Security number when he or she pays for any purchase by check.

such as banks, attempt to provide such a feature by using some ad hoc data element that an individual is likely to remember but is not common knowledge (e.g., mother's maiden name).

5. The SSN circulates widely, particularly in the finance industry. It is relatively easy to acquire someone's number and to parlay it into a false identity that supports fraud or other malicious or illegal actions.

6. There are often multiple holders of the same SSN, which introduces errors and clouds the records. Especially among less well-informed or immigrant households, the purpose of the number is not well understood or is colored by the role that a number might have played in another country or society. For example, all members of a household might use the same SSN because they believe it is intended to apply to all of them. Some numbers have achieved very wide use. The most famous is the "wallet incident" in which a replica of an SSN card complete with a number was included in an inexpensive, widely sold wallet; an appreciable number of people improperly believed that this SSN was to be used.

7. The SSN is closely related to the Medicare identifier, which identifies virtually all members of the population over age 65. For married people who receive SSA Title II benefits paid to an individual and the spouse on the basis of one person's earnings, the Medicare number of the primary beneficiary is the SSN followed by an A; for the spouse, the Medicare number is that same SSN followed by a B.

8. Not everyone needing health care has an SSN; for instance, foreign visitors, newborn infants, and the indigent or homeless are all likely to lack SSNs. This would require that health care providers be prepared to assign substitute numbers.

9. The crucial, almost overwhelming, objection to the SSN as a medical identifier, however, is that it has no legal protection, and because its use is so widespread, there is no chance of retroactively giving it such protection. As a data element, it is not characterized by law as confidential; hence, organizations that use it are under no legal requirement to protect it or to limit the ways in which it is used. For all practical purposes its use is unconstrained, this makes the risk of commingling health data with all other forms of personal data enormously high.

Confidentiality of Research Uses of HDO Databases

Through expenditures for medical research, the government and private sector indirectly contribute to third-party intrusions. Although epidemiological research was originally concerned with the causes and prevention of infectious diseases and focused chiefly on populations, such research has expanded to include chronic, noninfectious diseases with low rates of occurrence (PPSC, 1977a). Progression of such ailments may be slow, and because their causes are frequently insidious, their study often requires medical surveillance of a substantial population at widely disparate times.

In some cases, HDOs may serve research and statistical uses, and this raises consideration of how privacy interests might be affected. First, the benefits of such databases generally accrue not to the individual data subject but to society; this makes assessments of risks and benefits more complex because the person at risk is not the same as the beneficiary. Second, research databases depend on the voluntary cooperation of subjects, providers, or both in providing accurate and reliable information. If patients or clinicians distrust the ability or willingness of HDOs to protect the confidentiality of information, they may intentionally withhold or distort information. Third, it will become extremely important to understand the implications of differing methods of data collection and sources of data—for instance, abstraction of primary records and analysis of claims databases compared with patient responses to surveys fielded by the HDO. Each will have different sources of bias in the population reached, reasons for missing data, and accuracy.

With respect to research and statistical studies, Congress and agencies of the federal government have acted to protect the interests of individuals who are subjects of research and statistical records developed under federal authority or with federal funds (PPSC, 1977a). A report from the National Research Council (1993) analyzes available technical and administrative procedures that can be taken to protect confidentiality of data while permitting legitimate data use. A number of such disclosure limitation techniques are described: (1) collecting or releasing a sample of the data; (2) including simulated data; (3) "blurring" of the data by grouping or adding random error to individual values; (4) excluding certain attributes; (5) swapping of data by exchanging the values of certain variables between data subjects; (6) requiring each marginal total of the table to have a minimum count of data subjects; (7) using a "concentration rule" (described in Chapter 3); and (8) using controlled rounding of table entries (NRC, 1993). Whether these steps are sufficient in the HDO context requires reexamination.

Because HDO databases will include many elements of personal information collected for single, specific purposes and subsequently used for multiple, diverse purposes, they have the potential to conflict with the secondary use principle. If such secondary use does not, however, involve a decision about the individual, then the privacy threat is by no means as acute as it would be if the information were used to make a decision directly affecting the individual (USDHEW, 1973). Individuals' interests have not been compromised, for example, when these data are used anonymously for statistical or research purposes and not for administrative decision making that will affect them directly. Although the Harris/Equifax survey (1993) found that respondents objected to such use of their medical information without their express consent (64 percent of respondents), the IOM committee believes that individuals—and collectively, the public—may need to better understand the benefits of health services research using non-person-identifiable data and protections that are available for research use of person-identifiable data. Researcher access to HDO databases is addressed in the committee's recommendations.

RELEVANCE OF EXISTING LAWS TO HDOs

The committee examined existing law—constitutional, statutory, and common law—for its relevance to HDOs and its adequacy for protecting patient privacy. The committee also examined the way these laws might affect the design, establishment, and operation of HDOs.

It concludes that most of this body of law is unlikely to apply to HDOs. With the exception of laws regulating information considered sensitive, existing laws regulate recordkeepers and their recordkeeping practices; they do not regulate on the basis of either the content or the subject matter of a record. Current law thus seeks to regulate the information *behavior* of health care providers, government recordkeepers, insurers, consumer reporting agencies, quality assurance organizations, and researchers. For this reason, it is important to understand how HDOs are likely to be viewed by the legal system—that is, in what legal context their recordkeeping will be seen.

The committee believes that HDOs are unlikely to be treated as health care providers, payers, or quality assurance organizations. If they are treated as medical researchers, very little in the way of standards would apply. Some possibility exists that they will be subject to regulation as *consumer reporting agencies*—and they will probably want to avoid this—or as *insurance support organizations*, at least in states that have passed The National Association of Insurance Commissioners (NAIC) Information and Privacy Protection Model Act of 1981 (NAIC Model Act). Implications of being treated as either are described briefly below. HDOs may well have *governmental status*, and the legal implications of that status are described in more detail, with particular attention to the Privacy Act of 1974.

Laws Governing Insurance Support Organizations

The NAIC Model Act defines an insurance support organization as "any person who regularly engages, in whole or in part, in the practice of assembling or collecting information about natural persons for the *primary* purpose of providing the information to an insurance institution or agent for insurance transactions" (emphasis added). Because HDOs will likely provide information to insurance institutions on a regular basis in connection with insurance transactions (defined in the NAIC Model Act as a determination of an individual's eligibility for insurance coverage, benefit, or payment), it is possible they will be considered insurance support organizations.

In states that have passed the NAIC Model Act, an HDO would be subject to the following six requirements. First, the HDO could not disclose personal information about an individual without the written authorization of the individual or *unless* the disclosure was needed: to further an insurance function, provided there is no redisclosure; to a health care institution or health professional; to an insurance regulatory authority; to a law enforcement authority; in circumstances otherwise permitted or required by law; in response to compulsory process; for the purpose of a *bona fide* research study, provided that no individual can be identified in any subsequent research report; for marketing purposes; to consumer reporting agencies; to a group policyholder; to a professional peer review organization; or for a licensing activity.

Second, when subject consent is obtained, the HDO would have to assure that the consent has several properties: that it (1) is written in plain language; (2) is dated; (3) specifies the types of persons authorized to disclose information; (4) specifies the nature of the information authorized for disclosure; (5) names the institution authorized to disclose; (6) specifies the purposes for which the information is being disclosed; (7) specifies the length of time for which the authorization is valid; and (8) advises the individual whose information is the subject of the consent that the individual has a right to a copy of the consent form.

Third, the HDO would have to provide record subjects with a right of access to their records, either directly or through a health care professional designated by the individual. Fourth, the HDO would be required to provide individuals with rights of correction, amendment, and deletion. Fifth, the HDO could not maintain information concerning any previous adverse underwriting decision relating to the individual. Sixth, the HDO would be subject to the regulatory and investigatory powers of the state commissioner of insurance.

In states that have not adopted the NAIC Model Act, there is little or no statutory regulation of the information practices of insurance institutions or insurance support organizations (Trubow, 1991) to apply to HDOs. In theory, the above requirements might not apply at all in those states, or they might apply piecemeal by virtue of state-specific situations.

Laws Governing Consumer Reporting Agencies

It is possible, but by no means likely, that HDOs could be viewed as consumer reporting agencies under the federal Fair Credit Reporting Act

(FCRA) or state versions of the FCRA. These statutes regulate the collection, use, and dissemination of personal information by consumer reporting agencies. Federal law defines a consumer reporting agency as an organization that "regularly engages in whole or in part in the practice of assembling or evaluating consumer credit information or other information on consumers for the purpose of furnishing consumer reports to third parties" (FCRA 15 U.S.C. § 1681a[f]) for fees or on a cooperative, nonprofit basis. "Other information on consumers" includes medical record information.

The FCRA defines "consumer report" as any written or oral communication that bears on consumers' credit worthiness, credit standing, credit capacity, character, general reputation, personal characteristics, or mode of living when that report "is used or expected to be used or collected in whole or part for the purpose of serving as a factor in establishing the consumer's eligibility for: credit or insurance to be used primarily for personal, family or household purposes" or used "in connection with a business transaction involving the consumer" (FCRA 15 U.S.C. §§ 1681a(d) and 1681b(3)(E)).

If data from an HDO are used only in connection with insurance claims determinations, the HDO should not, at least by virtue of the insurance claims function, be classified as a consumer reporting agency. The Federal Trade Commission (FTC), which is charged with enforcing the FCRA, has stated that supplying data for insurance claims purposes does not constitute a consumer report.

If, however, HDOs were to acquire and supply personal financial information to health care providers to assist providers in making determinations about a patient's payment of a medical bill (including the acceptance of a consumer's credit card or check or the allocation of charges between the patient and various health care payment programs), HDOs would be providing information for use "in connection with a business transaction involving the consumer." Courts have held, for example, that providing financial information for point-of-sale determinations of whether to accept a consumer's check represents a disclosure in connection with a business transaction involving a consumer. This kind of action brings the party making the disclosure within the scope of the FCRA.

If, though highly unlikely, the FCRA were judged to be applicable to HDOs, then they would be subject to its provisions. These include limitations of the kind of personal information that could be collected and maintained; requirements with respect to consumer access to the database; restrictions on the disclosure of the information from the database; and a variety of administrative, civil, and criminal sanctions. Given the reach of the FCRA, the committee judged that HDOs will want to avoid action and responsibilities that will put them within the purview of the FCRA.

HDOs as Governmental Entities:
General Confidentiality Protections in Public Law

The governmental or private status of an entity that maintains or uses personal record information is particularly significant for recordkeeping. Constitutional principles, legislative charter, statutory law, and regulations must be considered separately.

Constitutional Law

If an entity has a governmental status, whether federal or state, constitutional privacy standards apply to the entity's handling of personal information. As noted earlier, various provisions of the U.S. Bill of Rights are aimed at protecting citizens from governmental abuse, and privacy rights are derived from limited case law (e.g., *Whalen v. Roe*). For federal or state constitutional protections to apply, an HDO would have to be operated by a governmental entity or pursuant to a governmental charter.

Legislative Charter

Even if HDOs are not operated by federal governmental entities, constitutional information privacy standards can affect their operations in two ways. First, HDOs may well operate under a state legislative charter. If that charter were to *require* the submission of personally identifiable medical record information (on the part of record subjects, providers, or others), this statutory requirement provides a basis for a challenge on constitutional privacy grounds, just as did the reporting requirements in *Whalen*.

Second, even if the HDOs are not statutorily chartered, constitutional information privacy concepts are used by the courts as benchmarks for assessing whether a privacy violation has occurred under common law or statute. Accordingly, if an HDO were challenged on tort or other common law or even statutory privacy theories, the extent to which the HDO violates constitutional informational privacy rights could well be influential in determining the outcome.

Freedom of Information Acts

In addition to any constitutional protections (which will be limited at best), a body of statutory law would also apply to HDOs if they were considered to be public agencies. For example, federal agencies and agencies in every state are covered by freedom of information (FOI) or public records acts. These statutes are intended to make records held by government agencies available to the public. The federal FOIA, however, contains express language that exempts from disclosure "personnel and medical files and similar files the disclosure of which would constitute a clearly unwarranted invasion of personal privacy" (5 U.S.C. § 552[b][6]). Most state freedom of information statutes include a similar exemption. Washington State's FOIA, for example, includes an exemption for medical records, pharmacy records, client records held by domestic violence programs, and various types of research data. The Washington courts have also held that medical records are exempt from disclosure under Washington's FOI statute.[16]

Fair Information Practices

In addition, the federal government and approximately one-third of the states have adopted fair information practices and statutes covering governmental agencies within each jurisdiction. The federal Privacy Act prohibits federal agencies, or contractors acting on behalf of an agency, from disclosing information accessible by personal identifiers and contained in a system of records without the prior written consent of the individual concerned.[17] The federal government and states that have adopted comprehensive privacy laws are also required by statute to make records relating to a record subject available upon request to that individual. Federal agencies and those in some states can, however, adopt special procedures that bar direct access to medical record data when officials have reason to believe that such access would be harmful to the subject (Cleaver, 1985; Andrussier, 1991).

The right to know about, challenge, control, and correct information about oneself are hallmarks of American privacy law. The elements of fair information practices derive from the report of the Secretary's Advisory Committee on Automated Personal Data Systems (USDHEW, 1973). The five principles in the original code are enumerated in that report (p. 41) as a Code of Fair Information Practices:

1.   There must be no personal data recordkeeping systems whose very existence is kept secret.

2.   There must be a way for an individual to find out what information about him is in a record and how it is used.

---

[16] Note, however, that FOIA would not necessarily exempt physician- or provider-specific information as discussed in Chapter 3.

[17] The federal Privacy Act contains 12 exceptions that permit disclosures without obtaining subject consent. One such exemption is for research purposes (*Federal Register*, 1991b). Personally identifiable health record information held by Medicare peer review organizations can be shared with authorized researchers without subject consent.

3. There must be a way for an individual to prevent information about him obtained for one purpose from being used or made available for other purposes without his consent.

4. There must be a way for an individual to correct or amend a record of identifiable information about him.

5. Any organization creating, maintaining, using, or disseminating records of identifiable personal data must assure the reliability of the data for their intended use and must take reasonable precautions to prevent misuse of the data.

The Privacy Act of 1974. The Privacy Act of 1974 (P.L. 93-579; 5 U.S.C. § 552a) concerns databases held by the federal government.[18] Along with FCRA and the Family Educational Rights and Privacy Act of 1974, this act invests record subjects with rights to see, copy, and correct their records, as well as with limited rights with respect to authorizing the collection and disclosure of information.

The Privacy Act of 1974 incorporated the five elements of the Code of Fair Information Practices as eight principles that are manifest as specific requirements (PPSC, 1977a):

1. There shall be no personal data recordkeeping system whose very existence is secret and there shall be a policy of openness about an organization's personal data recordkeeping policies, practices, and systems (The Openness Principle).

2. An individual about whom information is maintained by a recordkeeping organization in individually identifiable form shall have a right to see and copy that information (The Individual Access Principle).

3. An individual about whom information is maintained by a recordkeeping organization shall have a right to correct or amend the substance of that information (The Individual Participation Principle).

4. There shall be limits on the types of information an organization may collect about an individual, as well as certain requirements with re-

---

[18] Other federal laws address the use of personal information in an immense array of circumstances and settings: criminal justice information systems; student records and tests; tax information; financial information held by banks and other financial institutions including electronic transfers of funds; press offices; and identification of intelligence officers, bad debtors, cable service users, renters of videotapes, and rape victims. Confidentiality provisions also appear in statutes pertaining to the national census, Social Security, child abuse information, and federally supported drug and alcohol treatment facilities (OTA, 1986). Such protections are often filled with lists of exceptions, however, sometimes to the point of effectively negating the purpose of the legislation.

spect to the manner in which it collects such information (The Collection Limitation Principle).

5.   There shall be limits on the internal uses of information about an individual within a recordkeeping organization (The Use Limitation Principle).

6.   There shall be limits on the external disclosures of information about an individual a recordkeeping organization may make (The Disclosure Limitation Principle).

7.   A recordkeeping organization shall bear an affirmative responsibility for establishing reasonable and proper information management policies and practices that assure that its collection, maintenance, use, and dissemination of information about an individual is necessary and lawful and the information itself is current and accurate (The Information Management Principle).

8.   A recordkeeping organization shall be accountable for its personal data recordkeeping policies, practices, and systems (The Accountability Principle).

In addition to establishing privacy guidelines for federal databases, the Privacy Act also created the Privacy Protection Study Commission (PPSC), whose charter required it to examine recordkeeping practices in the private business sector and in selected federal domains (e.g., tax records).   The PPSC revisited the Fair Practices doctrine and reoriented the thrust of the Fair Practices somewhat by placing emphasis on promoting consent and participation rights, which it referred to as "fairness protections for individuals" (PPSC, 1977a, pp. 17-18). In fact, the majority of the commission's recommendations relate directly to fairness in recordkeeping. In the case of an individual, essential fairness protections include a right of access to records about oneself for reviewing, copying, and correcting or amending them as necessary, plus some control over the collection and disclosure of information about oneself.

The PPSC offered an illustrative revision of the Privacy Act to incorporate changes it suggested in its report. These modifications included steps in the following areas: amending records; limitations on disclosure; collecting and maintaining information; "propagating corrections" (which involves taking positive steps to correct information); uses for research or statistical records; notices about agency systems; policies and practices; rights of parents and legal guardians; agency implementation; civil remedies and criminal penalties; application to government contractors and grantees; archiving records; giving notice of new systems or alterations to old systems; reporting to the U.S. Congress; the effect of other laws; and prohibitions on selling or renting information for mailing lists (PPSC, 1977b).

A decade later, the Computer Matching and Privacy Protection Act of 1988 (P.L. 100-503) amended the Privacy Act to include a new section of conditions that must be met before computer matching would be permitted. Another new section pertained to computer matching and required: (1) verification of adverse administrative actions and provision for individuals to contest findings and (2) notification of the public and evaluation of the effect of new systems or matching programs.

OPTIONS FOR PROTECTING PRIVACY AND CONFIDENTIALITY OF HEALTH-RELATED DATA IN HDOs

Two assumptions should drive the policymaking process with respect to privacy protection strategies and options for the establishment and operation of HDOs. First, from both a public policy and a legal standpoint, privacy protection *will* be a material issue. Accordingly, the issue warrants careful attention. Second, because HDOs are not health care providers or federal entities, HDOs will escape the reach of most existing privacy law. Nevertheless, many of the entities contributing data *to* HDOs will be bound by confidentiality obligations, and these obligations may affect their ability to submit person-identifiable data to HDOs, particularly if HDOs do not adopt stringent protective measures. That is, entities contributing information to HDOs will *not* escape existing privacy law.[19]

The committee's prevailing assumption is that HDO policymakers will be under pressure to develop effective privacy protection safeguards. They will also enjoy some degree of flexibility in the development and implementation of those safeguards and will have a striking opportunity to develop internal safeguards in advance of public or legislative pressure. The development of computerized databases can be seen as—or can evolve into—a way of giving people greater confidence about and real control over their personal information. When considering policies about privacy that might be implemented, Gostin (1993) posed seven questions about the human rights impact of disclosure of information that should be addressed even before data are collected.

1. What is the purpose of the information?
2. Will collection achieve a compelling public health purpose?
3. Will collection result in effective health policy; that is, might it drive people underground if they fear the consequences of disclosure?

---

[19] Some state and federal laws will restrict the ability of providers to disclose medical record information *to* HDOs, at least in the absence of patient consent or a legislative mandate. In addition, in some states it may be difficult or impossible to word a patient consent to such disclosure that does not result in waiver of the physician-patient privilege.

4. Who will have access to the information? Can it be disclosed by force or law? What will be the effect of negligent disclosure?

5. What impact will it have on human rights—is there a stigma to individuals or communities?

6. Are there less invasive alternatives?

7. What safeguards are available to reduce the risks?

The committee views these points as useful considerations for fashioning a sensible approach to privacy protections and choosing among a range of options for protecting privacy and confidentiality. Threats to confidentiality and privacy might be seen as posing options within a series of "layers" of protection. Such layers could include: (1) uniform state or federal preemptive legislation; (2) enabling legislation and organizational articles of incorporation and bylaws; (3) limiting categories of information acquired or accessed by HDOs; (4) administrative rules and regulations including institutional and user codes of conduct and employee training; (5) comprehensive security safeguards in all automated systems and networks; (6) controlled access to databases; (7) techniques to reduce the risk of inferential identification, such as suppression of small cell sizes; and (8) enforceable administrative, civil, and criminal sanctions and penalties for misuse. At each level, more stringent efforts at security incur trade-offs of inconvenience for users and costs born by the parties—patients, users, supporting organizations, providers, researchers, and (perhaps) taxpayers.

In the remainder of this section, several options for addressing privacy protections are presented. The committee's recommendations—in effect, judgments about the seven questions posed by Gostin and choices among a set of options—appear in the next section of this chapter. They address uniform legislation establishing a clear set of rights, duties, administrative procedures, and remedies for all persons and institutions affected by the implementation and operation of HDOs. The recommendations also address administrative policies and procedures that HDOs should adopt.

Uniform Legislation

Federal Preemptive Legislation

The committee considered one important option to be enactment of federal preemptive legislation. Federal preemptive legislation refers to federal law that supersedes any state law or legislation that either covers the same matter or conflicts with the federal legislation. Such preemptive legislation in this area could establish uniform requirements for the preservation of confidentiality and protection of privacy rights for health data about individuals because health data, particularly in electronic form, will cross state boundaries when accessed and disclosed by HDOs.

As noted earlier, existing state laws pertaining to the actions of recordholders will likely not apply to HDOs, but HDOs might wish to comply with them. Yet, state protections for confidentiality of data contributed to HDOs may be lacking, inconsistent, or even in conflict from state to state. Where they exist, they create an extraordinary patchwork of regulations embedded in laws pertaining to a variety of recordkeepers such as hospitals, HMOs, nursing homes, state health departments, insurers, employers, and so forth. A brief review of state statutes indicated that in one state more than 50 different statutes and regulations pertain to the confidentiality of medical information. Compiling, understanding, and complying with conflicting or arcane regulations for each state would be virtually impossible for HDOs operating in numerous states. Making such policies clear to the public would likely be even more hopeless.

During the period of this study, a number of groups were examining the questions of privacy rights with electronic transfer of health information. Among the more significant was the Workgroup on Electronic Data Interchange (WEDI).

In its 1992 report, WEDI identified three principles for databases containing sensitive personal information that could be associated with identifiable persons; these principles involved computer system security, fair information practices, and privacy protection. To satisfy these principles, WEDI recommended federal preemptive legislation. Its proposals referring to the collection, storage, handling, and transmission of data were intended to facilitate and ensure the uniform, confidential treatment of person-identifiable information in electronic environments.

WEDI recommended that federal legislation include the following steps and provisions:

- establish uniform requirements for preservation of confidentiality and privacy rights in electronic health care claims processing and payment;
- apply these requirements to the collection, storage, handling, and transmission of individually identifiable health care data, including initial and subsequent disclosures in electronic transactions by all public and private payers, providers of health care, and all other entities involved in the transactions;
- exempt state public reporting laws;
- delineate protocols for secure electronic storage and transmission of health care data;
- specify fair information practices that ensure a proper balance between required disclosures, use of data, and patient privacy;
- require publication of the existence of health care data banks;
- establish appropriate protections for highly sensitive data, such as data concerning mental health, substance abuse, and communicable and genetic diseases;

- encourage use of alternative dispute resolution mechanisms where appropriate;
- establish that compliance with the act's requirements would be a defense to legal actions based on charges of improper disclosure;
- impose penalties for violations of the act, including civil damages, equitable remedies, and attorneys' fees where appropriate; and
- provide for enforcement by government officials and private, aggrieved parties.

As described earlier in this chapter, protections for data independent of the recordholder is an important option to consider, and federal legislation provides an opportunity to establish such protections.

Privacy advocates see two possible drawbacks to federal legislation. First, such legislation could *weaken* rather than strengthen protections if the federal legislation is less stringent than good state legislation—hence the need for *strong* federal law. If federal legislation leaves room for states to implement more stringent standards, multistate HDOs will still, however, be subject to conflicting requirements, and this may add to, rather than decrease, administrative cost and complexity.

Second, to the extent that federal legislation encourages uniform standards that foster interlinkage and creation of a national database, it will contribute to the development of national databases and, by linkage, to non-health-related databases, dossiers, and national identification systems. The committee's dim view of the development of national identification systems has already been noted.

Uniform State Legislation

The main alternatives to federal legislation would be the status quo or enactment of model state acts. Adoption of uniform state legislation would undoubtedly involve a lengthy and cumbersome process and would not ensure adoption by all states. Even if a uniform law were adopted by all the states, it would likely be adopted with variations by some states, much as in the case of the Uniform Commercial Code. Hence, the committee was not sanguine about the utility of this approach.

Options for Consent and Participation Rights

The discussion above related mainly to federal preemptive legislation. Whether or not such legislation is adopted, HDOs will need internal policies, although such organizational, administrative, and governance approaches would be informed by existing (if not new) federal or state law.

Consent and participation rights for record subjects are essential elements of the Privacy Act. They provide individuals with rights to see, copy, and correct their records, as well as grant limited rights to authorize the collection and disclosure of information. State statutes routinely give persons a right of access to data about themselves and a role in authorizing (or limiting) third-party disclosures. HDO designers will be able to select from a range of consent and participation options that run from weak to quite stringent, with middle-range strategies possibly a useful approach.

HDO Access to Data

Notification. At a minimum, HDOs could publish or give record subjects notice that information about them—including information that the individuals provide directly to participating health care providers, insurers, and employers—will be accessible by the HDO. They might also require notification by entities submitting data to HDOs. Presumably this notice would provide individuals with at least a cursory description of the manner in which HDOs or their agents might use their data.[20] They would have no further rights, however, in terms of access to the data. Under current law in many states, patient consent will be required to transmit data to or allow access by the HDO (see footnote 18).

General releases. HDOs could be designed so that individuals would simply be notified about their data being accessible to HDOs, but would also sign a general release authorizing participating providers, payers, and employers to share personal data with HDOs. The presumption, of course, is that such a release (and its implications) is well understood by those signing it. Such a general release might also be crafted to give the HDO a blanket authorization to redisclose.

From a *legal* standpoint, this approach, however modest it may seem, would be adequate except in the case of extremely sensitive health information such as alcohol and drug abuse, mental health treatment, and AIDS information. Extremely sensitive health record data (e.g., that just noted) generally could not be shared with the HDOs or redisclosed by the HDOs pursuant to general release under existing federal and state law.

Another option is for individuals to receive a complete and detailed written description of an HDO's permissible disclosures and other information practices and a complete description of their information rights.

Stronger options would allow individuals the right to revoke their authorization and, in any event, the authorization would be effective only for

---

[20] Notification is included as one of the recommendations of the IOM committee studying privacy and confidentiality protections in the genetics testing environment (IOM, 1993b).

a limited period. Even stronger options would require that individuals sign a specific consent form (described below) *each time* they provided data accessible to an HDO or to HDO participants. In this case, each data element might require separate authorization and expiration dates.

Other Consent and Participation Rights

Even if this approach were to meet minimum legal requirements, however, it is likely to be *politically* unacceptable for issues of database maintenance and disclosure *by* the HDO. Given the *comprehensiveness* and sensitivity of HDO databases and the high level of public concern about privacy, the committee expects that privacy advocacy groups, legislators, the media, and other public opinion leaders will insist that HDOs be brigaded with substantial consent and participation rights.

Participation. An HDO offering participation rights at the high end of the "protection spectrum" would have all or most of the following characteristics:

* Individuals would receive a complete and detailed written description of an HDO's permissible disclosures and other information practices and a complete description of their information rights.
* Record subjects would have a right of access to all data about themselves that are held in the HDO at a nominal charge. Access rights would include the right to receive a copy of their records, not merely a right to review their record.
* Persons would have a right to correct and amend their records and to add a rebuttal statement if the HDO refused to make a requested correction or amendment.
* Record subjects would have a right to inspect an "audit trail" that can identify all uses, disclosures, and other access events involving their own files.
* Alternatively, record subjects would receive notice in the mail each time the HDO discloses their data to third parties or, at the least, each time HDO data are used to make an adverse decision affecting the individual. This latter formulation is not dissimilar to current notice requirements in FCRA.

Disclosure Options

Rules about disclosure and confidentiality are at the heart of any information privacy policy. Here HDOs will enjoy a significant degree of legal flexibility. Under existing law, HDOs could adopt confidentiality policies that span a spectrum from a disclosure-oriented policy at one end to a strict confidentiality policy at the other. From a political standpoint, however, HDO proponents are likely to see advantages in opting for a confidentiality-sensitive policy for person-identifiable data.

Disclosure-Oriented Options (Weak Options)

Under a disclosure-oriented policy, all person-identified or person-identifiable data accessible to HDOs would be available to participating parties for any purpose and without specific subject authorization. Exceptions would apply to particularly sensitive kinds of data, such as records on substance abuse, AIDS, and genetic tests. Even under existing law most of these records cannot be made available without specific authorization. Adopting a disclosure-oriented approach would also make most person-identifiable information available to third parties, as long as the user had a legitimate business purpose for accessing the information.

Furthermore, under a disclosure-oriented policy HDOs would routinely make person-identifiable information available in response to subpoenas, other forms of compulsory process, or formal, voluntary requests from law enforcement or regulatory authorities. If a disclosure-oriented policy were adopted, the principal confidentiality restrictions would relate to the handling of sensitive subsets of health record information and to wholesale disclosures of identifiable information to the general public. The committee rejected this broad disclosure-oriented option as incompatible with its values and the effective implementation of HDOs.

Confidentiality-Oriented Options (Strong Options)

In contrast, a confidentiality-sensitive approach to disclosure would include some, if not all, of the elements listed below.[21]

- HDOs could release information only in non-person-identifiable formats except under very restricted circumstances.

---

[21] The Health Care Authority of Washington State issued draft recommendations for health information systems in September 1992 (6.7[4]; pp. 78-79). Among the draft recommendations were seven related to access to person-specific information. Access would be permitted only for the following specified purposes: use by the individual affected; use by service providers in the course of providing health services (subject to standards of client consent); use in payment, utilization review, and eligibility or plan membership processes; legally required reporting of births, deaths, communicable diseases, and other information; to carry out or cooperate with epidemiologic investigation of disease outbreaks by state or local public health authorities; for confidential research, when properly authorized by an institutional review board; and to establish linkage among data sources necessary to avoid duplicative data collection burden.

• HDOs could not release any information in personally identifiable form from an HDO database to third parties without a specific authorization, either signed or given electronically by the person in question.

• HDOs could opt never to release person-identifiable information even with subject consent, or to release information in a customized format that blocked parts of a subject's record, depending upon the user and use for which it was requested.[22]

• HDOs could refuse to provide person-identifiable information to third parties that intended or could use the information to make decisions about an individual's access to particular benefits (standard processing of health insurance claims would be an exception to this policy).

• HDOs could require users to sign "confidentiality agreements." These agreements would obligate users to safeguard information obtained from the HDO and use it only for the purpose for which it was provided. Violations of the agreement would give the HDO (and perhaps record subjects) a claim of either breach of contract or of confidentiality (or both) against the offending user.

• They would adopt a policy of refusing to comply with voluntary requests for access from law enforcement or regulatory agencies.

• In legal matters, HDOs could resist compliance with subpoenas or other forms of compulsory process, assert all available privileges, and notify record subjects of an access request so that they could contest production. (The Uniform Act noted earlier takes a similar approach with respect to compulsory process.)

Governance Options as an Approach to Privacy Protections

Issues relating to the structure and governance of an HDO will be critical to both the substance and the appearance of privacy protection and, therefore, to the HDO's political acceptability. In this context, the principal question will be the extent of government involvement in the operation of the HDOs. In the absence of federal preemptive legislation, state legislation might include a number of options. Although the laws in this section are all state oriented, if federal preemptive legislation is enacted, it would set confidentiality standards for HDOs and possibly preempt state statutes.

---

[22] Even if HDOs chose never to release person-identified or -identifiable data, and notwithstanding that the record subject had authorized release, HDOs would still be obliged to provide the person directly with a copy of his or her record. Nothing would stop that individual from personally delivering a copy of the record to a third-party requestor.

State-Based Systems

At one end of the governance spectrum, HDOs could be operated by state or local (but not federal) agencies. This kind of structure has privacy benefits. Constitutional privacy protections, for example, would attach if the HDOs were operated by public agencies. Further, governmental operation would increase the likelihood of effective public and regulatory oversight and accountability. Under this formulation, legislative hearings for budgetary and policy purposes could be expected to be a regular feature of the HDO process.

State or local agency operation of an HDO also carries significant dangers to privacy. This level of government involvement would exacerbate concerns about the linkage of HDOs with other sensitive government databases and the creation of a dossier system. Pressure for public access to HDO health record data means that HDOs will need to be exempted from state FOI laws.

Were an HDO to be operated by a state agency, it would resemble in several ways health data commissions now in place in a number of states. Because some of these have operated for some time, typical characteristics are worth reviewing here.

Iowa, for example, created a health data commission as a "statewide health data clearinghouse for the acquisition, compilation, correlation, and dissemination of data from health care providers, the state Medicaid program, third-party payers, and other appropriate sources." The Iowa statute gave the commission authority to require providers, payers, and others to submit medical record information in a person-identifiable format to the commission. It also provided that medical record data furnished to the commission would not constitute a public record and that all of the confidentiality protections available under the laws of Iowa would apply. Data releases suppress patient identifiers and suppress data in small cells. Early in 1993, bills introduced in the Iowa Senate and House called for implementation of a community health management information system (CHMIS) by the Health Policy Corporation of Iowa through its subsidiary, the Health Information Management Center. The main elements of CHMIS entities were given in Chapter 2.

Private-Sector Systems

At the other end of the governance spectrum, HDOs could be operated by purely private, for-profit or not-for-profit entities with no governmental status or legislative charter. Even in this posture, an HDO could take steps in structure and governance to maximize privacy protections. These steps could include:

- establishing a privacy ombudsman to respond to patient problems or complaints;
- establishing an advisory committee of representatives of organizations affected by the HDOs, including consumer, patient, and privacy advocacy groups;
- adopting a comprehensive privacy code to regulate all aspects of the collection, maintenance, use, and dissemination of person-identifiable data;
- designating a high-level employee to assure compliance with applicable privacy policies and standards and to prepare an annual "privacy status and compliance report" for submission to the boards of directors or advisory committees of HDOs;
- initiating a program of periodic audits to gauge compliance with privacy standards and a privacy impact audit of all new programs or functions; and
- creating an employee privacy training program.

Mixed Governance Systems

For privacy, an attractive governance approach is a middle ground, wherein the entity operating the HDO would be a private, not-for-profit organization with a legislative charter. Such an approach is under way in Washington State. A legislative charter could serve at least nine purposes in the protection of privacy.

First, a legislative charter could bring constitutional privacy protections to bear in some circumstances. Second, it could spell out a statutory cause of action for record subjects, which included remedies such as attorneys' fees and liquidated damages. Third, it could give statutory effect to the HDOs' confidentiality and other privacy standards. Fourth, a legislative charter would affect how federal law characterizes HDOs and help to dispel any confusion about the legal status of an HDO (by stating that the entity is not a health care provider, a payer, or a consumer reporting agency). Fifth, it could establish a "shield" to immunize the HDO databases from discovery and other forms of compulsory process in state courts and administrative proceedings. Sixth, it could criminalize egregious information practices such as intentional breaches of security or willful, unauthorized releases of information. Seventh, such a statute could charge the attorney general or some other appropriate state agency or official with oversight and enforcement responsibilities. Eighth, the statutory charter could institutionalize privacy safeguards such as auditing and training. Finally, it could require an annual report to a legislative committee detailing the HDO's compliance with privacy safeguards or otherwise establish an effective oversight mechanism for assisting the HDO in complying with privacy safeguards.

State charter and mixed governance options will continue to be hampered by the possibility that HDOs will operate in multistate areas. In the absence of federal legislation, this lack of uniformity of requirements or predictability of legal consequences of system design and operational characteristics would be major problems.

Other Administrative Options to Protect Privacy and Confidentiality

Security risks may be exacerbated for HDOs that have large numbers of remote on-line terminals. HDOs will need to implement comprehensive, state-of-the-art administrative, personnel, physical, and technological security safeguards; of special interest are employment agreements and security systems design. Whatever confidentiality policies HDOs adopt or are imposed by law, HDOs must be able to implement them and assure their effectiveness.

Employee agreements would, at a minimum, require employees to observe guidelines related to hard-copy reports, diskettes, and downloaded data and would instruct them about the dangers of altering, destroying, or revealing data and the penalties attached to infractions. For employees such steps include: requesting only reports needed for a given job; notifying a security administrator of changes in duties; safeguarding confidential materials; sharing information only with authorized users; using only approved user codes and passwords when requesting system access; not sharing such codes and passwords with anyone, employee or not; disposing of reports and materials in a secure manner; logging off and securing equipment when leaving a terminal; and reporting data and system misuse.

Features to limit insider and outsider threats include providing systems to conduct audit trails, having full-time security officers to enforce overall policy and monitor the system, employing expert systems to note unusual patterns of requests or employee behavior, assigning personal identification numbers (PINs) and passwords, and granting access to parts of records only on a need-to-know basis.

One option among many for addressing some of these problems is encryption (see OTA, 1993); in this process data are electronically coded so that only the dataholder and authorized users can decode the data. Medical records may require secured—that is, encrypted—communication because the inherent value of the records is very high.

Another option is the creation of a data integrity board. The Computer Matching and Privacy Protection Act of 1988 (P.L. 100-503) specified the creation of data integrity boards for federal agencies to oversee the implementation of computer matching programs. These boards were charged with overseeing a number of administrative requirements, which include the following: to issue annual reports on matching activities and any violations that have occurred; to serve as a clearinghouse for receiving and providing information on the accuracy, completeness, and reliability of records; to provide interpretations and guidance on requirements; and to review agency recordkeeping and disposal policies. These tasks illustrate what HDOs will need to oversee in their own operations.

COMMITTEE RECOMMENDATIONS

Overview and General Principles

In arriving at its set of recommendations concerning privacy and confidentiality protections, the committee reviewed federal and state statutes and regulations and common law that might apply to HDOs; it also took under advisement parallel studies related to these topics at the IOM and elsewhere. The committee ultimately arrived at a set of preferences among the various options described above, presented in the form of recommendations.

If HDOs are government entities or established by legislative charter, patients' rights embodied in federal, state, and local laws and statutes may apply to the acquisition and disclosure of person-identifiable data. Given: (1) the unprecedented *comprehensiveness* and *inclusiveness* of information in the files held by HDOs (as those terms were used in Chapter 2), (2) the generally scanty and inconsistent legal protections across geopolitical jurisdictions, and (3) the current public interest in and concern about privacy protections, *the committee believes that HDOs have both an obligation and an opportunity to fashion well-delineated privacy protection programs that will, at the same time, foster the realization of HDO goals.* Some of these protections, such as the establishment of data protection boards and organizational policies regarding security and access control, can be implemented in the short term. Others, such as passage of federal preemptive legislation, will likely require longer-term efforts.

Preemptive Legislation

RECOMMENDATION 4.1 PREEMPTIVE LEGISLATION

The committee recommends that the U.S. Congress move to enact preemptive legislation that will:

• establish a uniform requirement for the assurance of confidentiality and protection of privacy rights for person-identifiable health data and specify a Code of Fair Health Information Practices that ensures a proper balance among required disclosures, use of data, and patient privacy;

• **impose penalties for violations of the act, including civil damages, equitable remedies, and attorney's fees where appropriate;**
• **provide for enforcement by the government and permit private aggrieved parties to sue;**
• **establish that compliance with the act's requirements would be a defense to legal actions based on charges of improper disclosure; and**
• **exempt health database organizations from public health reporting laws and compulsory process with respect to person-identifiable health data except for compulsory process initiated by record subjects.**

The committee believes that both processes in the last item—public health reporting and responding to compulsory process such as subpoenas—should remain the continuing responsibility of the provider, as is now the case.

Arguments for Federal Legislation

The committee concludes that federal preemptive legislation is required to establish uniform requirements for the preservation of confidentiality and protection of privacy rights for health data about individuals because health data, particularly in electronic form, will cross state boundaries when accessed and disclosed by an HDO. In general, the committee subscribes to the positions laid out in the WEDI report (1992) and thus advocates federal preemptive legislation in preference to model state legislation or similar nonfederal approaches. It further advises that Congress enact such legislation as soon as possible. At a minimum, federal legislation should establish a floor and allow states or HDOs to implement more stringent standards so that it does not weaken state-imposed safeguards.

Attaching Privacy Protection to Data

Although current state protections often apply duties of confidentiality to the recordkeeper (e.g., the hospital), this protection is no longer in effect once the data have left the recordkeeper's control. This means that health data can be deprived of legal protection unless such protection is specified by another law; furthermore, such protection is likely to be left to the discretion of the organizations or individuals who acquire such information as secondary data. At the present time, that is little shelter indeed.

Therefore, legislation should clearly establish that the confidentiality of person-identifiable data is an attribute afforded to the data elements themselves, regardless of who holds the data. There is precedent for attaching umbrella protection to sensitive data either by regulation or by law. Examples include Executive Order 12356 (April 12, 1982), which gives defense agencies authority to establish levels of sensitivity and classify information in them; the Tax Reform Act of 1976 (P.L. 94-455), which stipulates that tax information is considered confidential, requires that the IRS and states protect it as such. According confidentiality protections to data, not to holders, would help to remedy the current lack of protections and to simplify the establishment of, compliance with, and communication of health information practices.

Uniform Requirements

The committee has concluded that ensuring an appropriate balance between the protection of confidentiality of health data about individuals and disclosures of database information requires several important features in legislation or implementing regulations. The first is the inclusion and observance of selected fair information practices, such as those found in the Privacy Act of 1974.[23] These practices—not yet available or understood in the health sector—are described in more detail in the following recommendation on data protection boards. Their significance lies (apart from historical precedent) in promulgating uniform expectations and protections for health data.

Second, federal legislation can be expected to encourage standard setting (e.g., connectivity and transmissions standards). As noted in Chapter 2, the lack of standard setting is a major obstacle to the development of automated medical records (GAO, 1991, 1993a); it will be no less a problem for advanced HDOs. Thus, the committee sees federal legislation as one more mechanism for addressing this problem for all computer-based systems dealing with health data.

Specific Elements of Federal Legislation

Good information practices[24] include the collection, transmission, and storage of only the information that is needed. They imply (if not explicitly demand) that data not be collected for unlawful purposes. Thus, proper preemptive legislation should also provide for enforcement by government

---

[23] When capitalized, the phrase "Fair Information Practices" refers to procedures established in the Privacy Act of 1974. When used without capital letters it is a generic phrase with a broader or narrower meaning, depending on the context.

[24] Good information practices include good security practices. A strong stance on privacy requires strong and comprehensive system and network security. Whether federal legislation would establish security practices and procedures or whether such policies would be left for promulgation by the HDOs, however, was considered by the committee to be beyond the scope of its charge.

officials and private aggrieved parties and should impose penalties for violations of the legislation. These might include civil damages, equitable remedies, and attorney's fees where appropriate. It will be important that the legislation clarify whether individuals have standing to bring suit.

HDOs may find themselves in complex legal thickets as demands mount for disclosure of various types of information, some of which may well include protected person-identifiable data. If it is likely that such disclosure will be deemed improper, HDOs may be understandably unwilling to release or disclose much information. This stance may in turn stifle the very contributions that HDOs can offer (as discussed in Chapters 2 and 3). To overcome this possible aversion to risk on the part of HDOs, the committee argues that compliance with requirements of any federal legislation in this area ought to be a straightforward and sufficient defense against legal actions based on charges of improper disclosure. In taking this position, however, the committee further stipulates its expectations that federal legislation will have strong privacy and confidentiality protections that meet, if not exceed, the usual provisions of fair information practices statutes or regulations.

Exemption from Compulsory Reporting and Compulsory Process

A special aspect of the committee recommendation concerns federal, state, and local public health reporting laws and compulsory process. Federal legislation should exempt HDOs from these types of requirements on the grounds that the primary dataholders or originators are the proper target for such laws and regulations. The issue may be especially acute where state laws specify reporting by providers or by "anyone who has knowledge of certain events" (e.g., a reportable communicable disease, a gunshot wound, or child abuse). The committee believes that HDOs ought not to be considered, for these purposes, either a provider or an "anyone" with knowledge of reportable events. To make this clear, the committee believes that HDOs should be directly exempted from such reporting requirements. It should be noted, however, that electronic transfer of such data from health providers to an HDO or its databases would facilitate independent reporting to the appropriate health agency *by the provider* and thus improve the completeness of those agencies' records.

In much the same way, the committee agrees that data that are essential for conduct of authorized activities by, for instance, the Internal Revenue Service, the Federal Bureau of Investigation, or legal authorities through subpoena or court order should be obtained from the primary recordholder, not the HDO. The committee believes that exemptions from compulsory reporting and compulsory process regarding third-party disputes will strengthen the claims regarding, and the actual protections accorded, the confidential person-identifiable health data held by HDOs. Compulsory process should apply, however, in disputes between HDOs and record subjects.

If federal (or state) legislation does not grant such exemptions to HDOs, then the committee's view is that HDOs should adopt a policy of refusing to comply with requests for access from law enforcement or regulatory agencies to the extent permitted by law, and it should actively seek exemptions in future federal and state legislation. They should also adopt policies of resisting compliance with subpoenas or other forms of compulsory process, asserting all available privileges, and notifying record subjects of an access request so that subjects would have an opportunity to contest production of such data.

Data Protection Units

HDOs will need clear, enforceable, written organizational policies and procedures in several areas: patients' rights regarding their own data; how to protect medical information and materials; how to ensure the accuracy of data; and how to know they have gained compliance with their policies. Members of the public should be able to request and receive clearly written materials describing these policies. Although precise policies cannot be written to cover every eventuality, they must be broad enough to address the most common situations, such as types of data, and potential requestors.

If an HDO is chartered by legislation, legislative language will undoubtedly describe its goals. HDO policies implementing these goals, however, must emanate from the top leadership of the organization. Leadership must delineate an "enforceable expectation of confidentiality" (as advocated by the PPSC, 1977a) and make clear that breaches will be rigorously addressed. Organizations should also make considerable efforts to educate (and reeducate) staff and the public (i.e., potential requestors) about these policies.

RECOMMENDATION 4.2 DATA PROTECTION UNITS

The committee recommends that health database organizations establish a responsible administrative unit or board to promulgate and implement information policies concerning the acquisition and dissemination of information and establish whatever administrative mechanism is required to implement these policies. Such an administrative unit or board should:

- **promulgate and implement policies concerning data protection and analyses based on such data;**
- **develop and implement policies that protect the confidentiality**

**of all person-identifiable information, consistent with other policies of
the organization and relevant state and federal law;**
   • **develop and disseminate educational materials for the general
public that will describe in understandable terms the analyses and their
interpretation of the rights and responsibilities of individuals and the
protections accorded their data by the organization;**
   • **develop and implement security practices in the manual and
automated data processing and storage systems of the organization;
and**
   • **develop and implement a comprehensive employee training program
that includes instruction concerning the protection of person-identifiable data.**

Establishing a Data Protection Board

The commitment of the governing body and executives of the HDO to
protection of confidentiality will be critical, and these objectives should be
written at the outset into the organization's bylaws. One useful mechanism
for accomplishing these goals is to establish a policy and oversight "data
protection" and "data integrity" unit or units to promulgate, publicize, oversee, and enforce formal policies and procedures concerning access to and
release of data. Such an entity within an HDO might be known generically
as a data protection board, and that is the term employed in this report.[25]
(Implementation of such policies and procedures would be the responsibility of specific operational arms of the organization, not the policy units
themselves.) Such policy boards and their formal policy statements should
be in place before HDOs begin operations, and regardless of whether such
policies are specified and enacted in federal preemptive legislation. Policies and procedures should explicitly deal with authorized and unauthorized
access to and authorized and unauthorized release of information from HDO
databases.

Functions and responsibilities. A data protection board would have
full authority to monitor data protection activities, intervene in potentially
harmful situations, make exceptions to privacy and confidentiality policies
on a case-by-case basis, address questions of new uses and new users of
information over time, and undertake other responsibilities that will fulfill
the spirit and the letter of the organization's policies.

---

[25] This term is used by some privacy advocates, and particularly in Europe, to mean a top-
level federal entity. It is also described in the proposal for the Health Security Act (1993). It is
used here in a more general sense and intended to refer to units that any type of HDO, of any
size, might create and support.

In terms of actions that HDO data protection boards might undertake, they should: (1) promulgate a code of fair *health* information practices (or implement one if included in federal or state legislation) and make that code available on request to any member of the public; (2) monitor compliance with such a code, audit for breaches of confidentiality, and respond in a timely way to public concerns; (3) establish, publicize, and implement formal policies and procedures concerning access to and release of data before full operation of their databases begins; and (4) ensure that such policies and procedures deal explicitly with authorized and unauthorized access to and authorized and unauthorized release of information from the database.

Drawbacks and limitations. The committee acknowledges that data protection boards will not provide a full solution without external (and probably federal) legislation and commitment from the governing boards and top leadership of HDOs. Moreover, this stance raises the issue of whether a data protection board should be a function of an HDO—which may be private, quasi-public, or public—or a governmental function applicable to all HDOs. Because of the limited powers of an HDO, particularly if it is private or quasi-public, the data protection board will be able to enforce its policies rigorously only within the organization; externally it can merely track the compliance of others that have contractual obligations to the HDO, but it will not have jurisdiction over them. In the absence of a law giving it added powers, the most that such a board could do about breaches of confidentiality by a party that received information would be to pursue legal remedies for breach of contract or any violation that may have occurred.

An additional problem with relying solely on contractual protections is that the real harm from improper disclosure of information will be suffered not by the HDO, but by persons who in all likelihood will not be a party to the contract with the HDO. (The exception might be when all such contracts name as third-party beneficiaries individuals whose information is on the system, but the committee regarded this as a remote possibility.) In the absence of legal action by such third-party beneficiaries, the liability for improper redisclosure may be minimal.

Developing Administrative Policies and Procedures

General administrative points. HDOs should develop and promulgate strong internal policies and procedures concerning the protection of health information with policies on public disclosure of information and evaluation studies. The committee further advises that such policies, which it assumes will be set by the data protection boards, specifically address the following administrative points:

• who in the organization has final responsibility for setting, monitoring, and enforcing policies and procedures;
• who inside the organization is authorized to have access to which data, and under what circumstances;
• who has authority to override policies (i.e., what are the unusual circumstances, to be decided on case-by-case basis, and who will make these decisions); and
• what are the penalties for unauthorized access or disclosure of protected information, and whether they will differ if disclosure is inadvertent, undertaken for financial gain, or for other inadmissible purposes.[26]

Implementation of such policies would likely be spread throughout the operating organization. For example, the electronic data processing department would be responsible for implementing security procedures, and the personnel department would likely carry out employee training in appropriate conduct. Some blend of oversight and operational officers would determine authorized uses of the data and rule on the exceptional case.

Policies should cover topics such as types and sources of data over time, notice to individuals about the databases accessed by the HDO, and similar matters. As a broad principle, the committee believes that HDOs must draw on the Privacy Act of 1974 and its principles of Fair Information Practices. This code and other significant issues that HDOs should address are discussed below.

Fair Health Information Practices. The committee strongly advises that HDOs include in their policies and procedures fair health information practices such as those provided for in the Privacy Act; it further urges that HDOs consider applicable revisions of the Privacy Act suggested by the PPSC and others. Any HDO should consider this code as the foundation of its privacy framework and depart from it only after careful consideration and explanation. There will be a direct relationship between, on the one hand, the extent to which record subjects are assured of notice, access, consent, and other rights with respect to information maintained in an HDO and, on the other hand, the political acceptability of HDOs as a concept or a reality in a given location. The committee thus sees such fair health information practices as critical elements in the eventual success of HDOs.

One procedural element of fair information practices is notice to subjects of their inclusion in a database. HDOs might provide for public notification in a variety of ways. At a minimum, periodic published notices

---

[26] If the HDO is not a governmental agency and is not authorized by law to do so, it cannot impose penalties.

in newspapers or public interest broadcast spots could alert individuals, indicate how more information could be obtained, and serve a public education function in explaining what HDOs do. Notice might also be given at the time a health service is provided or when enrolling in a health insurance or provider plan; a case in point is when authorization to access the HDO is given.

Types and sources of data. The committee believes that HDOs should collect only personal information that is necessary to achieve their publicly stated purposes and that they should identify, in writing, specific categories of personal information that they will not obtain under any circumstances. Information relating to an individual's exercise of First Amendment rights might be an example.

HDOs should agree to collect personal information to the fullest extent possible directly from record subjects and their health care providers. This stance reflects the approaches of both the Privacy Act and the PPSC.

Management of records over the long term. Databases cannot be permitted to grow without bounds. Given that the committee cannot foresee how the HDOs will function, it cannot be more specific than to urge that HDOs adopt policies and procedures for archiving records. HDO data protection boards will need policies to respond to an individual's request to purge or seal a record.[27]

Confidentiality agreements. HDOs should require those who are given access to HDO data to sign confidentiality agreements. These legal agreements would obligate users to safeguard information obtained from HDOs and use the information only for the purpose(s) for which it was provided. Violations of the agreement would give the HDO (and perhaps record subjects) a breach of contract and confidentiality claim against the offending user.

The effort to require recipients to protect confidentiality brings one squarely up against the limitations of contract provisions in this area. Without preemptive federal legislation that requires data recipients to protect the data they obtain in the same way that the HDOs are required to protect those data, no protection can be assured. First, HDOs would have to police the uses made of data by all recipients, and they would have to police

---

[27] This committee has proceeded on the assumption that HDOs will not be the repository of the primary medical record. If they were, then they would need to retain records for longer periods of time in order to defend against malpractice suits and, in some cases, to comply with state record retention requirements.

redisclosures. As a practical matter, these steps are impossible. Second, no mechanism such as a notarized affidavit would suffice, because such an instrument is merely a sworn statement and has no special status as a contract. A representation of intended use in a confidentiality agreement should be sufficient as a contract. In short, contractual protections are weak, so they should be used only as an adjunct to, and not as a substitute for, appropriate new federal legislation to protect the confidentiality of sensitive patient information held by HDOs.

Routine blocking of sensitive data. Legislation and organizational policies have sometimes distinguished among levels of sensitivity of various elements of health-related data in the belief that it is possible to identify categories of data that warrant special protection (IOM, 1991a; WEDI, 1992). For instance, laws protect data related to treatment in federal drug abuse treatment facilities that receive federal funds.

Despite precedent for adopting such a stance, this committee has decided otherwise. It has concluded that a given data element cannot always be reliably designated as inherently sensitive; rather, the sensitivity of data depends on the kinds of harm to which individuals are or believe themselves to be vulnerable if the information were known to others. Such assessments could differ dramatically from one person to another, one circumstance to another, one place to another, and over time as cultural attitudes change. Rather than recommending special protections for certain categories of data, the committee prefers that all data accessed by HDOs be afforded stringent, and essentially equal, protection.

Blocking divulgence by individuals of sensitive data. If no data are routinely to be considered "sensitive" and thus more stringently protected than other types of data, then might it be reasonable to permit individuals to block divulgence of particular kinds of information? That is, should persons be able to flag or label certain data as special or sensitive, so that those particular facts, specific to those individuals, would not be divulged to anyone? This could be accomplished either by: (1) permitting individuals to block information from disclosure without flagging that information as being so blocked or (2) by letting them block the information but labeling it as blocked. The committee concluded that neither of these options, although perhaps attractive from the point of view of autonomy and empowerment, was desirable as a means of protecting privacy.

The main reason for this position is that, unless care is taken in designing the system, flagging information as having been blocked might in some circumstance defeat or even exacerbate the challenge to privacy; such a label or flag would alert anyone reviewing the material that it includes sensitive data. More insidious from the viewpoint of a treating physician—

for whom this information may someday be a proxy medical record (as when information is unavailable by some other means)—it would compromise his or her ability to care for the patient. Furthermore, if blocked material is not so flagged or labeled, the consequences for treating physicians could be even more disastrous if that blocked information (e.g., the existence of a serious chronic condition or use of a particular medication) is directly relevant to clinical decisions. Although it is true that patients can always omit information in a face-to-face encounter, it would seem to defeat one of the purposes of a database to allow it to be intentionally incomplete. Thus, the committee does not subscribe to the view that specified material could be blocked (masked), whether labeled that way or not.

Overseeing Data Integrity

HDO data protection boards would oversee safeguards to prevent health information from being disclosed to unauthorized recipients. They may also need to be responsible for oversight of the protection of data from unauthorized alteration and for data accuracy and completeness. (These tasks might, alternatively, be assigned to a "data integrity" unit, board, or committee.)

At a minimum, this board would need to ensure that data and programs are changed only in a specified and authorized manner, and it would be responsible for assessing and reporting the accuracy of the HDO's data. Data integrity may be maintained by implementing security measures, by implementing procedural controls, by assigning responsibility, and by establishing audit trails as described earlier in this chapter.

Security requires proper *system design* driven by policies that have been determined and approved by the governing board, chiefly because software and hardware vendors are likely to implement only the level of security specified by the HDOs. Access must be limited to authorized users. Mechanisms and procedures must also be developed and implemented before the network becomes operational. These should address how data integrity will be maintained by preventing alteration or loss of data and what steps will be taken for authenticating users and maintaining records of communications with users. Procedures to ensure availability and recovery after unanticipated disruptions (e.g., power loss, fire) are also crucial, including assurance that the systems resume operation in a secure state and that data integrity is guaranteed.

Security in these environments presents special challenges, in part because it is only as adequate as that provided for the least secure database on the network. Further, remote access to computer systems, the possibility of accessing information over public telecommunications systems, and advances in standardization of data elements and transmission requirements will enhance the opportunities for data linkage, but they will also magnify the need for security protections. Data networks will become increasingly attractive to sabotage and access for financial gain and thus require special attention to manage these risks.

The basic intent is to provide assurance that the system, its resources, and information are protected against harm and that the information and resources are properly accessed and used by authorized users. The board should ensure that, at a minimum, the following list of security safeguards would be in place internally for a defined operational system and environment:

- a defined set of users;
- prescribed data and operational programs;
- defined network connections and interactions with other systems; and
- protection against defined threats against the system, its resources, and its data.

Safeguards might include policy guidance in several areas: procedures for granting access to systems and assigning passwords; administration and training of security officers for conduct of audits and disaster preparedness; and oversight of management review of safeguards and inspections.[28]

HDOs' resources will probably never be sufficient for all the activities and responsibilities envisioned for them. Long-term success is likely to be predicated in part on their ability to protect confidentiality of personal health data, and the committee believes that they will therefore have to devote adequate resources to some form of data protection board. It may well be that monetary or human resources sufficient to maintain *independent* data protection and data integrity units will not be available; those resource allocation decisions, however, are best left to individual HDOs.

Release of Person-identified Data

Policies Relating to Access and Disclosure

It is clear that the question of who *outside* the HDO has access to which data, under what circumstances, is supremely important; this is directly

---

[28] Specific concerns include physical risk management for disasters (e.g., fire, flood); memory protection and backup in case of hardware failure; design and use of audit trails, log-on procedures, antivirus protection for software; assignment and monitoring of badges and other mechanisms to control personnel access; logging and cataloging of magnetic tapes and floppy disks; destruction of paper containing sensitive printouts and other documents; and monitoring the system for unauthorized access.

related to questions of disclosure and is the essence of the privacy issue from the patient's point of view. The committee takes up these matters in a series of recommendations (presented below) that refer to person-identified or person-identifiable information only. As laid out in Chapter 3, this committee recommends release and disclosure of information that protects patient identity but provides reliable, valid, timely, and useful descriptive and evaluative information on a full range of health care providers and clinicians. It also acknowledges that some HDOs will have claims processing and payment functions that will require transmittal of person-identified claims information between the provider and payer.

RECOMMENDATION 4.3 RELEASE OF PERSON-IDENTIFIED DATA

The committee recognizes that there must be release of patient-identified data related to the processing of health insurance claims. The committee recommends, however, that a health database organization *not* release person-identifiable information in any other circumstances *except* the following:

- **to other HDOs whose missions are compatible with and whose confidentiality and security protections are at least as stringent as their own;**
- **to individuals for information about themselves;**
- **to parents for information about a minor child except when such release is prohibited by law;**
- **to legal representatives of incompetent patients for information about the patient;**
- **to researchers with approval from their institution's properly constituted Institutional Review Board;**
- **to licensed practitioners with a need to know when treating patients in life-threatening situations who are unable to consent at the time care is rendered; and**
- **to licensed practitioners when treating patients in all other (non-life-threatening) situations, *but only with the informed consent of the patient*.**

Otherwise, the committee recommends that health database organizations not authorize access to, or release of, information on individuals with or without informed consent.

Consent

In the last item, the committee has specifically recommended that consent for access to the database be a necessary and sufficient condition in only one circumstance: when needed by the treating practitioner. In such a situation it will be important that specific consent techniques be in place. The following requirements, similar to those in the Uniform Health Care Information Act, are based on PPSC recommendations for medical record information consent forms. Patient consent must:

- be in writing or electronically provided in an acceptable manner;
- be signed or authorized electronically by the individual on a date specified;
- be clear about the entities being authorized to disclose information;
- be specific about the nature of the information to be disclosed;
- be specific as to the institutions or persons to whom the information may be disclosed;
- be specific about the purposes for which the information may be used, both at the time of the intended disclosure and at any future time; and
- be specific as to the date when the authorization expires.

Requirements of signed and written consent, which arose at a time when all records were kept on paper, are still valid, but they will require modification to permit consent by computer, such as by keypad attached to a terminal in a treating physician's office.

The Uniform Act expressly states that the signing of an authorization is *not* a waiver of any privacy rights that the patient may have under other statutes, rules of evidence, or common law. It further requires that providers (or, in this case, HDOs) retain a copy of each authorization and provides that an authorization may not permit the release of health record information relating to health care that is to be provided more than 90 days in the future. (Exceptions are made for disclosures to third-party payers, but they would be irrelevant for HDOs.) Finally, the Uniform Act states that a patient may revoke a disclosure authorization in writing at any time. Even if consent and participation rights are in place, privacy protection is not ensured, because strategies used to obtain consent, in particular, are fallible. As discussed earlier in this chapter, for example, patients experience substantial pressure to sign authorizations and waivers in order to facilitate both access to and payment for health care.

Release of Person-identified Data

In the seven cases listed in Recommendation 4.3, the committee believes that values other than confidentiality justify access to person-identifiable information with or without consent, and that there exist adequate safeguards for the protection of data in these very limited circumstances. Those values include autonomy for patients in accessing their records, fiduciary responsibility for those unable to care for themselves or make health decisions for themselves, beneficence in providing health care in acute situations, and the social benefits of epidemiologic and health services research. The rationale for each case is described below.

The Standing of Other HDOs

HDOs will need to acquire information about out-of-area care provided to persons in their databases and should be able to do so for those specific circumstances. For example, one HDO might ask another to provide information for state residents of given zip codes who have been hospitalized in other states. The committee concludes that if the requesting HDO has confidentiality and security protections that are at least as stringent as those of the HDO that would be releasing the information, the data should be released. Such HDOs might be in adjoining states (e.g., when Vermont residents are hospitalized in New Hampshire) or within a single state; in other cases they might include overlapping geographical areas such as one or more states and a metropolitan area. In all such cases, individuals might be expected to be found in several different HDOs, and in their best interest (insofar as needed health care is concerned), their data ought to be shared or transferred.

The Standing of Persons, Parents, and Legal Representatives

The second case cited in Recommendation 4.3 is self-evident—when information about themselves is sought by individuals. The third and fourth cases reflect the need to care for minors and persons who are legally incompetent to give consent for themselves.

One important case concerns the parents of a minor child except when certain actions are protected by state law. Such exceptions include, for instance, family planning services. *Emancipated minors* are those who live away from home or are in the armed forces and manage their own financial affairs. *Mature minors*, although still dependent on their parents, are judged to be mature enough to understand the treatment or issue in question and to give informed consent for their own care. The committee believes that privacy and confidentiality for emancipated and mature minors should have the same protection as that given to adults. Parental involvement should be related to the age and development of the minor. Current state laws regarding emancipated or mature minors do not consistently protect such information, and uniform federal legislation is desirable.

The other important case involves legal representatives of incompetent patients. Such legal or personal representatives include guardians as well as individuals who are named in advance directives and granted durable power of attorney.

The Special Standing of Research

The fifth case in Recommendation 4.3—researchers with approval from relevant human subjects committees or institutional review boards (IRBs)—is a different category. In this case person-identified information is not being sought *by* the patient or *for care of* the patient, but to conduct studies that in some fashion are regarded to be in the public's interest. Such uses of the databases are considered by this committee to be central and vital to the effective implementation of HDOs. For this reason, researchers whose research design and study plans are deemed appropriate and approved by a review panel—typically but not necessarily an IRB at the lead researcher's university or institution—should be permitted access to person-identified or person-identifiable data in the HDO files.

An IRB is a specially constituted review body established to protect human subjects, usually those recruited for biomedical and behavioral research, when that research is conducted under the auspices of the institution (USDHHS, 1993b). Review and approval by an IRB is required for research that is conducted by investigators supported by a department or agency subject to federal policy. IRBs function under policies set by federal legislation (45 CFR 46 for Department of Health and Human Services; *Federal Register*, 1991a) and by policies of the institution. Members of the IRB carefully weigh the likely risks and benefits of the proposed research and the procedures and protections for the research subjects.

When research involves only the review of records, such as those in HDOs, the IRB is encouraged to determine that an institutional approval or an expedited review is sufficient. It may do so if it is persuaded: (1) of the significance of the research and that use of data in personally identifiable form is necessary, (2) that any risk of harm to subjects is minimal, (3) that adequate safeguards will be implemented to protect the record or information from unauthorized disclosure, and (4) that removal and destruction of identifiers will be carried out when the research is complete. The committee urges institutions to review applications when requested by serious investigators who many not be affiliated with an institution. Alternatively, such requests might be considered as exceptions by the Data Protection Board on a case-by-case basis.

The committee believes it will usually *not* be necessary for researchers to obtain consent from record subjects for access to *person-identified* or *-identifiable* material, but methods should be incorporated for protecting a record subject's privacy, including notification by the HDO of the uses that may be made of the records.

Contacting potential subjects to obtain further information is a more sensitive matter. It requires careful attention and sensitivity to who would make initial contact and what information would be conveyed to potential subjects or their relatives in the course of the contact. The information conveyed should include the purpose of the study and the kind of data that would be collected, the identity of the persons who will have access to the data, the safeguards that will be used to protect the data from inappropriate disclosure, and the risks that could result from disclosure. Such negotiations should also give written assurance that any publications that result will present the data only in aggregate form so that individuals are not identifiable. Research subjects should also be told if they will be contacted in the future (USDHHS, 1993b).

Special Patient Care Considerations

The sixth case in Recommendation 4.3 involves treating licensed practitioners with a need to know in life-threatening situations, whom the committee believes ought to be able to access data about a patient. This requires that the patient be unable to consent at the time care is rendered. A patient in a situation that threatens loss of life or limb sometimes cannot provide coherent but needed medical information because of mental impairment, stress, or substance abuse and is not considered to be a "reliable historian." In such cases the committee believes it appropriate to access such data, if available, through the HDO. When the patient cannot be identified, access to the HDO might be particularly helpful if biometric (nonvolitional) identifiers are part of the database.

The committee has chosen the term "licensed practitioner" advisedly, a broader concept than "physician." Circumstances justifying access might occur in a hospital emergency department, in an intensive care unit, or outside the hospital when a health care professional is present and determines that in his or her judgment obtaining certain health information is crucial. All such cases presume that a primary medical record is not available and that no one (patient, family, or friend) can reliably provide needed health information in a timely way.

The seventh case—the release of data to licensed practitioners when treating patients in all other (non-life-threatening) situations, but only with the informed consent *of the patient*—is the only case in which the committee has recommended the use of informed consent to release of person-identifiable information. Such a circumstance might occur when a treating physician wishes to access the HDO database in addition to the medical records he or she keeps. For example, information on medications prescribed by other practitioners might be pertinent. In such cases, the treating practitioner should obtain explicit consent of the patient. As discussed earlier, consent might be given electronically and might be time limited.

Prohibition on Access to Person-identifiable Data

The committee recommended that HDOs not authorize access to or release of health information on individuals, with or without the informed consent of the individual, in any situation or to any requestor other than those stated above.

To ensure that individuals (i.e., patients, parents of minor children, or legal representatives) are not placed in an untenable situation concerning release of information, the committee has opted for a position that does not rely on consent procedures in most uses or disclosures of data. It prefers to rely on stringent policies against disclosure or release of personal information on individuals. It should be noted that the consent procedures described in this recommendation are for release of information by the HDO. Patients will always be able to consent to release of information by each of their care providers. Nevertheless, in some circumstances the committee envisions that consent procedures will be invoked before HDOs will release person-identifiable information.

The importance of consent as a concept, and adequate procedures for implementing consent, is accentuated by the multiplicity of uses of HDOs. Given this multiplicity, it is difficult to argue that, by providing information, record subjects have implied their consent to subsequent uses and redisclosures. It may well turn out that record subjects will have little or no idea of the number or variety of disclosures that could be made from an HDO.

Implications of Recommendations Denying Access

The reason for prohibiting broad disclosure following patient consent is that HDOs may contain a longitudinal record about all health care delivered to a patient and many personal details about the patient. Permitting the same ritual of consent to authorize disclosure of this information will result in an increased abridgment of patient privacy.

The prohibition on access to person-identifiable information is very broad. If this limitation is enacted into law or such a policy is promulgated by the HDO, it would have several consequences. For example, employers could not obtain information about "out-of-health-plan" use by their employees even for case management purposes. No access for law enforcement would be permissible through compulsory process (if prohibited by federal preemptive legislation). Attorneys could not access the database to build a case on behalf of clients except through compulsory process in accordance with governing law. Secret service agents seeking information about a person suspected of being a security threat to an elected official could not seek information from the HDO.

Prohibiting access could result in some disadvantage or inconvenience to the recordholder as well as possible harm to society. Nevertheless, the committee believes that risks to individual privacy and the importance of a clear and unambiguous policy for HDOs outweigh such possible disadvantages.

In some circumstances, the committee foresees difficult situations that seem to present a conflict between policies. For example, an individual might wish to obtain a copy of his information in the database that he could then supply to an attorney who needs it for a malpractice case or to an employer who demands it for determining new assignments or for case management purposes. The committee, as noted elsewhere, sees little way to "protect" patient information when the individual requests the information from an HDO and then transfers it as he or she sees fit.

Employer Access

RECOMMENDATION 4.4. RESTRICTING EMPLOYER ACCESS

The committee recommends that employers not be permitted to require receipt of an individual's data from a health database organization as a condition of employment or for the receipt of benefits.

Special circumstances exist in the health sector of particular concern to the committee. One involves the current practice of extensive exchange of medical information between employer and payer, with little control by providers or patients. This practice has dramatic implications for patients whose information is accessed by an HDO if the employer and payer are readily able to tap into data in the network. HDOs could make such exchanges of information more harmful to patients because the information exchanged could cover all encounters the patient has with the health care system (not just those covered by insurance or by the employer's health plan).

The committee acknowledges the danger and inappropriateness of these practices. It thus concurs with a recent IOM report (IOM, 1993e) that urged that access to information collected in connection with employment-based health benefits be limited through provisions analogous to those contained in the Americans with Disabilities Act of 1990 (P.L. 101-336).

In Recommendation 4.4, the committee attempts to prohibit the use of HDOs by employers for employment-related decisions about employees. In particular, it seeks to constrain access to person-identifiable data and prevent employers from coercing employees to provide such data about themselves or their families as a condition of employment (e.g., promotion, placement, retention, or termination). This recommendation applies only to the HDO and would not, of course, prevent employers or others from acquiring health information from other sources—examination, a treating physician, an insurer, and so forth.

Employees might wish, however, to provide access to their records to their employer's case managers in circumstances relating to needed health care. To account for this, the committee advises that there be a clear and enforceable division of functions between employment and personnel decisions of an employer and the employer's health benefits administration and case management. In the absence of state or federal legislation limiting access and threatening liability, employers should at least promulgate and enforce such internal policies.

Universal Person Identifiers

Unique, individual person identifiers are essential to facilitate the efficient operation and data interchange of HDOs. The committee also recognizes the strong arguments against the use of the SSN as that unique identifier. The great majority of the committee agreed on the need for a *new* unique identifier of the grounds that the SSN offers too many opportunities to breach confidentiality. The creation of a new number would: (1) permit legislative protection of that number, (2) offer the possibility of greater protection for health information than is possible with the SSN, and (3) could occur at the time of implementation of universal health care coverage, which will, if enacted, require some scheme for unique identification.

COMMENT

In this report the committee has addressed its views and concerns about a new entity in health care delivery and recordkeeping—the HDO. Little is really understood about how HDOs will function, what effects they will really have as opposed to the benefits they are expected to offer, and how they will evolve over the next decade or so. These matters will be worked out in an environment of change and stress, as the nation sorts out its posture toward health care and health reform. This report, therefore, must be seen as laying the groundwork for the context in which HDOs come into being and function. It cannot be read as providing answers to all HDO issues that may arise, but neither could the committee ignore the future completely.

In matters of privacy, the unique aspects of the HDO are two: (1) the concentration of medical information about very large numbers of individuals, coupled with (2) the large number of end users who have authorized access to some or all of an individual's record. The HDO will inevitably lead to much more varied use of health care information, and therein is a privacy issue of substantial significance for the future.

Undoubtedly, both anticipated and innovative uses of HDO databases will be evolutionary. In an operational sense, this is probably wise and unavoidable; in matters of privacy, it is risky because a small number of seemingly innocuous uses can cumulatively create a substantial privacy risk. Some uses that arise will prove repugnant to society and will be impermissable; others will be considered annoying, but will be tolerated. Some could be so discriminatory or otherwise distasteful that they might well be proscribed by law.

The committee notes that the privacy dimension of medical records, regional databases, and HDOs is not a matter that can be examined once and thereafter ignored. New dimensions of privacy will arise, as will extensions of old concerns, new threats to privacy, and new uses of data that prove unwise. From time to time, perhaps every few years in the beginning of the "HDO movement," the privacy issue needs to be revisited and reevaluated. New mechanisms for assuring privacy may need to be invented; new actions by Congress may be needed.

Security safeguards that protect the confidentiality of data and the automated systems themselves have similar characteristics. New threats will materialize; penetrators will become more skilled; new motivations for surreptitiously acquiring health data will appear. From time to time, the safeguards will need upgrading and strengthening.

The New Privacy

Privacy concerns have centered historically on the use of information about an individual that governs some decision about her (e.g., a right, entitlement, or privilege) or some action taken for or against her. The benefit or harm as well as the risk of information misuse applies to the same individual.

With the growth of an information industry that deals widely with information about people, the benefit-risk aspect has changed; the benefit has turned toward organizations and society, but the risk has remained for the individual. The traditional recordkeeping characterization of privacy is far too limited given the intense pace of automation in recordkeeping and the electronic linkages of systems of all kinds.

Conflicts have already begun to appear with regard to medical data. The most frequently quoted anecdote is that of the pharmaceutical company that uses patient drug use as the basis for targeted mailings and advertising. Some people will tolerate such nonmedical use of health data as an annoyance; others will feel strongly about it; some will be harmed because a mailing can reveal a medical condition that was being concealed. Employer use of health data also brings two motivations into conflict: that of the employer who, having paid for the health care in whole or in part, feels it is entitled to have the data for more efficient management of the organization and that of the individual who considers that health data are personal and to be shared only as he sees fit.

Other conflicts will arise, and the concentration of so many kinds of information in an HDO will be a stimulus to their further creation. Looking well to the future, therefore, a Code of Fair *Health* Information Practices is likely to be necessary. It need not be exactly like the one in the federal Privacy Act; indeed, it would probably have additional provisions for controlling the use of health data.

For example, society has not yet expressed its view on how very sensitive kinds of medical information can be used; genetic data is a case in point. It may be decided that prohibitions against particular uses of information will be accepted. If so, then one mechanism for implementation is incorporation of the prohibition, possibly stated in a very general way, into a fair code; another is to cast it into law. There is precedent for such prohibitions; for example, personnel forms cannot ask certain kinds of questions such as those dealing with religion or sexual orientation.

For the most part, privacy law in this country has been formulated under the assumption that holders of information about people may generally do with it what they please, constrained only by corporate ethics and the good taste of business, societal acceptance (or outrage), occasional attention by the government, pressures of consumer activist groups, and the consequences of legal actions brought by individuals or consumer groups. This historical view may prove inappropriate or even dangerous in regard to health data. There is now evidence that the American public agrees. Westin has found high medical privacy concerns among 48 percent of respondents and high privacy concerns in general among 25 percent of survey respondents whom he terms Privacy Fundamentalists. This group would seek sharp limits on organized data collection and legal protection for privacy. Another 57 percent of the public has been termed Privacy Pragmatists. He describes this group as examining each situation to see whether information is really needed for a legitimate societal function and whether safeguards are being followed. The final group he calls Privacy Unconcerned. This small group is not apprehensive about the use of personal data (Harris/Equifax, 1993).

Our society and country are designed to operate with what the engineer would call feedback, or what society would call controls, weakly defined and often *ad hoc* or *de facto*. The country, its people, its government, and its institutions have survived thus far under this paradigm. With the coming concentration of health information about huge numbers of people in the

HDO, is this an acceptable national posture for information that is potentially the most sensitive of all data ever collected about people?

It is difficult to attempt answers to a question such as this because the near future of health care is so poorly defined. Events under way—for example, national health care reform—will have a major impact on the motivations of managers in charge of health care providers.

The country might be safe with the perception and handling of privacy as it has been done for over two decades, but it might not. There can easily arise distasteful practices in the way health care information is exploited for other than delivery and payment of care. It is simply not known which uses of health care information will be acceptable to society, will wisely serve the needs of society and the health care industry, and will strike an acceptable balance between the desires of a profit-oriented health care industry (which may be ever more prevalent in the future) and the invasion-of-privacy consequences for patients. In short, the privacy dimension of health care information is dynamic, and it must be treated accordingly.

SUMMARY

The committee has examined sources of concerns about informational privacy and the confidentiality of health-related information and security, and it defines each in the context of health information. After a review of privacy rights, confidentiality obligations and disclosure policies, and disclosure as it is treated by law and in practice, the committee concluded that there was much basis for concern about confidentiality, but little applicable legal guidance for HDOs. It reviewed options related to uniform legislation, consent and participation rights, disclosure policies, and governance, and advanced a set of recommendations favoring strong federal preemptive legislation and responsible organizational policies to protect privacy and confidentiality of person-specific information.

In the context in which "confidential" is a designation given data to be protected in terms of security and access, the committee has made a number of recommendations that would help HDOs achieve these ends. First, confidentiality is addressed by a recommendation for preemptive federal legislation that all health care data be confidential, protected as such, and access to it controlled.

Second, the committee recommends the establishment of data protection and data integrity boards to provide oversight of security and access in HDOs. To implement protection of health care data, the committee has addressed security and recommended that automated systems and networks supporting HDOs have comprehensive system and network security that reflect the state of the art.

Third, to address patient privacy rights, the report has recommended that patients can have access and other rights regarding their records, and be dealt with through a code of fair health information practices. To accommodate patient expectations of privacy, the committee recommended that patients have certain legally assured rights to recover damages and force compliance if health care information is misused, abused, or improperly released to unauthorized parties.

Fourth, to address privacy—the issue of access to personal information—the committee has made recommendations concerning who should and should not have access to person-identified information and under what circumstances.

References

ACS (American College of Surgeons) Fact Sheet. The National Trauma Registry of the American College of Surgeons (Draft). Chicago: American College of Surgeons, 1992.

Adler, N.E., Boyce, T., Chesney, M.A., et al. Socioeconomic Inequalities in Health. No Easy Solution. *Journal of the American Medical Association* 269:3140-3145, 1993.

AHCPR (Agency for Health Care Policy and Research). *AHCPR Purpose and Programs.* Rockville, Md.: Department of Health and Human Services, Public Health Service, AHCPR, 1990a.

AHCPR. *Program Note. Medical Treatment Effectiveness Research.* Rockville, Md.: Department of Health and Human Services, Public Health Service, AHCPR, 1990b.

Allen, A. *Uneasy Access: Privacy for Women in a Free Society.* Totowa, N.J.: Rowman and Allanheld, 1987.

AMA (American Medical Association). Principles of Medical Ethics, *Current Opinions of the Council on Ethical and Judicial Affairs of the AMA Including the Principles of Medical Ethics and Rules of the Council on Ethical and Judicial Affairs.* 1992.

AMPRA (American Medical Peer Review Association). *Managed Competition and the Role of Quality Oversight.* Washington, D.C.: AMPRA, 1993.

Anderson, H.J. Managing Data in a New Era. *Medical Claims Management* 1(4):29-36, 1993.

Andrussier, S.E. The Freedom of Information Act in 1990: More Freedom for the Government; Less Information for the Public. *Duke Law Journal* 729:753-801, 1991.

Aronow, D.B., and Coltin, K.L. Information Technology Applications in Quality Assurance and Quality Improvement, Part II. *Journal on Quality Improvement* 19:465-477, 1993.

Ayanian, J.Z. Heart Disease in Black and White [editorial]. *New England Journal of Medicine* 329:656-658, 1993.

Ayanian, J.Z., and Epstein, A.M. Differences in the Use of Procedures between Women and Men Hospitalized for Coronary Heart Disease. *New England Journal of Medicine* 325:221-225, 1991.

Baker, N.A. Medicare PROs and Assessment of Quality: Should Physician-Specific Data be Released? *Utilization Review* 21(16):4-6, 1992.

Ball, M.J., and Collen, M.F. *Aspects of the Computer-Based Patient Record.* Computers in Health Care Series. New York: Springer-Verlag, 1992.

Barnes, B.A., O'Brien, E., Comstock, et al. Report on Variation in Rates of Utilization of Surgical Services in the Commonwealth of Massachusetts. *Journal of the American Medical Association* 254:371-375, 1985.

Batalden, P.B., and Buchanan, E.D. Industrial Models of Quality Improvement. Pp. 113-155 in: *Providing Quality Care: The Challenge to Clinicians.* N. Goldfield and D. Nash, eds. Philadelphia: American College of Physicians, 1989.

Beauchamp, T., and Childress, J. *Principles of Biomedical Ethics.* New York: Oxford University Press, 1989.

Becker, L.B., Han, B.H., Meyer, P.M., et al. Racial Differences in the Incidence of Cardiac Arrest and Subsequent Survival. *New England Journal of Medicine* 329:600-606, 1993.

Belair, R.R. *Regional Health Data Networks: Privacy Law and Policy.* Paper prepared for the Institute of Medicine Committee on Regional Health Data Networks. Washington, D.C.: Kirkpatrick & Lockhart, 1993.

Benn, S. Privacy, Freedom, and Respect for Persons. In *NOMOS XIII: Privacy.* J. Pennock and J. Chapman, eds. New York: Atherton, 1971.

Bennett, C.J. *Regulating Privacy: Data Protection and Public Policy in Europe and the United States.* Ithaca, N.Y.: Cornell University Press, 1992.

Berwick, D.M. Sounding Board. Continuous Improvement as an Ideal in Health Care. *New England Journal of Medicine* 320:53-56, 1989.

Berwick, D.M., Godfrey, A.B., and Roessner, J. *Curing Health Care. New Strategies for Quality Improvement.* San Francisco: Jossey-Bass, 1990.

BI (Benton International). *CHMIS. Community Health Management Information System. General Overview.* New York: BI, 1991a.

BI. *CHMIS. Community Health Management Information System. CHMIS Overview.* New York: BI, 1991b.

BI. *CHMIS. Community Health Management Information System. Generic Specification.* New York: BI, 1992.

Bloustein, E.J. Privacy as an Aspect of Human Dignity: A Reply to Dean Prosser. In *Philosophical Dimensions of Privacy: An Anthology.* New York: Cambridge University Press, 1984.

Blum, J.D., Gertman, P.M., and Rabinow, J. *PSROs and the Law.* Germantown, Md.: Aspen, 1977.

Blumenthal, D. Total Quality Management and Physicians Clinical Decisions. *Journal of the American Medical Association* 269:2775-2778, 1993.

Borbas, C., Stump, M.A., Dedeker, K., et al. The Minnesota Clinical Comparison and Assessment Project. *Quality Review Bulletin* 16:87-92, 1990.

Braveman, P., Oliva, G., Miller, M.G., et al. Adverse Outcomes and Lack of Health Insurance Among Newborns in an Eight-County Area of California, 1982-1986. *New England Journal of Medicine* 321:508-513, 1989.

Brook, R.H. *Quality of Care Assessment: A Comparison of Five Methods of Peer Review.* DHEW Pub. No. HRA 74-2100. Rockville, Md.: Department of Health, Education, and Welfare, National Center for Health Services Research and Development, 1973.

Brook, R.H., and Appel, F.A. Quality-of-Care Assessment: Choosing a Method for Peer Review. *New England Journal of Medicine* 288:1323-1329, 1973.

Brook, R.H., and Lohr, K.N. Efficacy, Effectiveness, Variations and Quality: Boundary-Crossing Research. *Medical Care* 23:710-722, 1985.

Bulger, R.J. The Search for a New Ideal. Pp. 9-21 in *In Search of the Modern Hippocrates.* R.J. Bulger, ed. Iowa City: University of Iowa Press, 1987.

Burnham, D. *The Rise of the Computer State.* New York: Random House, 1983.

Burnum, J.F. The Misinformation Era: The Fall of the Medical Record. *Annals of Internal Medicine* 110:482-484, 1989.

Burstin, H.R., Lipsitz, S.R., and Brennan, T.A. Socioeconomic Status and Risk for Substandard Medical Care. *Journal of the American Medical Association* 268:2383-2387, 1992.

California Office of Statewide Health Planning and Development. *Health Data Catalog.* Sacramento: State of California, January 1991.

Chassin, M.R. Quality of Care. Time to Act. *Journal of the American Medical Association* 266:3472-3473, 1991.

Chassin, M.R. Explaining Geographic Variations. The Enthusiasm Hypothesis. *Medical Care* 31:YS37-YS44, 1993a.

Chassin, M.R. The Missing Ingredient in Health Reform. Quality of Care [editorial]. *Journal of the American Medical Association* 270:377-378, 1993b.

Chassin, M.R., Brook, R.H., Park, R.E., et al. Variations in the Use of Medical and Surgical Services by the Medicare Population. *New England Journal of Medicine* 314:285-290, 1986a.

Chassin, M.R., Kosecoff, J., Park, R.E., et al. Does Inappropriate Use Explain Geographic Variations in the Use of Health Care Services? A Study of Three Procedures. *Journal of the American Medical Association* 258:2533-2537, 1987.

Chassin, M.R., Park, R.E., Fink, A., et al. *Indications for Selected Medical and Surgical Procedures—A Literature Review and Ratings of Appropriateness.* R-3204/2-CWF/HF/HCFA/PMT/RWJ. Santa Monica, Calif.: The RAND Corporation, 1986b.

Chassin, M.R., Park, R.E., Lohr, K.N., et al. Differences among Hospitals in Medicare Patient Mortality. *Health Services Research* 24:1-31, 1989.

Chlapowski, F. Note: The Constitutional Protection of Informational Privacy. *Boston University Law Review* 71:133-145, 1991.

CHQC (Cleveland Health Quality Choice). *Cleveland-Area Hospital Quality Outcome Measurements and Patient Satisfaction Report.* Volumes I and II. Cleveland, Ohio: CHQC, 1993.

Chueh, H.C., and Barnett, G.O. Client-Server, Distributed Database Strategies in a Healthcare Record System for a Homeless Population. *Proceedings. Seventeenth Annual Symposium on Computer Applications in Medical Care,* October 30-November 3, 1993. New York: McGraw-Hill, 1994.

Cleaver, C.M. Privacy Rights and Medical Records. *Fordham Urban Law Journal* 13:165, 184, n.133, 1985.

Cooley, T.M. *A Treatise on the Law of Torts, or, the Wrongs Which Arise Independent of Contract.* Chicago: Callaghan & Co., 1880.

Couch, J.B., ed. *Health Care Quality Management for the 21st Century.* Tampa, Fl.: Hillsboro, 1991.

Darby, M. Minnesota Guideline Project Hinges on Local Networks. *Report on Medical Guidelines and Outcomes Research* 3(4):8-9, 1992.

Darby, M. New HCFA Chief Reconsiders Hospital Mortality Reports. *Report on Medical Guidelines and Outcomes Research,* 4(13):1-2, 5, 1993.

Densen, P.M., Fielding, J.E., Getson, J., et al. The Collection of Data on Hospital Patients— The Massachusetts Health Data Consortium Approach. *New England Journal of Medicine* 302:171-173, 1980.

Department of Justice. *Report of the Federal Advisory Committee on False Identification: Criminal Use of False Identification.* Washington, D.C.: U.S. Department of Justice, 1976.

Des Harnais, S. Current Uses of Large Data Sets to Assess the Quality of Providers. Construction of Risk-Adjusted Indexes of Hospital Performance. *International Journal of Technology Assessment in Health Care* 6:229-238, 1990.

Donabedian, A. Evaluating the Quality of Medical Care. *Milbank Memorial Fund Quarterly* 44:166-203, 1966.

Donabedian, A. *Explorations in Quality Assessment and Monitoring.* Volumes 1-3. Ann Arbor, Mich.: Health Administration, 1980, 1982, 1985.

Doyle, E. Physicians Worried by Requests to Turn Over Data Bank Reports. *ACP Observer* 12(9):6, 1992.

Dubois, R.W. Inherent Limitations of Hospital Death Rates to Assess Quality. *International Journal of Technology Assessment in Health Care* 6:220-228, 1990.

Dubois, R.W., Brook, R.H., and Rogers, W.H. Adjusted Hospital Death Rates: A Potential Screen for Quality of Medical Care. *American Journal of Public Health* 77:1162-1166, 1987a.

Dubois, R.W., Moxley, J.H., Draper, D., et al. Interpreting Hospital Mortality: Is it a Predictor of Quality? *New England Journal of Medicine* 317:1674-1680, 1987b.

DVA (Department of Veterans Affairs). *VA Databases Resource Guide.* M.C. Beattie, R.M. Swindle, and L.A. Tomko, eds. Palo Alto, Calif.: HSR&D Center for Healthcare Evaluation, Department of Veterans Affairs Medical Center, 1992.

DVA. *Decentralized Hospital Computer Program.* Veterans Health Administration, Medical Information Resources Management Office, August 1993.

Dworkin, R. *Taking Rights Seriously.* Cambridge, Mass.: Harvard University Press, 1977.

Eaton, J.W. *Card-Carrying Americans: Privacy, Security and the National I.D. Card Debate.* Totowa, N.J.: Rowman and Littlefield, 1986.

Eddy, D.M. Variations in Physician Practice: The Role of Uncertainty. *Health Affairs* 3(Summer):74-89, 1984.

Elison, L.M., and Nettiksimmons, D. The Right of Privacy. *Montana Law Review* 48:1-52, 1987.

Equifax. *Harris-Equifax Consumer Privacy Survey, 1992.* Atlanta: Equifax, 1992.

Faden, R. Maintaining the Balance Between the Privacy of Private Sector Health Records and the Need for Information: An Overview. Address given at a conference, "Health Records: Social Needs and Personal Privacy," sponsored by the Task Force on Privacy, the Department of Health and Human Services, Washington, D.C., February 11-12, 1993.

Federal Register. Federal Policy for the Protection of Human Subjects: Notices and Rules. 56:28002-28032, June 18, 1991. (For FDA policy, see *Federal Register* 56:28025-28029, June 18, 1991a.)

Federal Register. Health Care Financing Administration. Privacy Act of 1974; System of Records (proposing the Uniform Clinical Data Set). 56:67078-67080, December 27, 1991b.

Fleming, C., Wasson, J.H., Albertsen, P.C., et al. A Decision Analysis of Alternative Treatment Strategies for Clinically Localized Prostate Cancer. *Journal of the American Medical Association* 269:2650-2658, 1993.

Fried, C. Privacy. *Yale Law Journal* 77:475-493, 1968.

Gable, C.B. A Compendium of Public Health Data Sources. *American Journal of Epidemiology* 131:381-394, 1990.

Gallagher, S.S., Finison, K., Guyer, B., and Goodenough, S. The Incidence of Injuries Among 87,000 Massachusetts Children and Adolescents: Results of the 1980-81 Statewide Childhood Injury Prevention Program Surveillance System. *American Journal of Public Health* 74:1340-1346, 1984.

GAO (General Accounting Office), Information Management and Technology Divison (IMTEC).

Medical ADP Systems: Automated Medical Records Hold Promise to Improve Patient Care. GAO/IMTEC-91-5. Washington, D.C.: U.S. Government Printing Office, 1991.

GAO, IMTEC. *Automated Medical Records. Leadership Needed to Expedite Standards Development.* GAO/IMTEC-93-17. Washington, D.C.: U.S. Government Printing Office, 1993a.

GAO, IMTEC. *Health Care Information Systems. National Practitioner Data Bank Continues to Experience Problems.* GAO/IMTEC-93-1. Washington, D.C.: U.S. Government Printing Office, 1993b.

Gardner, E. UB-82 Forms Offer Wealth of Information, Misinformation. *Modern Healthcare* 20(38):18-29, 1990.

Gates, M. Rochester Pioneers New Frontier with Cost and Quality Reform Model. *Report on Medical Guidelines and Outcomes Research* 4(18):11-12, 1993a.

Gates, M. Patient Outcomes Take on Long-Term Implications at Henry Ford. *Report on Medical Guidelines and Outcomes Research* 4(20):6-7, 1993b.

Gavison, R. Privacy and the Limits of Law. *Yale Law Journal* 89:421-471, 1980.

Gellman, R.M. Prescribing Privacy: The Uncertain Role of the Physician in the Protection of Patient Privacy. *North Carolina Law Review* 62:255-294, 1984.

Gerety, T. Redefining Privacy. *Harvard Civil Rights-Civil Liberties Law Review* 12:233-296, 1977.

Goldfield, N., and Nash, D.B., eds. *Providing Quality Care: The Challenge to Clinicians.* Philadelphia: American College of Physicians, 1989.

Gosfield, A.G. *PSROs: The Law and the Health Consumer.* Cambridge, Mass.: Ballinger, 1975.

Gostin, L. Consequences to the Individual of Data Collection and Information Use and Individual Rights and Expectations and Societal Needs. Panel presentation at a conference, "Health Records: Social Needs and Personal Privacy," sponsored by the Task Force on Privacy, the Department of Health and Human Services, Washington, D.C., February 11-12, 1993.

Gostin, L.O., Brezina, J.T., Powers, M., et al. Privacy and Security of Personal Information in a New Health Care System. *Journal of the American Medical Association* 270:2482-2493, 1993.

Greenfield, S. Adjusting for Severity: Variations in Outcomes. Paper presented at a conference, "Measuring, Managing, and Improving Quality in the ESRD Treatment Setting," sponsored by the Institute of Medicine, Washington, D.C., September 21-22, 1993.

Greenfield, S., Aronow, H.U., Elashoff, R.M., and Watanabe, D. Flaws in Mortality Data. The Hazards of Ignoring Comorbid Disease. *Journal of the American Medical Association* 260:2253-2255, 1988.

Hand, R., Sener, S., Imperato, J., et al. Hospital Variables Associated with Quality of Care for Breast Cancer Patients. *Journal of the American Medical Association* 266:3429-3432, 1991.

Hannan, E.L., Bernard, H.R., O'Donnell, J.F., et al. A Methodology for Targeting Hospital Cases for Quality of Care Record Reviews. *American Journal of Public Health* 79:430-436, 1989a.

Hannan, E.L., Kilburn, H., Bernard, H., et al. Coronary Artery Bypass Surgery: The Relationship Between In-Hospital Mortality Rate and Surgical Volume After Controlling for Clinical Risk Factors. *Medical Care* 29:1094-1107, 1991a.

Hannan, E.L., Kilburn, H., Lindsey, M.L., et al. Clinical Versus Administrative Data Bases for CABG Surgery. Does It Matter? *Medical Care* 30:892-907, 1992.

Hannan, E.L., Kilburn, H., O'Donnell, J.F., et al. Adult Open Heart Surgery in New York State: An Analysis of Risk Factors and Hospital Mortality Rates. *Journal of the American Medical Association* 264:2768-2774, 1990.

Hannan, E.L., Kilburn, H., O'Donnell, J.F., et al. Interracial Access to Selected Cardiac Procedures for Patients Hospitalized with Coronary Artery Disease in New York State. *Medical Care* 29:430-441, 1991b.

Hannan, E.L., O'Donnell, J.F., Kilburn, H., et al. Investigation of the Relationship Between Volume and Mortality for Surgical Procedures Performed in New York State Hospitals. *Journal of the American Medical Association* 262:503-510, 1989b.

Harris/Equifax. *Health Care Information Privacy. A Survey of the Public and Leaders.* Conducted for Equifax. New York: Louis Harris and Associates, 1993.

HCFA (Health Care Financing Administration), U.S. Department of Health and Human Services. *Medicare Hospital Mortality Information, 1986.* Washington, D.C.: U.S. Government Printing Office, 1987.

HCFA. *Medicare Hospital Mortality Information, 1990.* Washington, D.C.: U.S. Government Printing Office, 1991.

Health Affairs. Special Issue: Variations in Medical Practice. 3(2):6-148, 1984.

Health Pages. Green Bay/Madison/Milwaukee Edition. 1(1):1-68, 1993.

Health Pages. St. Louis Edition. 1(1):1-64, 1994.

Hendricks, E. Hacker "Manual" Tells Wannabes How to Penetrate TRW Database. *Privacy Times* 12(15):1-2, 1992.

Herdrich, M.A. *California v. Greenwood:* The Trashing of Privacy. *The American University Law Review* 38:993, 999-1002, 1989.

Hibbert, C. *What To Do When They Ask for Your Social Security Number.* Available at: hibbert@xanadu.com, 1992.

Hospital Inpatient Care. *Washington Consumers' Checkbook* 8(3):22-36, 1992.

HSA (Health Security Act). Washington, D.C.: U.S. Government Printing Office, 1993.

Iezzoni, L.I. Measuring the Severity of Illness and Case-mix. Pp. 70-105 in *Providing Quality Care: The Challenge to Clinicians.* N. Goldfield and D.B. Nash, eds. Philadelphia: American College of Physicians, 1989.

Iezzoni, L.I., Foley, S.M., Saley, J., et al. Comorbidities, Complications, and Coding Bias. Does the Number of Diagnosis Codes Matter in Predicting In-Hospital Mortality? *Journal of the American Medical Association* 267:2197-2203, 1992.

Inquiry. Special Issue on Quality of Care. 25:423-468, 1988.

IOM (Institute of Medicine). *Access to Medical Review Data.* Washington, D.C.: National Academy Press, 1981.

IOM. *Medicare: A Strategy for Quality Assurance.* Volumes I and II K.N. Lohr, ed. Washington, D.C.: National Academy Press, 1990.

IOM. *The Computer-Based Patient Record: An Essential Technology for Health Care.* R.S. Dick and E.B. Steen, eds. Washington, D.C.: National Academy Press, 1991a.

IOM. *Kidney Failure and the Federal Government.* R.A. Rettig and N.G. Levinsky, eds. Washington, D.C.: National Academy Press, 1991b.

IOM. *Guidelines for Clinical Practice: From Development to Use.* M.J. Field and K.N. Lohr, eds. Washington, D.C.: National Academy Press, 1992a.

IOM. *Setting Priorities for Health Technology Assessment. A Model Process.* M.S. Donaldson and H.C. Sox, Jr., eds. Washington, D.C.: National Academy Press, 1992b.

IOM. *Access to Health Care in America.* M.A. Millman, ed. Washington, D.C.: National Academy Press, 1993a.

IOM. *Assessing Genetic Risks: Implications for Health and Social Policy.* L.B. Andrews, J.E. Fullarton, K.E. Hanna, N.A. Holtzman, and A.G. Motulsky, eds. Washington, D.C: National Academy Press, 1993b. Prepublication copy.

IOM. *Assessing Health Care Reform.* M.J. Field, K.N. Lohr, and K.D. Yordy, eds. Washington, D.C.: National Academy Press, 1993c.

IOM. *Emergency Medical Services for Children.* J.S. Durch and K.N. Lohr, eds. Washington, D.C.: National Academy Press, 1993d.

IOM. *Employment and Health Benefits: A Connection at Risk.* M.J. Field and H.T. Shapiro, eds. Washington, D.C.: National Academy Press, 1993e.

IOM/CBASSE (Commission on Behavioral and Social Sciences and Education). *Toward A National Health Care Survey. A Data System for the 21st Century.* G.S. Wunderlich, ed. Washington, D.C.: National Academy Press, 1992.

Isikoff, M. Theft of U.S. Data Seen as Growing Threat to Privacy. *Washington Post*, December 28, 1991, p. A1.

Kahn, K.L., Draper, D., Keeler, E.B., et al. *The Effects of the DRG-Based Prospective Payment System on Quality of Care for Hospitalized Medicare Patients—Final Report.* R-3931-HCFA. Santa Monica, Calif.: The RAND Corporation, 1992.

Kaiser Permanente. *1993 Quality Report Card.* Oakland, Calif.: Kaiser Permanente, 1993a.

Kaiser Permanente. *1993 Quality Report Card Supplement. Performance Measure Methodologies.* Oakland, Calif.: Kaiser Permanente, 1993b.

Kane, R.L., and Lurie, N. Appropriate Effectiveness: A Tale of Carts and Horses. *Quality Review Bulletin* 18:322-326, 1992.

Keeler, E.B., Kahn, K.L., Draper, D., et al. Changes in Sickness at Admission Following the Introduction of PPS. Pp. 24-43 in *The Effects of the DRG-Based Prospective Payment System on Quality of Care for Hospitalized Medicare Patients. Final Report.* K.L. Kahn, et al., eds. R-3931-HCFA. Santa Monica, Calif.: The RAND Corporation, 1992a.

Keeler, E.B., Rubenstein, L.V., Kahn, K.L., et al. Hospital Characteristics and Quality of Care. *Journal of the American Medical Association* 268:1709-1714, 1992b.

Keller, J. The Vermont Program for Quality Health Care (mimeo handout). Burlington, Vt., National Health Policy Forum, June 7, 1993.

Krakauer, H., and Jacoby, I. Predicting the Course of Disease. *Inquiry* 30:115-127, 1993.

Kratka, J. *For Their Eyes Only. The Insurance Industry and Consumer Privacy.* Boston: Massachusetts Public Interest Research Group, 1990.

Lasovich, D., White, E., Thomas, D.B., et al. Underutilization of Breast-Conserving Surgery and Radiation Therapy among Women with Stage I or II Breast Cancer. *Journal of the American Medical Association* 266:3433-3438, 1991.

Leape, L.L., Hilborne, L.H., Kahan, J.P., et al. *Coronary Artery Bypass Graft. A Literature Review and Ratings of Appropriateness and Necessity.* RAND/JRA-02. Santa Monica, Calif.: The RAND Corporation, 1991.

Lohr, K.N. Commentary: Professional Peer Review in a "Competitive" Medical Market. *Case Western Reserve Law Review. The Legal Implications of Health Care Cost Containment: A Symposium* 36(4):1175-1189, 1985-86.

Lohr, K.N., Grossman, J.H., and Cassel, C.K. From the IOM. Issues in Measuring and Assuring Quality of Care for Health Care Reform. *Journal of the American Medical Association* 270:1911, 1993.

Longo, D.R., Bohr, D.A., Miller, L., and Miller, J. *Inventory of External Data Demands Placed on Hospitals.* A Report of the Quality Measurement and Management Project. Chicago: The Hospital Research and Educational Trust, 1990.

Luft, H.S., and Romano, P.S. Chance, Continuity, and Change in Hospital Mortality Rates: Coronary Artery Bypass Graft Patients in California Hospitals, 1983 to 1989. *Journal of the American Medical Association* 270:331-337, 1993.

Lu-Yao, G.L., McLerran, D., Wasson, J., et al. An Assessment of Radical Prostatectomy. Time Trends, Geographic Variation, and Outcomes. *Journal of the American Medical Association* 269:2633-2636, 1993.

McCloskey, H.J. Privacy and the Right to Privacy. *Philosophy* 55:17-38, 1980.

McNeil, B.J., Pederson, S.H., and Gatsonis, C. Current Issues in Profiling Quality of Care. *Inquiry* 29:298-307, 1992.

McPherson, K., Strong, P.M., Epstein, A., et al. Regional Variations in the Use of Common Surgical Procedures: Within and Between England and Wales, Canada and the United States of America. *Social Science and Medicine* 15A:273-288, 1981.

Marquis, M.S. *Consumers' Knowledge About Their Health Insurance Coverage.* R-2753-HHS. Santa Monica, Calif.: The RAND Corporation, 1981.

Marquis, M.S., Kanouse, D.E., and Brodsley, L. *Informing Consumers about Health Care Costs. A Review and Research Agenda.* R-3262-HCFA. Santa Monica, Calif.: The RAND Corporation, 1985.

Martin, J. *Managing the Database Environment.* Englewood Cliffs, N.J.: Prentice Hall, 1983.

Mayo Foundation. Index to Medical Records Access Policy. Internal Document, May 1991.

Merrick, N.L., Brook, R.H., Fink, A., et al. Use of Carotid Endarterectomy in Five California Veterans Administration Medical Centers. *Journal of the American Medical Association* 258:2531-2535, 1986.

MIB (Medical Information Bureau). MIB Fact Sheet. Boston: MIB, 1989.

Miller, M. Patients' Records Are Treasure Trove for Budding Industry. *Wall Street Journal,* February 27, 1992.

Moses, L.E. Framework for Considering the Role of Data Bases in Technology Assessment. *International Journal of Technology Assessment in Health Care* 6:183-193, 1990.

NAHDO (National Association of Health Data Organizations). *NAHDO Resource Manual.* Falls Church, Va.: NAHDO, 1988.

NAHDO. *The State Health Data Resource Manual: Hospital Discharge Data Systems.* Falls Church, Va.: NAHDO, 1993.

Nash, D.B. Is the Quality Cart Before the Horse? [editorial]. *Journal of the American Medical Association* 268:917-918, 1992.

National Conference of Commissioners on Uniform State Laws. *Uniform Laws Annual* 9(1):475. St. Paul, Minn.: West Publishing Co., 1988.

NCHS (National Center for Health Statistics). *National Health Interview Survey, 1991. Public Use Data Tape.* NTIS Order No. PB93-500700. Springfield, Va.: National Technical Information Service, 1993.

Newhouse, J.P., and Insurance Experiment Group. *Free for All? Lessons from the RAND Health Insurance Experiment.* Cambridge, Mass.: Harvard University Press, 1993.

NRC (National Research Council). *Private Lives and Public Policies: Confidentiality and Accessibility of Government Statistics.* G.T. Duncan, T.B. Jabine, and V.A. de Wolf, eds. Washington, D.C.: National Academy Press, 1993.

OTA (Office of Technology Assessment). *Federal Government Information Technology: Electronic Record Systems and Individual Privacy.* OTA-CIT-296. Washington, D.C.: U.S. Government Printing Office, 1986, p. 15.

OTA. *The Quality of Medical Care: Information for Consumers.* OTA-H-386. Washington, D.C.: U.S. Government Printing Office, 1988.

OTA. *Protecting Privacy in Computerized Medical Information.* OTA-TCT-576. Washington, D.C.: U.S. Government Printing Office, 1993.

Palmer, R.H. *Ambulatory Health Care Evaluation: Principles and Practice.* Chicago: American Hospital Association, 1983.

Palmer, R.H., and Adams, M.M.E. (Commissioned Paper). *Quality Improvement/Quality Assurance Taxonomy: A Framework.* Rockville, Md.: Agency for Health Care Policy and Research, 1993.

Parent, W.A. Privacy, Morality, and the Law. *Philosophy and Public Affairs* 12:269-288, 1983.

Patrick, D.C., Madden, C.W., Diehr, P., et al. Health Status and Use of Services Among Families With and Without Health Insurance. *Medical Care* 30:941-949, 1992.

Paul, J.E., Weis, K.A., and Epstein, R.A. Data Bases for Variations Research. *Medical Care* 31:S96-S102, 1993.

PHCCCC (Pennsylvania Health Care Cost Containment Council). *Hospital Effectiveness Report: A Model Report*. HE 5—Volume I. Harrisburg: PHCCCC, 1989.

PHCCCC. *A Consumer's Guide to Coronary Artery Bypass Graft Surgery*, Harrisburg: PHCCCC, 1992.

Piller, C. Privacy in Peril. How Computers are Making Private Life a Thing of the Past. *Macworld* 10(7):124-130, 1993.

Pipko, S., and Pucciarelli, A.J. The Soviet Internal Passport System. *International Lawyer* 19:915-919, 1985.

Powers, M. Legal Protections of Confidential Medical Information and the Need for Anti-Discrimination Laws. Pp. 221-255 in *AIDS, Women and the Next Generation*. R. Faden, G. Geller, and M. Powers, eds. New York: Oxford University Press, 1991.

Powers, M. Privacy and the Control of Genetic Information. In *The Genetic Frontier: Ethics, Law, and Policy*. M.S. Frankel and A.H. Teich, eds. Washington, D.C.: American Association for the Advancement of Science Press, 1993.

PPRC (Physician Payment Review Commission). *Annual Report to Congress*. Washington, D.C.: PPRC, 1992.

PPRC. *Annual Report to Congress*. Washington, D.C.: PPRC, 1993.

PPSC (Privacy Protection Study Commission). *Personal Privacy in an Information Society*. Washington, D.C.: U.S. Government Printing Office, 1977a.

PPSC. *Appendix 4. The Privacy Act of 1974: An Assessment*. Washington, D.C.: U.S. Government Printing Office, 1977b.

Rachels, J. Why Privacy Is Important. *Philosophy and Public Affairs* 4:323-333, 1975.

Raskin, I.E., and Maklan, C.W. Medical Treatment Effectiveness Research. A View from Inside the Agency for Health Care Policy and Research. *Evaluation & the Health Professions* June:161-186, 1991.

Raz, J. *The Morality of Freedom*. Oxford, England: Oxford University Press, 1986.

Reiman, J.H. Privacy, Intimacy, and Personhood. *Philosophy and Public Affairs* 6:26-44, 1976.

Roos, L.L., Cageorge, S.M., Austen, E., et al. Using Computers to Identify Complications After Surgery. *American Journal of Public Health* 75:1289-1295, 1985.

Roos, L.L., Roos, N.P., Cageorge, S.M., et al. How Good Are the Data? Reliability of One Health Care Data Bank. *Medical Care* 20:266-276, 1982.

Roos, L.L., Sharp, S.M., Cohen, M.M., and Wajda, A. Risk Adjustment in Claims-Based Research: The Search for Efficient Approaches. *Journal of Clinical Epidemiology* 42:1193-1206, 1989.

Roos, N.P. Hysterectomy: Variations in Rates Across Small Areas and Across Physicians' Practices. *American Journal of Public Health* 74:327-335, 1984.

Roos, N.P., Black, C., Frolich, N., et al. Assessing the Relationship Between Health Care Use and the Health of a Population: Seeking Levers for Policy Makers. *Daedalus* 1993, in press.

Roos, N.P., and Roos, L.L. High and Low Surgical Rates: Risk Factors for Area Residents. *American Journal of Public Health* 71:591-600, 1981.

Roper, W.L., Winkenwerder, W., Hackbarth, G.M., et al. Effectiveness in Health Care: An Initiative to Evaluate and Improve Medical Practice. *New England Journal of Medicine* 319:1197-1202, 1988.

Rothfeder, J. *Privacy for Sale*. New York: Simon and Schuster, 1992.

Schoeman, F.D. Privacy: Philosophical Dimensions of the Literature. In *Philosophical Dimensions of Privacy: An Anthology*. F.D. Schoeman, ed. New York: Cambridge University Press, 1984.

Shattuck, J. In the Shadow of 1984: National Identification Systems, Computer-Matching and Privacy in the United States. *Hastings Law Journal* 35:991-1005, 1984.

Shils, E. Privacy: Its Constitution and Vicissitudes. *Law and Contemporary Problems* 31:281, 282, 1966.

Smith, S. NHIS Electronic Data Products. *Public Health Reports* 108:409, 1993.

Stern, R.S. Record Linkage. A Powerful Tool for Epidemiological Analysis [editorial]. *Archives of Dermatology* 122:1383-1384, 1986.

Steven, C. Good Medicine. *Washingtonian* 29:90-114, 1993.

Tanouye, E. Merck Will Exploit Medco's Database. *Wall Street Journal*, August 4, 1993, p. B1.

Thomson, J.J. The Right to Privacy. *Philosophy and Public Affairs* 4:295-314, 1975.

Tillmann, I.A., and Sullivan, S. Quality and the Future of American Health Care. In *Building Blocks for Change: How Health Care Reform Affects Our Future.* J.A. Meyer and S. Silow-Carroll, eds. Washington, D.C.: The Economic and Social Research Institute, 1993.

Tribe, L. *American Constitutional Law.* Mineola, Minn.: Foundation, 1978.

Trubow, G.B. (ed.) *Privacy Law and Practice.* New York: Bender, 1991.

Turkington, R.C. Legal Protection for the Confidentiality of Health Care Information in Pennsylvania: Patient and Client Access; Testimonial Privileges; Damage Recovery for Unauthorized Extra-Legal Disclosure. *Villanova Law Review* 32:259, 269, 1987.

USDHEW (U.S. Department of Health, Education and Welfare). Secretary's Advisory Committee Report on Automated Personal Data Systems. *Records, Computers and the Rights of Citizens.* DHEW Pub. No. (OS)73-97. 1973.

USDHHS. *Report to Congress: The Feasibility of Linking Research-Related Data Bases to Federal and Non-Federal Medical Administrative Data Bases.* AHCPR Pub. No. 91-0003. Rockville, Md.: Agency for Health Care Policy and Research, 1991.

USDHHS. *Literature Review. Automated Data Sources for Ambulatory Care Effectiveness Research.* M.L. Grady and H.A. Schwartz, eds. AHCPR Pub. No. 93-0042. Rockville, Md.: Agency for Health Care Policy and Research, 1993a.

USDHHS. *Protecting Human Research Subjects. Institutional Review Board Guidebook.* Washington, D.C.: U.S. Government Printing Office, 1993b.

U.S. News & World Report. 1991 Survey on America's Best Hospitals. August 5, 1991.

U.S. News & World Report 1992 Annual Guide on America's Best Hospitals. June 15, 1992.

U.S. News & World Report 1993 Annual Guide on America's Best Hospitals. 115(2):68-94, 1993.

U.S. Senate, Subcommittee on Courts, Senate Committee on the Judiciary. Federal Identification Systems: Hearings on S. 1706 before the Subcommittee on Courts, Senate Committee on the Judiciary. 98th Congress, 1st Session 5, July 19, October 5, 21, 1983, p. 169.

VanAmringe, M., and Shannon, T.E. Commentary: Awareness, Assimilation, and Adoption: The Challenge of Effective Dissemination and the First AHCPR-Sponsored Guidelines. *Quality Review Bulleting* 18:397-404, 1992.

Waller, A.A. Appendix B. Legal Aspects of Computer-Based Patient Records and Record Systems. In *The Computer-Based Patient Record: An Essential Technology for Health Care.* R.S. Dick and E.B. Steen, eds. Washington, D.C.: National Academy Press, 1991.

Waller, A.A. Confidentiality Issues in Electronic Data Interchange. Conference on Electronic Data Interchange: If You Are a Health Care Provider, It Applies to You! Bloomington, Minn., November 20, 1992.

Ware, W. The New Faces of Privacy. *The Information Society* 9:195-211, 1993.

Warren, S.D., and Brandeis, L.D. The Right to Privacy. *Harvard Law Review* 4:193-220, 1890. (*See further, Katz v. United States* 389 U.S. 347; 1967.)

Webster's New World Dictionary of the American Language. 2nd ed. D.B. Guralnik, ed. New York: Simon and Schuster, 1980.

WEDI (Workgroup for Electronic Data Interchange). *Report to Secretary of U.S. Department of Health and Human Services,* 1992.

Weissman, J.S., Gatsonis, C., and Epstein, A.M.   Rates of Avoidable Hospitalization by Insurance States in Massachusetts and Maryland. *Journal of the American Medical Association* 268:2426-2427, 1992.

Welch, W.P., Miller, M.E., Welch, H.G., et al.   Geographic Variation in Expenditures for Physicians' Services in the United States. *New England Journal of Medicine* 328:621-627, 1993.

Wennberg, J.E.   Dealing with Medical Practice Variations: A Proposal for Action. *Health Affairs* 3:6-32, 1984.

Wennberg, J.E.   Small Area Analysis and the Medical Care Outcome Problem. Pp. 17-206 in *AHCPR Conference Proceedings: Research Methodology: Strengthening Causal Interpretations of Nonexperimental Data.* L. Sechrest, E. Perrin, and J. Bunker, eds. DHHS Pub. No. (PHS) 90-3454, Rockville, Md.: Department of Health and Human Services, 1990.

Wennberg, J.E., and Gittelsohn, A.   Variations in Medical Care Among Small Areas. *Scientific American* 246:120-134, 1982.

Wennberg, J.E., Barnes, B.A., and Zubkoff, M.   Professional Uncertainty and the Problem of Supplier-Induced Demand. *Social Science and Medicine* 16:811-824, 1982.

Wennberg, J.E., McPherson, K., and Caper, P.   Will Payment Based on Diagnosis-Related Groups Control Hospital Costs? *New England Journal of Medicine* 311:295-300, 1984.

Wenneker, M.B., and Epstein, A.M.   Racial Inequalities in the Use of Procedures for Patients with Ischemic Heart Disease in Massachusetts. *Journal of the American Medical Association* 261:253-257, 1989.

Wenneker, M.B., Weissman, J.S., and Epstein, A.M.   The Association of Payer with Utilization of Cardiac Procedures in Massachusetts. *Journal of the American Medical Association* 264:1255-1260, 1990.

Westin, A.F. *Privacy and Freedom.* New York: Atheneum, 1967, p. 39.

Westin, A.F. *Databanks in a Free Society. Computers, Record-Keeping and Privacy.* (Report of the Project on Computer Databanks of the Computer Science and Engineering Board, National Academy of Sciences.) New York: Quadrangle, 1972.

Westin, A.F. *Computers, Health Records, and Citizen Rights.* Washington, D.C.: U.S. National Bureau of Standards, 1976.

Whittle, J., Conigliaro, J., Good, C.B., and Lofgren, R.P.   Racial Differences in the Use of Invasive Cardiovascular Procedures in the Department of Veterans Affairs Medical System. *New England Journal of Medicine* 329:621-627, 1993.

Wilensky, G., and Jencks, S. The Health Care Quality Improvement Initiative: A New Approach to Quality Assurance in Medicare. *Journal of the American Medical Association* 268:900-903, 1992.

William M. Mercer, Inc. *CHMIS Information Repository. Hartford Foundation Grant. Initial Analytic Framework Deliverable for Task 7.* Seattle: William M. Mercer, Inc., 1993.

Williamson, J.W. *Assessing and Improving Outcomes in Health Care: The Theory and Practice of Health Accounting.* Cambridge, Mass.: Ballinger, 1978.

Winslow, C.M., Kosecoff, J.B., Chassin, M., et al. The Appropriateness of Performing Coronary Artery Bypass Surgery. *Journal of the American Medical Association* 260:505-509, 1988a.

Winslow, C.M., Solomon, D.H., Chassin, M.R., et al. The Appropriateness of Carotid Endarterectomy. *New England Journal of Medicine* 318:721-727, 1988b.

Work Group on Computerization of Patient Records. *Toward a National Health Information Infrastructure.* Report of the Workgroup to the Secretary of the U.S. Department of Health and Human Services, April 1993.

Zinman, D.   Heart Surgeons Rated.   State Reveals Patient-Mortality Records. *Newsday*, December 18, 1991, p. 3.

Appendixes

A
Fact-Finding for the Committee on Regional Health Data Networks

This appendix briefly documents the organizations and individuals who contributed to the committee's efforts at data collection and fact-finding during the first parts of the project. Listed below are participants and guests at committee meetings, including experts who gave special briefings to the committee. Following that is material on the committee's site visits.

PARTICIPANTS AND GUESTS AT COMMITTEE MEETINGS

Expert Presentations and Briefings

John A. Baker, Senior Vice President, Equifax, Inc.
Robert Belair, J.D., formerly Kirkpatrick and Lockhart; currently Mullenholz and Brimsek
John P. Fanning, LL.B., OHPE/OASH/Department of Health and Human Services
Marilyn J. Field, Ph.D., Senior Program Officer, Institute of Medicine
Jane Fullarton, Senior Program Officer, Institute of Medicine
William Goss, Health Care Management Program, General Electric
Edward J. Hinman, M.D., Lincoln National
H. Jefferson Smith, Ph.D., Georgetown University School of Business Administration
Robin Stults, R.R.A., University of Maryland Medical System
Bert Tobin, Benton International

Invited Guests and Observers

Lois Alexander, Special Assistant to the Commissioner, Social Security Administration

Leslie Alexandre, Government Affairs Representative for Health Policy, Office of Government Affairs, Electronic Data Systems

Marjory Blumenthal, Ph.D., Staff Director, Computer Science and Telecommunications Board, Committee on Physical Sciences, Mathematics, and Applications, National Research Council

Moses Boyd, Committee on Commerce, Science, and Transportation, U.S. Senate

Paula Bruening, J.D., Office of Technology Assessment

Mark Epstein, Executive Director, National Association of Health Data Organizations

J. Michael Fitzmaurice, Ph.D., Director, Office of Science and Data Development, Agency for Health Care Policy and Research

Kathleen Frawley, R.R.A., J.D., Director, Washington, D.C., Office, American Health Information Management Association

Robert Gellman, J.D., Chief Counsel, Subcommittee on Government Information, Justice, and Agriculture, Committee on Government Operations, U.S. House of Representatives

Michael Hash, Subcommittee on Health and the Environment, Committee on Energy and Commerce, U.S. House of Representatives

Stephen Jencks, M.D., Health Standards and Quality Bureau, Health Care Financing Administration

Judith Miller Jones, Director, National Health Policy Forum, George Washington University

Charles N. Kahn III, J.D., Committee on Ways and Means, U.S. House of Representatives

Rene C. Kosloff, Ph.D., Vice President, Kunitz and Associates, Inc.

Selma Kunitz, Ph.D., President, Kunitz and Associates, Inc.

Donald A. B. Lindberg, M.D., Director, National Library of Medicine, National Institutes of Health

Richard S. Sharpe, Program Officer, The John A. Hartford Foundation

Nicole Simmons, Office of Legislation and Policy, Health Care Financing Administration

Joan Turek-Brezina, Ph.D., Director of Technical and Computer Support, Office of the Assistant Secretary for Planning and Evaluation, Department of Health and Human Services

Institute of Medicine Staff

Enriqueta Bond, Ph.D., Executive Officer
Jane Durch, Staff Officer

Kenneth I. Shine, M.D., President
Karl D. Yordy, M.P.A., Director, Division of Health Care Services

SITE VISITS

This section gives the location and dates of the committee's site visits and lists the organizations or groups of individuals with whom the committee met.

Memphis, Tennessee: July 26-28, 1992

Baptist Memorial Hospital
Blue Cross and Blue Shield of Memphis
International Paper Company
Memphis and Shelby County Medical Society
Memphis Business Group on Health, Confidentiality Task Force
Memphis Business Group on Health, Inc.
Methodist Health Systems
Regional Medical Center (County Medical Center)
Sharpe Manufacturing Company, Personnel Department

Cleveland, Ohio: August 2-4, 1992

Academy of Medicine
Blue Cross/Blue Shield of Cleveland
Board of County Commissioners
Centerior Energy
The Cleveland Clinic Foundation
Cleveland Health Quality Choice
Council on Small Enterprises
Greater Cleveland Hospital Association
Health Action Council
Lubrizol Corporation
University Hospitals of Cleveland

Des Moines, Iowa: August 26-28, 1992

Blue Cross and Blue Shield of Iowa
Health Policy Corporation of Iowa
Iowa Bankers Insurance Service
Iowa Hospital Association
Iowa Medical Society
Iowa Methodist Medical Center
Iowa State Education Association

Pioneer Hi-Bred, Human Resources Department
Principal Financial Group
Practicing Physicians

Seattle, Washington: September 9-11, 1992

The Exchange System
Foundation for Health Care Quality (FHCQ)
Health Care Purchasers Association
Group Health of Puget Sound
Overlake Hospital Medical Center, Employees
State of Washington, Department of Health
State of Washington, Office of the Governor
University of Washington, Faculty
Washington State Health Care Authority
Washington State Hospital Association and Task Force on Administrative
    Reform
Washington State Medical Association
Weyerhaeuser Company, Health Management Services

Rochester and Albany, New York: September 21-23, 1992

Albany

Albany Medical Society
Hospital Association of New York State
New York State Department of Health (NYDOH)

Rochester

Consumer Representatives
Integrated Mental Health Services
Physicians Network
Rochester Health Information Group

Basic Findings of Site Visits

During the site visits, IOM committee members and staff were able to learn in some detail about current and planned initiatives under the auspices of numerous groups as well as about a great variety of issues, concerns, and suggestions from these groups and a broad cross-section of people in urban and rural areas.

The site visits included three sites where CHMISs were being developed (both state-mandate and business coalition models in Washington State, Des Moines, and Memphis) and three where they are not (Rochester, Albany, and Cleveland). Questions raised frequently by hosts were as follows:

1. Who would run and administer such a database, and who would own the data?

2. What would this effort cost and who would finance it, in terms of both fixed costs (for example, for computer equipment) and variable costs (over the short and long run, such as staff/personnel costs for data entry)?

3. What is in it for me or what will this do to me (particularly from physicians in private practice and from employers with national interests whose health policies were set at a corporate level somewhere else)?

4. Who would have access to patient-identified and provider-specific data? Interestingly, not everyone was worried about privacy of patient data, believing either that such information could be protected (so the question was moot) or that not much harm would come from judicious release to, for example, employers. Consumers understood the potential value of such databases, but they were also worried about access to patient-level data, especially concerning insurability.

5. Could analyses about quality of care realistically be done (in contrast to analyses of cost or charges data or analyses of utilization patterns)?

The visiting committee members, in turn, tried to learn as much as possible about ways—in practice or in theory—groups in these various areas meant to realize the benefits of such databases, to minimize or prevent the exacerbation of current risks to the confidentiality of patient-level data, to improve database security, and to promote appropriate data collection, valid analyses, and useful dissemination of data.

B
Committee on Regional Health Data Networks Biographical Sketches

ROBERT H. BROOK, M.D., Sc.D., F.A.C.P., is a Corporate Fellow at RAND and the Director of RAND's Health Sciences Program. He led the Health and Quality Group on the $80 million. RAND Health Insurance Experiment, and he was co-principal investigator on the Health Services Utilization Study, which developed a method to assess appropriateness of care and applied it to carotid endarterectomy, coronary angiography, and endoscopy. He was the co-principal investigator on a joint activity of 12 academic medical centers, the AMA, and RAND, the purpose of which was to develop appropriateness criteria and parameters for the use of procedures. At UCLA, Dr. Brook is the Director of the Robert Wood Johnson Clinical Scholars Program. He is also professor of Medicine and Health Services, UCLA Center for Health Sciences. His special research interests include quality assessment and assurance, the development and use of health status measurements in health policy, the efficiency and effectiveness of medical care, and the variation in use of selected services by geographic area. He is a member of the Institute of Medicine, the American Society for Clinical Investigation, and the American Association of Physicians. He was awarded the Baxter Foundation Prize for excellence in health services research, the Rosenthal Foundation Award of the American College of Physicians for contributions to improving the health of the nation, and the Distinguished Health Services Research Award of the Association of Health Services Research. Dr. Brook is the author of over 250 articles on quality of care.

ROGER J. BULGER, M.D., is currently President and Chief Executive Officer of the Association of Academic Health Centers. Before his appointment in 1988, Dr. Bulger served for 10 years as President of the University of Texas Health Science Center at Houston, professor of medicine at the University of Texas Health Medical School at Houston, and professor of public health at the University of Texas School of Public Health at Houston. Earlier he served as the second dean of the University of Massachusetts School of Medicine and chancellor of the University of Massachusetts Medical Center campus at Worcester. He was the first executive officer of the Institute of Medicine, serving that organization during its first formative years. Dr. Bulger has served on numerous government and private advisory committees on issues related to health policy and higher education, including the Board of Directors of Georgetown University, the Board of the Association for Health Services Research (of which association he was president in 1992-1993), the Advisory Committee on Scientific Integrity of the Assistant Secretary of Health, and the Special Medical Advisory Group of the Department of Veterans Affairs. Dr. Bulger also chaired the Institute of Medicine's Committee to Study Medical Professional Liability and the Delivery of Obstetrical Care. He has written numerous articles in the fields of infectious diseases, internal medicine, and human values and public policy related to health and medicine. The two most recent of his books on health policy are *In Search of the Modern Hippocrates* and *Technology, Bureaucracy and Healing in America: A Post Modern Paradigm.* Dr. Bulger is a member of the Institute of Medicine, a fellow in the American College of Physicians, a fellow of the Infectious Diseases Society of America, a member of the Society of Medical Administrators, and a fellow in the Royal Society of Medicine, London.

ELLIOTT S. FISHER, M.D., M.P.H., is Associate Professor of Medicine and Community and Family Medicine in the Center for the Evaluative Clinical Sciences (CECS) at Dartmouth Medical School and the Department of Veterans Affairs Medical Center in White River Junction, Vermont. He directs the VA Outcomes Group, which conducts policy-related research for the Department of Veterans Affairs and is co-director of the VA General Medicine Faculty Development Fellowship. He is also co-director of the Health Policy curriculum in Dartmouth's newly established postgraduate program in the Evaluative Clinical Sciences. He received his undergraduate and MD degrees from Harvard and his Masters of Public Health from the University of Washington, where he was a Robert Wood Johnson Clinical Scholar. His primary research interests are in the measurement of health system performance, the development of methods for resource allocation, and the use of administrative databases for health care research.

SPENCER FOREMAN, M.D., is president of Montefiore Medical Center in the Bronx, New York. As chairman of the Association of American

Medical Colleges (AAMC), Dr. Foreman is committed to broadening the social commitment of academic medical centers, enabling them to use their considerable resources to help alleviate problems of poverty, isolation, and community disintegration. Dr. Foreman was chairman of the Administrative Board of the AAMC Council of Teaching Hospitals and served on its Task Force on Graduate Medical Education. He served on the Task Force on Graduate Medical Education of the Hospital Association of New York State; on the Accreditation Council on Graduate Medical Education, the accrediting body for residency training in the United States; and on the Liaison Committee on Medical Education, which accredits United States and Canadian medical schools. He is board chairman of the League of Voluntary Hospitals, chairman of the Board of Governors of the Greater New York Hospital Association, and is a member of the Board of Directors of the Hospital Association of New York State. Before assuming leadership of Montefiore in 1986, Dr. Foreman was president of Sinai Hospital in Baltimore. He received his doctor of medicine degree in 1961 from the University of Pennsylvania. Dr. Foreman's medical training included internship at the Henry Ford Hospital in Detroit, residency in internal medicine at the U.S. Public Health Service Hospital in New Orleans, and a fellowship in pulmonary disease at Tulane University. He is certified by the American Board of Internal Medicine and Subspecialty Board of Pulmonary Diseases, and is a fellow of the American College of Physicians and the New York Academy of Medicine. He is professor of Medicine and professor of Epidemiology and Social Medicine at the Albert Einstein College of Medicine. For 11 years Dr. Foreman served as a commissioned officer in the United States Public Health Service, achieving a rank equivalent to the United States Navy rank of captain.

JANLORI GOLDMAN is director of the Project on Privacy and Technology of the American Civil Liberties Union. Her work on the Project involves researching the ways technology impacts on access to information and individual privacy. She has testified before Congress and appeared on panels on numerous privacy issues, including the federal Privacy Act, telecommunications, video and library lists, credit records, criminal justice systems, and drug testing. Prior to her work with the Project on Privacy and Technology, Ms. Goldman was legal counsel to the Minnesota affiliate of the ACLU. The priority for the Project on Privacy and Technology for the 103rd Congress has been passage of legislation to create a privacy right in personal health care records.

CLARK E. KERR is Vice President, Government Relations, at the Bank of America, where he manages corporate policy development and advocacy for state and federal health care reform legislation. He is president of the California Business Group on Health, and chairs the California Health Policy and Data Advisory Commission. Mr. Kerr is a commissioner on the Prospective Payment Assessment Commission, and a member of the board of directors of the Washington Business Group on Health, the National Committee for Quality Assurance, and the Bay Area Business Group on Health.

JOHN W. KIRKLIN, M.D., has been professor of Surgery at the University of Alabama at Birmingham since 1966. Earlier he occupied that same position at the Mayo Clinic. He is a member of the Institute of Medicine and has previously served on Institute committees. Dr. Kirklin had a 38-year career in academic cardiac surgery, to which he made many contributions. Since his retirement from active cardiac surgery in 1989, he continues to work in a number of areas, including outcomes research, multi-institutional studies, the chairmanship of the Cardiac Advisory Committee of the State of New York, and most recently the development and installation of a paperless computer-based medical record concomitantly with the application of a unique computer architecture at the University of Alabama at Birmingham Medical Center.

ANTHONY M. KOTIN, M.D., is currently the National Medical Director for Marketing and Specialty Products at the Travelers companies. He also serves as the Travelers' National Medical Quality Officer. Dr. Kotin received his bachelor of science, magna cum laude, from the University of Illinois in 1975. He attended Rush Medical College and graduated, Alpha Omega Alpha, in 1977. After completing an internal medicine internship and residency at Rush-Presbyterian St. Luke's Medical Center he entered private practice. In 1983, he cofounded the Highland Health Care IPA and served as its Medical Director until 1988, at which time he left to become the medical director for Metlife HMO of Illinois and Wisconsin. In 1990, he joined the Travelers as Midwest Regional Medical Director.

ROBERT M. KRUGHOFF, J.D., is Founder and President of the Center for the Study of Services in Washington, D.C. The center is a nonprofit organization studying local services and publishing two local *Consumer Reports*-like magazines entitled *Washington Consumers' Checkbook* and *Bay Area Consumers' Checkbook*, which rate Washington and San Francisco area services firms. Prior to that position, he was the Director of the Office of Research and Evaluation Planning in the Office of the Secretary of the Department of Health and Human Services. Mr. Krughoff received his B.A. from Amherst College and his J.D. from the University of Chicago Law School. He has published numerous articles and reports. Mr. Krughoff served as a member of the earlier Institute of Medicine Committee on Professional Standards Review Organization Disclosure Policy from 1980 to 1981, and as a member of the Advisory Panel for the Study of Medical Technology Under Competitive Proposals for the Office of Technology Assessment.

RENE LERER, M.D., is Senior Vice President for Corporate Development at Value Health Sciences. Dr. Lerer received his undergraduate degree from Oberlin College and his medical degree from the State University of New York at Buffalo. Dr. Lerer is board-certified in internal medicine and practiced in the Hartford area for approximately five years. Prior to joining Value Health Sciences, Dr. Lerer was chief medical officer for the Travelers Managed Care and Employee Benefits operations. He had responsibility for the development and implementation of the Travelers managed care strategy as well as its medical management strategy in the indemnity environment. At VHS, Dr. Lerer is responsible for the introduction of all new products, for support of large accounts, and for all marketing and sales operations.

ELENA O. NIGHTINGALE, M.D., Ph.D., is Special Advisor to the President and Senior Program Officer of the Carnegie Corporation of New York, Adjunct Professor of Pediatrics at Georgetown University, and a lecturer in Social Medicine at Harvard University. She received an A.B. degree in zoology, summa cum laude, from Barnard College of Columbia University (1954), a Ph.D. in microbial genetics from The Rockefeller University (1961), and an M.D. from New York University School of Medicine (1964). Dr. Nightingale is a member of the Institute of Medicine and is a fellow of both the American Association for the Advancement of Science and the New York Academy of Sciences. She is the coauthor of *Before Birth: Prenatal Testing for Genetic Disease*, coeditor of *Prenatal Screening, Policies and Values: The Example of Neural Tube Defects*, *The Breaking of Bodies and Minds: Torture, Psychiatric Abuse and the Health Professions*, and *Promoting the Health of Adolescents: New Directions for the Twenty-first Century*, and author of numerous articles on health, health policy, and human rights.

MADISON POWERS, J.D., D.Phil., has written on legal, ethical, and public policy aspects of informational privacy, and has made numerous presentations and participated in panel discussions of privacy and health care. He is coeditor of *AIDS, Women and the Next Generation*, and has written on privacy, discrimination, and reproductive decision making in legal, medical, and philosophical journals. He is the author of several forthcoming papers on genetic privacy, and has completed commissioned papers for the Department of Health and Human Services and the Department of Energy on both conceptual and policy aspects of genetic privacy. In addition, Dr. Powers has served as a consultant to the president's Health Care Reform Task Force, and is coauthor of the task force policy position paper on privacy.

EDWARD H. SHORTLIFFE, M.D., Ph.D., is professor of Medicine and of Computer Science at Stanford University. After attending Harvard College (1970), he earned a Ph.D. in Medical Information Sciences (1975) and an M.D. at Stanford (1976). During the early 1970s, he was principal developer of the medical expert system known as MYCIN. He then served medical residencies at Harvard and Stanford. As a member of Stanford's internal-medicine faculty since 1979, he has directed an active research program in medical expert systems and has spearheaded the formation of a degree program in medical informatics. He is currently Chief of the Division of General Internal Medicine and Associate Chair of Medicine for Primary Care. Dr. Shortliffe is a member of the Institute of Medicine, the American Society for Clinical Investigation, the American Association of Physicians, the American Clinical and Climatological Association, the American College of Medical Informatics, and is a fellow of the American Association for Artificial Intelligence. He has served on the Computer Science and Telecommunications Board (National Research Council), the Federal Networking Advisory Committee (National Science Foundation), the Biomedical Library Review Committee (National Library of Medicine), and was recipient of a research career development award from the last named agency. In addition, he received the Grace Murray Hopper Award of the Association for Computing Machinery in 1976 and has been a Henry J. Kaiser Family Foundation Faculty Scholar in General Internal Medicine.

ELLIOT M. STONE has been Executive Director of the Massachusetts Health Data Consortium since it was established in 1978 as a private, nonprofit corporation and a politically neutral setting for the collection and analysis of the state's large health care databases. The consortium publishes annual reports to a broad constituency of health care organizations and business coalitions. Previously, Mr. Stone served as director of the state's Center for Health Statistics in the Massachusetts Department of Public Health. Massachusetts provided data to the federal government through the Cooperative Health Statistics System (CHSS) of the National Center for Health Statistics (NCHS). Mr. Stone has been an advisor to the AHCPR, NCHS, HCFA, and the Robert Wood Johnson Foundation on state health statistics issues. Mr. Stone is a board member of the Massachusetts Peer Review Organization and chairman of its Data Committee. He is an active member of the National Association of Health Data Organizations (NAHDO) and the Association for Health Services Research (AHSR). Mr. Stone received his bachelors and masters degrees at Boston University. He attended an executive program in health care management at Yale University.

ADELE A. WALLER, J.D., is a partner who practices health law with the Chicago law firm of Gardner, Carton & Douglas. A substantial portion of her law practice involves advising clients on issues related to health information and the use of information technology in health care. Ms. Waller has spoken extensively on health information issues for organizations such as the American Medical Association, the National Health Lawyers Association, the American Academy of Hospital Attorneys, the American Health Information Management Association, and the National Managed Health Care Congress. She has published numerous articles and book chapters on health information topics. She cochairs the Workgroup on Confidentiality, Privacy, and Legislation of the Computer-Based Patient Record Institute and is a member of the Advisory Board of *Computers in Healthcare*. Ms. Waller has been an adjunct faculty member for the Health Law Institute at Chicago's School of Law, Loyola University, and is a frequent guest lecturer in the graduate health information management program of the University of Illinois at Chicago.

WILLIS H. WARE is a senior computer scientist with RAND in Santa Monica, California. His academic degrees include Ph.D. (Princeton University), S.M. (MIT), and B.S. (University of Pennsylvania)—all in electrical engineering. He joined RAND in 1952 and has held several staff and managerial positions. His career has been devoted to all aspects of computer science—hardware, software, architectures, software development, federal agency and military applications, management of computer-intensive projects, public policy, and legislation. In the late 1960s he developed a research interest in the security of computer systems, and shortly thereafter, a corresponding interest in the personal privacy consequences of recordkeeping systems. He has written extensively on both topics, testified to Congress, and been active professionally as speaker and conferee. In the early 1970s, he chaired the "HEW Committee" whose report was the foundation for the Federal Privacy Act of 1974. President Ford appointed him to the subsequent Privacy Protection Study Commission, whose report remains the most extensive examination of private-sector recordkeeping practices. Dr. Ware is a member of the National Academy of Engineering, a Fellow of the Institute of Electronic and Electrical Engineers, and a Fellow of the American Association for the Advancement of Science.

Glossary

Access control Information use policy to determine who can have access to what data (both organization personnel and persons external to the organization) and policies and procedures preventing access by those who are not authorized to have it.

Accuracy Magnitude of errors in data resulting from miscoding or misrepresenting facts, maintaining out-of-date findings, or commingling of data from more than one person.

Comprehensiveness Completeness of records in patient care events. Amount of information one has on an individual in the population both for each patient encounter with the health care system and for all of a patient's encounters over time.

Computer-based patient record See **Patient record, computer-based.**

Connectivity The potential of the (computer-based) record or record system to establish links to or interact effectively with any sort of provider or database (IOM, 1991a).

Database A collection of data in a computer, organized so that it can be expanded, updated, and retrieved rapidly for various uses.

Data confidentiality Status accorded to data or information indicating that it must be protected. Protection includes maintaining the integrity of the data and access control.

Data-exchange standards Standards that govern the collection, aggregation, transmission, dissemination, and exchange of health data (across disparate systems) and that foster the use of more consistent medical vocabulary (IOM, 1991a).

Data integrity Quality or state of being unimpaired such that data are not altered or destroyed accidentally or intentionally.

Data linkage Bringing together two separately recorded pieces of information concerning a particular individual, family, provider, facility, or other record subject.

Data network See **Network, data.**

Data reliability A measure of the consistency of data items based on their reproducibility and an estimation of their error of measurement.

Data reuse Use of data that have been gathered for another purpose (such as patient care, billing, or research) and that are employed for purposes for which they were not necessarily intended but which may generate new knowledge.

Data security Protection of data, especially sensitive data, from accidental or intentional disclosure to unauthorized persons and from unauthorized alteration by techniques such as software and hardware protections, physical measures, and informed, alert staff. (See also **Data confidentiality.**)

Disclosure, public Communication, or publication and dissemination, of certain kinds of information to the public at large.

Feedback Making available to providers and practitioners the data for or results of evaluative studies about themselves and their peers.

Generalizability The proposition that information on one dimension of health care delivery and performance will in some fashion predict or otherwise relate to other dimensions of performance.

Global index A composite score intended to represent the performance of an entire hospital, plan, or individual provider.

Health database organization The administrative and operational structure for regional health databases. A data organization that has as its mission the public release of data and results of analyses done on the databases under its control. It (1) operates under a common authority; (2) obtains health-related information from a wide variety of sources and puts databases to multiple uses; (3) contains person-identifiable data; (4) serves a specific, defined geographic area; (5) has inclusive population files; (6) has comprehensive data; (7) manipulates data electronically; and (8) supports electronic access.

Health status Information typically from individuals themselves, on domains of health such as physical functioning, mental and emotional well-being, cognitive functioning, social and role functioning, and perceptions of one's health in the past, now, and for the future and/or compared with that of one's peers (also called health-related quality of life).

Inclusiveness The extent to which entire populations or defined groups are intentionally included in a database.

Longitudinal record of care All the care provided for a discrete course of illness or injury, regardless of site or setting.

Network, data A set of databases that are hosted on several computer systems interconnected with one another and to terminals and that serve some community of users. Such a network will typically have the following attributes: (1) The databases are dispersed over several machines; each one or group resides on one or more computer systems. (2) The computer systems are often, but not necessarily, physically distant from one another. (3) All the machines in the network are linked by some means so that information can be transmitted from one machine to another. (4) Each machine has software to permit exchange of information among individual systems in the network, and in turn to allow individual users of the network to query the many databases and to receive, analyze, and aggregate data from them.

Outcomes What happens to a person as a result of health care. Outcomes include measures of the individual's health status and quality of life (or health-related quality of life), as well as numerous other measures such as presence or absence of disease, readmission to hospital, repeat surgery, and death (USDHHS, 1991).

Patient record, computer-based An electronic patient record that resides in a system specifically designed to support users by providing accessibility to complete and accurate data, alerts, reminders, clinical decision support systems, links to medical knowledge, and other aids (IOM, 1991a).

Patient record, primary That health care/medical record used by health care professionals while providing patient care services to review patient data or document their own observations, actions, or instructions (Ball and Collen, 1992).

Patient record, secondary Patient-identifiable data taken from the primary patient record to satisfy the needs of specific users (Ball and Collen, 1992).

Person-identifiable Any information that could be uniquely associated with the individual to whom it pertains; such inferential identification is greatly enhanced by computer cross-matching. *Person* is not intended to include physicians or other individual caregivers in their caregiver roles. (See also **Person-identified**.)

Person-identified Information that definitely or probably refers to specific persons. Person-identified information is associated with names, Social Security numbers, alphanumeric codes, or other unique (or nearly unique) information assigned to an individual. *Person* is not intended to include physicians or other individual caregivers in their caregiver roles. (See also **Person-identifiable**.)

Personal identification code A short code entered by a patient, probably on a keypad, at the time of health care services that permits access to his or her database.

Primary data See under **Data, primary**.

Primary patient record See under **Patient record, primary**.

Privacy The right of the individual to be left alone, to withdraw from the influence of his environment, to be secluded, not annoyed, and not intruded upon by extension of the right to be protected against physical or psychological invasion or against the misuse or abuse of something legally owned by an individual or normally considered by society to be his or her property (Westin, 1976). (See also **Privacy, information**.)

Privacy, information The interest of an individual to control the dissemination and use of information that relates to himself or herself or to have information about oneself be inaccessible to others.

Quality assessment Measurement of technical and interpersonal aspects of health care, including access to and outcomes of that care.

Quality assurance A cycle of activities and systems for maintaining the quality of patient care. Programs of quality assurance can be internal or external to an organization.

Quality improvement Efforts to improve the level of performance of a key process, which involves measuring the level of current performance, finding ways to improve that performance, and implementing new and better methods.

Reliability See **Data reliability**.

Secondary data See **Data, secondary**.

Secondary patient record See **Patient record, secondary**.

Security See **Data security, System security**.

System security Protection from unauthorized access, including provisions for hardware, software, communications, and system users, and use determinations based on organizational computer security programs

(Martin, 1983). Also, the measures taken to keep computer-based information systems safe from unauthorized access and other harm (IOM, 1991a).

Third-party payers Companies that administer health benefit plans, maintain records of eligibility and payment, adjudicate, and pay claims. The first and second parties are the patient and the provider (clinician or institution). (When the health plan is administered by the company, they are called **third-party administrators.**)

Unique identifier A code (usually numeric or alphanumeric) that refers to one, and only one, person at any one time, does not change for that person over time, and permits positive (or probable) identification of that individual. The term may apply to codes assigned to data subjects and to practitioners. (See also **Universal identifier.**)

Universal identifier A single code used in all health databases to refer to an individual. Such a code would allow linkage among health databases. (See **Data linkage.**)

Validity The extent to which data correspond to the actual state of affairs or an instrument that measures what it purports to measure.

Internal validity The degree to which one can support a causal relationship between treatment and outcome, given the way they are measured by the data.

Construct validity The degree to which one can generalize from one analysis to broader theories or models.

External validity The degree to which one can generalize from a finding (of causal relationship) to alternative measures of the treatment and outcome and across different types of individuals, sites of care, and times. (See also **Generalizability.**)

Acronyms

ADA	Americans with Disabilities Act
AHCPR	Agency for Health Care Policy and Research
AHIMA	American Health Information Management Association
AIDS	Acquired immunodeficiency syndrome
AMA	American Medical Association
ANSI	American National Standards Institute
ASTM	American Society for Testing and Materials
ATM	Automated teller machine
BCBSA	Blue Cross and Blue Shield Association
CABG	Coronary artery bypass graft
CHMIS	Community Health Management Information System
CPR	Computer-based patient record
DRG	Diagnosis-related group
DVA	Department of Veterans Affairs
EDS	Electronic Data Systems
EFT	Electronic funds transfer
ERISA	Employment Retirement Insurance Security Act
ESRD	End-stage renal disease

FCRA	Fair Credit Reporting Act
FOIA	Freedom of Information Act
FOIL	Freedom of Information Law

HCFA	Health Care Financing Administration
HDO	Health database organization
HIC	Health Insurance Claim (number, for Medicare beneficiaries)
HIV	Human immunodeficiency virus
HMO	Health maintenance organization
HSA	Health Security Act

ICD-9-CM	International Classification of Diseases, ninth revision, clinical modifications (for use in the United States)
ID	Personal identifier
IOM	Institute of Medicine
IPA	Independent practice association
IRB	Institutional review board
IRS	Internal Revenue Service
MEDTEP	Medical Treatment Effectiveness Program (of AHCPR)

NAHDO	National Association of Health Data Organizations
NAIC	National Association of Insurance Commissioners
NCHS	National Center for Health Statistics
NRC	National Research Council

OTA	Office of Technology Assessment

PHCCCC	Pennsylvania Health Care Cost Containment Council
PIC	Personal identification code
PIN	Personal identification number
PORT	Patient Outcomes Research Team (in MEDTEP program)
PPO	Preferred provider organization
PPRC	Physician Payment Review Commission
PPSC	Privacy Protection Study Commission
PRO	(Medicare) Peer Review Organization

QA/QI	Quality assurance/quality improvement

RHIG	Rochester Health Information Group

SPARCS	Statewide Planning and Research Cooperative System
SSA	Social Security Administration
SSN	Social Security number

TPA	Third-party administrator
TPP	Third-party payer
UB-82	Uniform Bill (1982) (a HCFA-mandated claim form for inpatient care)
UB-92	Uniform Bill (1992)
UCDS	Uniform Clinical Data Set
UHDDS	Uniform Hospital Discharge Data Set
UPIN	Universal physician identification number
USDHEW	U.S. Department of Health, Education, and Welfare
USDHHS	U.S. Department of Health and Human Services
VHCA	Vermont Health Care Authority
WEDI	Workgroup for Electronic Data Interchange

Index

A

Academic organizations, 64, 81, 98
Access control (to data), 3, 36, 37, 152, 153,
    154-155, 162, 239
Access to health care, 61, 65, 70, 80
Account numbers, 52
Accuracy of data, 5-6, 7, 8, 11, 12-13, 31,
    36, 50, 85-90 *passim*, 95, 107-108,
    161, 239
Acquired immunodeficiency syndrome
    (AIDS), 149
Administration on Aging, 64
Administration on Children and Families, 64
Administrative information, 3, 33, 44, 45,
    54, 75-76, 88
    data sets, 29, 54, 70, 87n
Adopted children, 75
Age and date of birth, 44, 51
Agency for Health Care Policy and Research
    (AHCPR), 43, 87n. *See also* National
    Center for Health Services Research
Allergies, 46, 74
Alliances, *see* Networks and alliances
    (provider)
Ambulatory care, 30, 63, 73, 86, 99
American College of Surgeons National
    Trauma Registry, 68, 80

American Health Information Management
    Association, 34n
American National Standards Institute, 89
Americans with Disabilities Act (ADA), 79,
    159
Analysis consultants, 115n
Analytic methods, 7, 8, 12-13, 36, 113
Ancillary facilities, 78
Antitrust issues, 31, 78, 111-112
Appropriate health services, 1, 62, 72, 88, 114
Artificial intelligence, 77
Assessment, *see* Comparative data; Needs
    assessment; Quality assessment;
    Technology assessments
Associations, *see* Business coalitions;
    Consumer interest groups;
    Professional associations
Attorneys, 37, 65, 82, 141, 207

B

Behavioral risks, 44, 80
Benefits, 76n. *See also* Insurance coverage
    and terms
Benton International (BI), 59
Bill collectors, 65, 82
Billing, 59, 70, 76

Reuse, *see* Data reuse
Risk adjustment, 2, 13, 113, 127
Rochester Area Hospital Corporation
    (RAHC), 56-57
Rochester Healthcare Information (RHI)
    Group, 56, 57

S

St. Louis metropolitan area, 97-98
Sampling frames, 72
Satisfaction with services, 3, 33, 46, 47, 54,
    60, 96*n*, 97-98
Science Applications International
    Corporation, 34*n*
Scorecards, *see* Report cards
Screening procedures, 46, 74
Secondary patient records, 5, 37, 42, 42*n*,
    141, 241
Secondary use, 158-160, 171
Security, *see* Data security; System security
Selective contracting, 77, 78, 79, 119
Self-insured health plans, 37, 64, 75, 78-79,
    152, 159-160
Severity adjustment, 2, 46, 113
Sexual preference, 154
Side effects, 46
Small-area variations, 65, 70
Social functioning, 46, 99
Social Security numbers (SSN), 19, 25, 52,
    165, 167-170, 209
Social service agencies, 65, 80, 141
Socioeconomic status, 37, 44, 65
Southeast Organ Procurement Foundation, 74
Soviet Union, 164
Staff management, 73, 74, 79
Standards and standardization
    of coding and definitions, 6, 7, 31, 76,
        87, 89
    data exchange, 31, 43*n*, 89, 239-240
    obstacles to, 31, 76
    privacy safeguards, 21, 139-140*n*
State laws, 6, 32, 35, 37, 50, 51, 60, 79*n*,
    107, 182
    privacy, 17, 140, 147, 149, 151, 152,
        159, 186-189, 191
Statewide databases, 29-30, 32, 35, 43, 50,
    55, 70, 80-81
    and mortality rate studies, 71-72
    public disclosure, 96-97, 98
Statistical disclosure limitation, 101-102*n*, 171

Stigmatization, 157, 161, 162
Strategic planning, 73, 77-78
Substance abuse, 82, 149
Surgical procedures, 46, 71-74, 79, 96, 98,
    99, 119, 123-135
Surveys and questionnaires, 41, 51, 60, 97-
    98, 171
    national, 30, 42, 43, 47, 84
    on privacy concerns, 137, 156, 159,
        164, 171-172, 211
Sweden, 164
Symbolic data presentation, 104, 105
Systematic error, 86*n*
System security, 153, 154-155, 242-243
    of HDOs, 22, 36, 189, 200-201

T

Task Force on Privacy, 139
Tax Reform Act, 168, 192
Technology assessments, 32, 62, 72-73*n*
Telecommunications, and privacy, 138, 152,
    157, 200-201
Telephone Consumer Protection Act, 138
Terminology, 31, 89
Therapeutic procedures, 46, 119, 153
Therapists, 99
Third-party administrators (TPAs), 37, 64,
    76, 77, 159, 243
Third-party payers (TPPs), 64, 70, 77, 141,
    243
    precertification programs, 76-77, 141
    See also Insurance claims; Insurance
        premiums; Insurers
Timeliness of data, 33, 49-50, 54, 62
    limitations of databases, 31, 84
    in public release, 3, 8, 11, 12, 91, 92,
        106, 118
Training programs, 64
Transaction systems, 59, 60
Transmission of data, 59, 76
    medical histories, 2, 32
    privacy issues, 137-138, 141, 142, 151-
        152, 157, 200-201
    standardization, 31, 89
    See also Networks (data)
Transplantation, 79, 80
Transportation barriers, 65
Trauma
    identification of victims, 52
    registries, 42, 68, 79-80